To Jean, Lincoln, Andy, Carol, and Jeremy

Investing Online

BENTON E. GUP

Blackwell
Publishing

© 2003 by Benton E. Gup

350 Main Street, Malden, MA 02148-5018, USA
108 Cowley Road, Oxford OX4 1JF, UK
550 Swanston Street, Carlton South, Melbourne, Victoria 3053, Australia
Kurfürstendamm 57, 10707 Berlin, Germany

The right of Benton E. Gup to be identified as the Author of this Work has been asserted in accordance with the UK Copyright, Designs, and Patents Act 1988.

First published 2003 by Blackwell Publishing Ltd

Library of Congress Cataloging-in-Publication Data

Gup, Benton E.
    Investing online/Benton E. Gup.
        p. cm.
Includes bibliographical references and index.
    ISBN 0–631–23155–2 (hbk: alk. paper) – ISBN 0–631–23156–0 (pbk: alk. paper)
1. Electronic trading of securities. 2. Investments – Computer network
resources. 3. Investments – Computer network resources – Directories.
4. Web sites – Directories. 5. Portfolio management. 6. Investment
analysis. I. Title.
    HG4515.95.G87 2003
    332.6'0285'4678—dc21
                                                        2002012480

A catalogue record for this title is available from the British Library.
Set in 10/12½ Galliard
by Newgen Imaging Systems (P) Ltd, Chennai, India
Printed and bound in the United Kingdom
by MPG Books, Bodmin, Cornwall

For further information on
Blackwell Publishing, visit our website:
http://www.blackwellpublishing.com

Contents

Introduction   vii

Part I: Getting Started Online

1: Understanding the Suitability of Online Investment
   Recommendations   3

2: The Changing Securities Markets and Regulation   19

3: Dealing with Brokers and Dealers Online   44

Part II: Types of Securities

4: Stocks   65

5: Debt Securities   81

6: Investment Companies and Mutual Funds   96

Part III: Making Investment Decisions

7: Analyzing Investment Opportunities Online   113

8: Interpreting Financial Data   133

9: Valuation Models   153

10: Portfolio Management   171

Directory of Websites   185

Index   194

Introduction

In 2001, there were more than 93 million individuals (more than 48 percent of all households) owning stock directly, or through mutual funds, retirement savings accounts, or defined contribution pension plans, almost double the number of shareowners in 1989.[1] Technology changed during this period. In the 1980s, broker-dealers began offering direct dial-up services for their customers. In 1995, the first Internet-based trading system was introduced. By 2000, the use of online trading had grown to 7.8 million individuals making 807,000 trades per day![2] And there are now more than 200 broker-dealers offering online services.

The major difference between the traditional means of investing (talking to a broker) and investing online is the overwhelming volume of information that is readily available over the Internet. This book focuses on *investing online*. It explains what individual investors should know before, during, and after investing online. Chapter 1 explains how you can determine what investments are suitable for you. Chapters 2 and 3 are about securities markets and regulations, and dealing with brokers and dealers online. Chapters, 4, 5, and 6 explain various aspects of stocks, bonds, and mutual funds. Next we turn to analyzing investments online (Chapters 7 and 8) and then how to determine their value (Chapter 9). Finally, we put it all together in a discussion of managing an investment portfolio. Each chapter contains relevant websites and a directory of websites that are useful to investors is presented at the back of the book.

Each chapter contains "Investor Insights" boxes that provide unique perspectives or insights that you can use. The end-of-chapter questions are designed to help you make sense of the information in the chapters and to steer you to relevant websites.

NOTES

1 Based on data from the Investment Company Institute (www.ici.org) and the New York Stock Exchange (www.nyse.com), and the US Census Bureau, *Statistical Abstract of the United States, 2000.*
2 Securities and Exchange Commission, "Examinations of Broker-Dealer Offering Online Trading: Summary of Findings and Recommendations," January 25, 2001.

PART ONE

Getting Started Online

1. Understanding the Suitability of Online Investment
Recommendations   3
2. The Changing Securities Markets and Regulation   19
3. Dealing with Brokers and Dealers Online   44

1 Understanding the Suitability of Online Investment Recommendations

Key Concepts

Asset allocation
Beta coefficient
Bid price
Blue-chip stock
Bond
Broker
Dealer
Diversification
Intrinsic value
Investing
Junk bonds (speculative grade bonds, high-yield bonds)
Liquidity
Market coefficient
Market risk
Mortgage-backed securities
Municipal bonds
National Association of Securities Dealers (NASD)
New York Stock Exchange (NYSE)
Offered price
Securities and Exchange Commission (SEC)
Shingle theory
Stock
Suitability
Systematic risk
Trading
Unsystematic risk
US Treasury bills

The distinction between online and full-service brokerages is disappearing as traditional full-service firms, such as Merrill Lynch & Co., offer competitive online services in order to avoid losing income and market share. Meanwhile, traditional online brokers, such as Charles Schwab & Co., Inc., have opened offices throughout the country to serve client needs. Other types of financial institutions, such as Fidelity Investments and T. Rowe Price (major mutual funds families), and Prudential Insurance, offer brokerage and other investment services online.[1] A Securities and Exchange Commission report said the following about online investing:[2]

> Online brokerage has significantly changed the dynamics of the marketplace, causing one of the biggest shifts in individual investors' relationships with their brokers since the invention of the telephone. Online trading was introduced in 1995, and by 2001 there were more than 200 broker-dealers offering online retail investment services.[3] For the first time ever, investors can – from the comfort of their own homes – access a wealth of financial information on the same basis as professionals, including breaking news developments and market data. In addition, online brokerage provides investors with tools to analyze this information, such as reports, calculators, and portfolio analyzers. Finally, online brokerage enables investors to act quickly on this information.

This chapter deals with the "suitability" doctrine that concerns brokers' recommendations to their customers. The first part of the chapter examines the source of this doctrine and how it applies to recommendations. The second part presents a six-step paradigm that individual investors can use to determine the investments that are suitable for them.

SUITABILITY

Look before you leap

Why should this book start with a discussion of suitability? The answer to that question lies in two old sayings. The first is: "If you don't know where you are going, it does not make any difference what road you take to get there." The analogy in investments is that you must have some understanding of the types of investments and advice that are suitable for your particular needs, or you may be making bad investment decisions – which is another way of saying losing money. Let's try to avoid that outcome.

The second saying is: "Look before you leap." Just because a broker or someone else tells you that "this is a great investment" does not make it so. You have a duty to yourself to investigate the quality and future prospects of that investment. Some of the chapters in this book explain how to do that.

Suitability refers to the doctrine that a broker-dealer's obligation is to recommend only those investments that are suitable for a customer. The doctrine is triggered when a registered representative, commonly called a stockbroker, makes an investment recommendation to his or her customer. The suitability doctrine is based on rules from the National Association of Securities Dealers (NASD), the New York Stock Exchange (NYSE), and on the "shingle theory" of law.

NASD and NYSE requirements

The **National Association of Securities Dealers** is the principal self-regulatory organization (SRO) of the securities industry. More information about the NASD is presented in Chapter 2. The NASD requires members, firms to have certain knowledge about their customers prior to making transactions.[4] The information includes the customer's: (1) financial status, (2) tax status, (3) investment objectives, plus (4) any other details the broker considers pertinent to making a recommendation. And with respect to the specific investment that is being recommended: (5) "an adequate and reasonable basis" for any recommendation made.

New York Stock Exchange Rule 405 requires brokers to know their customers and use diligence when opening accounts and accepting orders for transactions. The **New York Stock Exchange** is the USA's largest stock exchange. It is a marketplace for the securities of more than 3,000 domestic and foreign companies. It too is discussed in the next chapter.

INVESTOR INSIGHTS

NASD AND NYSE RULES

NASD Rule 2310 (a): Recommendations to Customers[5]
"In recommending to a customer the purchase, sale or exchange of any security, a member shall have reasonable grounds for believing that the recommendation is suitable for such customer upon the basis of facts, if any, disclosed by such customer as to his other security holdings and as to his financial situation and needs."

NYSE Rule 405: Diligence as to Accounts[6]
"Every member organization is required to . . . Use due diligence to learn essential facts relative to every customer, every order, every cash or margin account accepted or carried by such organization and every person holding power of attorney over any account accepted or carried by such organization."

The shingle theory

The **shingle theory** comes from common law. It provides that by virtue of "hanging out his shingle," a broker-dealer firm makes an implied representation to its customers that it will deal with them fairly in accordance with professional standards. Part of this legal obligation is to determine what is a suitable investment for the customer. Another part requires the broker-dealer to have a reasonable basis for recommending the specific investment. In other words, the broker-dealer must investigate the investment itself, before recommending it to customers.

There is a difference between brokers and dealers. A **broker** is any person who is engaged in the business of effecting securities transactions for others.[7] Brokers do not own the securities that are traded. They receive a commission for executing orders on behalf of the customers. In that sense they are similar to real estate brokers who receive a commission from bringing together homebuyers and sellers.

A **dealer** is in the business of buying and selling securities for his or her own account. The dealer profits from buying and selling at favorable prices. Many securities firms are both brokers and dealers. However, a firm cannot act as a broker and dealer in the same transaction – it can do one or the other, but not both at the same time. For convenience, the term "broker" will be used to refer to both, unless there is some reason to make the distinction between the two.

Suitability online

What constitutes an "investment recommendation" is difficult to determine in an environment where online firms provide personalized information to clients. The issue is the distinction between making a recommendation and providing information. The issue is complicated by the fact that in some cases, both the brokers and their customers can determine what personalized information they receive. The following hypothetical situations from a **Securities and Exchange Commission (SEC)** report on online brokerage helps to clarify the situation.[8] The SEC is the primary overseer and regulator of US securities markets. Its mission is to protect investors and to maintain the integrity of the securities markets.

1. *An online broker provides only order execution services.*
   Assuming that the firm is only an order taker, a customer-specific suitability review is not required.

2. *An online broker provides order execution services and allows all customers to obtain investment information from its "virtual library." The virtual library contains research reports, etc.*
   This type of activity should not trigger a customer-specific suitability review. Nevertheless, the broker must have a reasonable basis for assuming that the investment information is appropriate for at least some of its customers.

3. *In addition to scenario 2, the customer can personalize the information received on the firm's website – tracking quotes in specified stocks, alerts about research in those stocks or sector they are in. The customers identify themselves as a particular type of investor – conservative, growth, speculative.*
   If the customer has personalized information, is identified as a particular type of investor, and is following stocks that may be inappropriate, the firm has a suitability obligation to advise the customer in writing before executing transactions in securities that are not consistent with the investor's (e.g. conservative) investment strategy.

4. *The online broker classifies its customers into categories based on their account balance, securities holdings, trading activity, etc.*

   If the firm makes recommendations based on the information gathered about a specific customer, the firm has a customer-specific suitability obligation. This would probably not be the case if the customer selects the investment categories and requests to receive information appropriate for that category.

5. *In addition to the services provided in scenario 2, the online broker-dealer pushes selected information to the customer based on observations that the firm has made when the customer was online. For example, she buys blue-chip stocks after the price has declined. The firm sends her information about similar stocks.*

   The broker has a customer-specific suitability obligation.

6. *In addition to the services provided in scenario 2, the online broker helps the customer manage her portfolio by providing benchmarks that should be met or by advising about the asset allocation of the portfolio (the percentage invested in stocks, bonds, and cash).*

   The broker has a customer-specific suitability obligation.

Although these hypothetical situations help to clarify the issues, what constitutes a recommendation online that triggers suitability is yet to be determined by the regulators and the courts.

Some brokers have "Use Agreements" with their customers. These agreements state that none of the information or research reports provided to customers constitute

INVESTOR INSIGHTS

A PROFILE OF ONLINE INVESTORS

Are you a typical online investor? Compare your profile to the information from a survey about online investors that was made by the Investment Company Institute and the Securities Industry Association:

- Median age: 41 years.

- Median household income: $73,800.

- Median household financial assets: $229,000.

- Equity investments: $127,600.

- Most are college educated.

Source: Investment Company Institute and Securities Industry Association, *Equity Ownership in America*, Fall 1999.

a recommendation that any particular security should be bought or sold; nor does the broker or the providers of the research reports assess for their customers the suitability of any particular investment. The message here is *caveat emptor* – let the buyer beware. Next we examine how to determine what investments may be suitable for you.

DETERMINING WHAT INVESTMENTS MAY BE SUITABLE FOR YOU

Investment recommendations are based on available data and projections about the future prospects for a firm. The amount of investment data that investors can receive from online and print sources is overwhelming. The problem is to select only the data needed to make suitable investment decisions.

The remainder of this chapter presents a six-step paradigm of how to organize data to make suitable investment decisions, including analysis, implementation, and review.

Before examining the six steps, consider the returns and risk on different types of investments during the 1926–2000 period. The standard deviation is a measure of risk. The data shown in Table 1.1 reveal that there is a positive relationship between risk and returns. During the period under review, small company stocks had the highest returns and the highest risk when measured annually. If the risk and returns are measured over a longer time span, such as 10-year periods, stocks are relatively less risky. **Stocks** represent an ownership interest in a company. At the other end of the risk–return spectrum, US Treasury bills had the lowest returns and lowest risk. **Treasury bills** represent short-term government securities. The returns on Treasury bills barely exceed the rate of inflation. The returns on corporate and government **bonds**, representing long-term debt, were higher than Treasury bills, but lower than the returns on stocks. Although there is no guarantee that history will repeat itself, the relationships between risk and returns shown here will probably hold in the future as well – high expected returns are associated with high risks.

Table 1.1   Investment returns and risk (1926–2000)

Investment	Annual arithmetic return (%)	Standard deviation (%)
Small company stocks	17.3	33.4
Large company stocks	13.0	20.2
Long-term corporate bonds	6.0	8.7
Long-term government bonds	5.7	9.4
Intermediate-term government bonds	5.5	5.8
US Treasury bills	3.9	3.2
Inflation	3.2	4.4

Source: Ibbotson Associates, *Stocks, Bonds, Bills, and Inflation 2000 Yearbook* (Chicago, IL: 2001).

Table 1.2 Investment objectives and degrees of risk

Investment objectives	Low risk	Medium risk	High risk
Income			
Balanced income and growth of capital			
Growth of capital			

Step 1: Determine investment objectives and risk preference

The first step in evaluating suitability is to determine the investment objectives and the degree of risk that the investor is willing to assume. Simply stated, if you don't know where you are going, it does not make any difference what road you take to get there. It follows that if you don't know your investment objectives and risk preferences, it does not make any difference what security you buy. Step 1 is part of determining where you are going in terms of investments.

The simplified matrix shown in Table 1.2 includes three investment objectives (income, a balanced combination of income and growth, and growth of capital), and three degrees of risk (low, medium, and high).

Risk can be measured by statistics, such as the standard deviation of returns. However, risk is also subjective. An experienced investor may not consider buy options to buy or sell stocks (calls and puts) risky, whereas a novice investor may consider them very risky. There is no way to measure each investor's perceptions of risk. Therefore, we use risk in the statistical sense of the word.

Step 2: Determine the types of securities to be considered

The second step is to determine the types of securities that are consistent with the investor's objectives and risk parameters. Selected types of securities are listed in the cells of the investment objective/risk matrix shown in Table 1.3. The list of securities shown here is not complete. It is presented only to illustrate how to use the investment objective/risk matrix. Other types of investments, such as commodities and options, are discussed in later chapters in the book. Although not listed separately, an investor's tax status must be taken into account. Some debt securities issued by state and local governments (i.e. **municipal bonds**) are exempt from state income taxes.

Table 1.3 reveals that investors seeking income and low risk may consider Federal Deposit Insurance Corporation (FDIC) insured certificates of deposit (CDs), US government Treasury bills, and money market funds whose principal investment is short-term, high-grade securities.[9]

Those willing to take a high degree of risk may consider **high-yield bonds** (also called **junk bonds** or **speculative grade bonds**). They are bonds with credit ratings of BBB/Baa or below. The highest credit ratings are AAA/Aaa. The AAA rating means that the bonds have the highest credit rating assigned by Standard & Poor's Corporation. Aaa is the equivalent credit rating assigned by Moody's Investor Service.[10]

Investors also can consider mortgage-backed securities, and mutual funds that invest in high-yielding income producing debt and equity instruments.[11] **Mortgage-backed securities** are backed by pools of mortgage loans that can pay investors interest, principal, or both. More will be said about these securities in Chapter 5 in connection with bond investments.

Those who want balanced income and growth with a low degree of risk can choose income mutual funds and blue-chip stocks. **Blue-chip stocks** refer to those that have a national reputation for high quality and financial strength.

Table 1.3   Investment objectives and degrees of risk and selected investments

Investment objectives	Low risk	Medium risk	High risk
Income	Short-term CDs; Treasury bills; money market funds	Medium-term CDs; Treasury bonds; investment grade corporate and municipal debt issues; selected income mutual funds	Junk bonds; foreign bonds; mortgage-backed securities; high-yield bond mutual funds; high-yield stocks
Balanced income and growth of capital	Dividend paying blue-chip stocks; Treasury, corporate, and municipal bonds; balanced mutual funds	Dividend paying stocks; corporate and municipal bonds; balanced and growth mutual funds	Junk bonds; foreign bonds; high-yield mutual bond funds; convertible bonds; dividend paying stocks
Growth of capital	Growth mutual funds; blue-chip stocks	Growth mutual funds; sector mutual funds; growth stocks; stock index funds	Growth stocks; aggressive growth and sector mutual funds; stock index funds

Investors who want growth and who are willing to take on a high degree of risk may consider growth stocks, aggressive growth funds, and stock index funds.[12] Aggressive growth mutual funds seek maximum capital gains as their objective. Index funds mimic the performance of various stock market indexes and sectors. By specifying the investment objectives and the degree of risk, the number of alternative investments that must be evaluated is reduced to a manageable number.

INVESTOR INSIGHTS

TRADING OR INVESTING?

"Increased activity in buying and selling stocks highlights an important difference between *trading* and *investing*. Trading is buying on the hunch that the stock price will rise – regardless of what the buyer actually thinks it's worth. It's simply a game of placing bets. As the number of momentum traders increases and market volatility soars, trading today is more like playing a lottery. While studies show that the more times you trade the less profit you make, there's nothing wrong with such a strategy as long as you understand the risks.

"Investing for the long term means focusing on the fundamentals that make up a solid company – no matter what the market environment, no matter how revolutionary change is. Ask questions such as does the company have a vision, a business plan model that works, a strong management team or a quality product? Is it well-positioned to embrace new technology or innovation? Does it use its resources to become a better company? P/E ratios and other traditional metrics may not be as helpful for some of today's Internet and technology companies, but these time-honored fundamental questions will always have relevance."

Source: Arthur Levitt, "Investing With Your Eyes Open," speech by the SEC Chairman, February 12, 2000; see www.sec.gov/news/speeches/spech345.htm (visited 2/16/00).

Step 3: Establish a time horizon

The third step is to determine the time horizon for the investment. The data required by a day-trader who buys a stock at 10 a.m. and sells it by 10:30 is different than the data required by an investor who buys a stock as a long-term investment. The day-trader needs up-to-the-minute data about the price at which the stock is being offered for sale (**offered price**) and the price that buyers are willing to pay to buy the stock (**bid price**), the number of buy and sell orders, the volume of trading, and charts. It is estimated that less than 1% of people investing online are day-traders.

Table 1.4   Time horizons and information required for investment decisions

Investment time horizon	Selected examples of data required
One-day	New information that has an immediate impact on the stock price. Current (and historical) stock price (bid and ask price) and volume of trading. Daily charts.
Short-term (1 year or less)	Current economic data and short-term projections. Changes in management, marketing, products, sales, etc. Firm's financial data. Earnings projections.
Long-term (1 year or more)	The firm's strategies for growth. Projections of major trends affecting the firm, such as changes in demographics, technology, laws, etc. Firm's financial data. Earnings projections.

In contrast, both short-term and long-term investors are concerned about future earnings and dividends. Therefore, the long-term investor needs data about the future demand for the firm's products, its strategy, its financial condition, and so on. The primary focus in this book is on the needs of investors rather than day-traders.

For the purposes of illustration, the time horizons shown in Table 1.4 are divided into three categories: one-day, short-term, and long-term. The one-day period suits the day-traders. The short-term and long-term are better suited for longer-term investors. Selected examples of the type of data that are required to determine the intrinsic value of a stock – its theoretical worth – are listed in the table. This listing of data required to make investment decisions is not complete.

Step 4: Organizing data to make investment decisions

The next step is to organize the data into a format that can be used to make investment decisions. Two types of investment decisions and data formats are presented here. The first one deals with the selection of a debt security, and the second with determining the intrinsic value of a stock. The **intrinsic value** is the theoretical value of a security – what you think it's worth after analyzing all of the facts. Various models, presented in later chapters, are used to estimate the intrinsic value. The examples presented below reveal that different types of investment decisions require different formats.

A caveat is in order at this point. There is more than one way to organize data used to make any investment decision. The formats presented here are those that we have

Table 1.5 Selected debt securities

Security	Yield	Characteristics	Tax status
Treasury bond	5.8%	Highly liquid; interest paid semi-annually	Exempt for state and local taxes
Corporate bond AAA/Aaa rated	6.0%	More risk than Treasury; interest paid semi-annually	No tax exemption
Municipal bond AAA/Aaa rated	4.2% tax-free (6.0% tax equivalent yield)	More risk than Treasury; interest paid semi-annually	Exempt from federal and in some cases state taxes
CD	5.6%	Interest paid quarterly	No tax exemption

found useful. We acknowledge, however, that there may be better ways to do the same things.

Selecting a debt security The first decision involves a risk-averse investor who wants income, and she has a 5-year time horizon. Two additional constraints are added here. First, she may need **liquidity**, the ability to sell the investment quickly and at or near the current market price. Second, she is in the 40% income tax bracket. Based on those additional constraints, she has limited her choices to Treasury bonds, AAA rated corporate and municipal bonds, and certificates of deposit (CDs). In order to make her decision, she listed their yields, selected investment characteristics, and tax exemptions. She considered the advantages and disadvantages of each of the securities, as shown in Table 1.5, and then she made her decision as to which security to buy. Which one would you choose? Why?

Determine intrinsic value of a stock The second investment decision concerns an investor who wants to determine the intrinsic value of a stock that he is thinking about buying. If the intrinsic value is more than the market price of the stock, it is undervalued and the investor may buy it. Conversely, if the intrinsic value is less than the market price of the stock, it is overvalued and he definitely will not buy it.

Some of the things to be considered in evaluating the firm are the major factors that affect the future demand for its products (such as changes in technology or changes in law), the rate of economic growth, competition, the firm's strategies, financial condition, and other factors. Both historical and current data are examined to obtain insights about the firm's past and current performance. In addition, the firm's data must be compared with its competitors' data to evaluate the relative performance of the firm.

After all of this is done, there are several valuation models that can be used to estimate the intrinsic value. The models are based on expected earnings and other factors that are explained in later chapters.

Step 5: Portfolio considerations

A stock may be undervalued, but it may not be a suitable investment at the current time because of portfolio considerations such as diversification, taxes, or liquidity. **Diversification** of investments simply means not putting all of your eggs in one basket. Specifically, it means holding assets whose returns are not perfectly positively correlated. By way of illustration, a portfolio consisting of shares of General Motors, Ford, and Daimler/Chrysler is not well diversified because all three are automotive companies and their returns are closely related. They are all affected by similar factors in the economy. In contrast, a portfolio consisting of General Motors, McDonald's, and Amazon.com would be well diversified because the returns on these are not related.

Systematic risk is another important part of understanding diversification. The total returns of a stock consist of systematic risk and unsystematic risk. **Systematic risk**, also known as **market risk**, is that portion of a firm's total risk that cannot be eliminated by diversification. Systematic risk is measured by a stock's **beta coefficient**, also called **beta** or **market coefficient**. It refers to the extent to which the returns of a particular stock are related to the returns of a particular stock market index, such as the Standard & Poor's 500 stock index. The average beta for the stock market index is 1. Stocks with a beta of greater than 1 have more systematic risk than those with betas less than 1. **Unsystematic risk** is risk that is unique to the firm. A flood in the Ohio river valley that affects one firm in that valley is an example of unsystematic risk. It can be eliminated by diversification.

The extent of diversification and asset allocation depends on the investor's willingness to assume risk and other factors. Risk-taking investors may prefer not to be diversified. Risk-averse investors may want to minimize risk. It's a personal choice.

Asset allocation refers to the allocation of the portfolio in asset classes such as stocks, bonds, real estate, commodities, etc. Each class of assets has its own risk and return characteristics. By way of illustration, the assets might be allocated 40% in stocks, 20% in bonds, 30% in real estate, and 10% in short-term savings and liquid accounts.

Asset allocation is a dynamic process because investment requirements change over time. A young aggressive investor might have 80% of his or her assets in stocks, while an older richer investor might have 35% in stocks and the remainder in real estate, bonds, and other assets. There is no one magic mix of stocks and bonds that is suitable for everyone because everyone's needs differ. More will be said about asset allocation in Chapter 10.

Step 6: Taking action and monitoring results

Securities are to be bought, sold, or held after all of the previous steps have been taken into account. Keep in mind that most investment data concerns buying stocks or bonds. Brokers don't like giving advice to sell. Nevertheless, if stocks or other securities do not meet your investment objectives in the specified time horizon, they should be sold. A common mistake is keeping a stock that has declined in value, hoping that it will "come back." Wishful thinking does not produce financial results. If a security does not meet the objectives, sell it!

The investment process does not stop here because security prices and interest rates change over time. Equally important, investment objectives and risk preferences, asset allocation, and the need for cash may change as well. Therefore, it is necessary to monitor the portfolio and rebalance it – buy or sell securities when it is appropriate to do so. Monitoring stocks is easy to do because of the stock screeners that are available from online brokers and other sources – such as Bloomberg.com (www.bloomberg.com); CNNmoney (CNNmoney.com); *Fortune* magazine online (www.fortuneinvestor.com), and others – that will track and analyze your portfolio of stocks.

All six of these steps must be considered in determining what is a suitable investment for you. What is suitable changes over time as a result of aging, changes in income, and so on. Therefore, determining suitability is a dynamic, never-ending process.

CONCLUSION

The first step in investing is to determine your investment needs and what investment advice or recommendations you should request and receive. The suitability doctrine is of concern to investors who want to avoid making bad investment decisions based on misguided information. Suitability also is of concern to investment brokers because it refers to the doctrine that sets out their obligation to recommend only those investments that are suitable for a customer. The dramatic growth of online investing, which includes access to research reports and personalized information, has brought increasing attention to the suitability doctrine because there is a very thin line between making investment recommendations and providing research reports stating that particular securities are good investments at this time.

While the suitability doctrine is aimed at brokers, the ultimate decision is up to the individual investor – he or she needs to determine where a particular investment recommendation is suitable. Investors must understand their own needs and risk preferences.

The process of making suitable investment decisions includes the six steps listed below. In general terms, they begin with determining the investor's objectives, risk preferences, and time horizon. Then the securities that fit those criteria are evaluated to determine their intrinsic value, and their suitability in the investor's portfolio. Next, securities are bought or sold. Finally, the portfolio must be monitored and responsive to changes in the investor's needs and changes in the values of the securities held.

1. Determine the investor's objectives and risk preferences.

2. Determine the types of securities to be considered.

3. Establish a time horizon.

4. Organize the data needed to make investment decisions.

5. Consider the portfolio in terms of diversification, risk, and asset allocation.

6. Take action and monitor results.

This paradigm provides a continuous process for the analysis, implementation, and review of investments.

SELF-TEST QUESTIONS

The following questions are designed to illustrate the wide range of investment-related information that can be obtained online. Answers to most of the questions can be found at the websites listed. Note that the answers to some of the questions are based on current developments, and may change every time the website is visited.

1. Describe the type of investor information that is available from the following web-sites: Merrill Lynch (a full service broker), www.ml.com; Charles Schwab Corp. (a discount broker), www.schwab.com; Fidelity Investments (mutual funds), www.fidelity.com, Prudential Insurance (insurance), www.prudential.com.

2. How does the NASD define suitability? To answer this question go to the NASD's web page, www.nasd.com, then click on "Glossary," and then the letter "S."

3. The New York Stock Exchange is the largest stock exchange in the US. How large is it? To answer this question go the NYSE website at www.nyse.com. Click on "Market Information" and then on "Quick Facts."

4. FDIC insured certificates of deposit (CDs) are safe investments. What interest rates are available on CDs in your market area? How can you explain the difference in rates offered by various institutions? To answer this question go to the Bankrate.com website, www.bankrate.com, click on "Savings – CDs," then select the state and market area.

5. Are the CD rates better than the rates being paid on US government savings bonds? See: www.savingsbonds.gov.

6. There are mutual funds that can meet a wide variety of investment needs. According to the Investment Company Institute, what is the difference between a money market mutual fund and a bond fund? To answer this question go to the ICI website, www.ici.org, and click on "Essential Information," or click on the "Mutual Fund Fact Book."

7. What are the current rates on Treasury bills, notes, and bonds? To answer this question, go to the Bloomberg.com website, www.bloomberg.com/welcome.html and click on "US Treasuries."

8. Standard & Poor's and Moody's Investor Service give credit ratings to corporate debt securities. What is the difference between a "B" rated security, a "C" rated security, and a "D" rated security? To answer this question, go to Standard & Poor's web page, www.standardpoor.com, click on "Corporate Ratings," then click on "Ratings Definitions."

9. Stock prices can be volatile. What is the stock market doing today, and which stocks are most active? What factors affected stock prices today? To answer these questions, go to the CNNmoney website, CNNmoney.com. Click on "Markets and Investing," and then click on "Most Actives."

10. What percentage of your salary do you have to save to have the funds you want when you retire? To answer this question, use the T. Rowe Price Retirement Planning Worksheet at www.troweprice.com. Click on "Tools & Insights," then click on "Retirement Planning Worksheet" and fill in the blanks.

NOTES

1   Merrill Lynch, www.ml.com; Charles Schwab Corp., www.schwab.com; Fidelity Investments, www.fidelity.com; T. Rowe Price, www.troweprice.com; Prudential Insurance, www.prudential.com. The websites of many of the firms and organizations mentioned in this and other chapters can be found in the "Directory of Websites" at the back of this book.

2   Laura S. Unger, "On-Line Brokerage: Keeping Apace of Cyberspace," US Securities and Exchange Commission, November 22, 1999. See www.sec.gov/news/studies/cybexsum.htm (visited 11/23/99).

3   US Securities and Exchange Commission, "Examinations of Broker-Dealer Offering Online Trading: Summary of Findings and Recommendations," January 25, 2001.

4   NASD Rule 2310, "Recommendations to Customers (Suitability)," *NASD Manual* (Chicago, IL: Commerce Clearing House, 1999).

5   *NASD Manual* (Chicago, IL: Commerce Clearing House, 1999).

6   *New York Stock Exchange, Inc. Constitution and Rules* (Chicago, IL: Commerce Clearing House, September 1999). Only an excerpt of the rule is shown here.

7   The terms broker and dealer are defined in 15 U.S.C. 78c. The definition excludes banks and individuals trading on their own behalf.

8   Laura S. Unger, "On-Line Brokerage: Keeping Apace of Cyberspace," SEC, November 22, 1999, 32–4. See www.sec.gov/news/studies/cybexsum.htm.

9   Not all FDIC insured CDs are equal with respect to investment risk. Some long-term CDs offered by brokers are "callable." That means when interest rates decline, the broker can redeem high-yielding CDs, and the customer must look for alternative investments. Likewise, the FDIC does not insure all securities offered by banks. For example, Bank of America InterNotes[sm] are unsecured debt of Bank of America Corporation, and they are not insured by the FDIC.

10 For more information, see www.moodys.com; and www.standardpoor.com.

11 The various types of mutual funds are defined in the *Mutual Fund Fact Book* (Washington, DC: Investment Company Institute, annual). The website for the ICI is www.ici.org. High-yield bond funds maintain at least two-thirds of their portfolios in bonds rated Baa or BBB or lower; balanced funds tend to invest conservatively, pay income, and promote growth.

12 Although not discussed here, investors may consider using options and futures contracts instead of investing in the underlying security.

2 The Changing Securities Markets and Regulation

Key Concepts

Alternative trading systems (ATSs)
American Stock Exchange (Amex)
Asked price
Asset-backed securities
Auction market
Bid price
Block (of stock)
Blue sky laws
Bond
Capital market
Commodity Futures Trading Commission (CFTC)
Continuous market
Dealer
EDGAR
Electronic communications networks (ECNs)
Futures contract
Government-sponsored enterprise (GSE)
Initial public offering (IPO)
Inside market
Insider
Insider Trading and Fraud Act of 1988
Intermarket Trading System (ITS)
Investment Advisor Act of 1940
Investment bankers
Investment Company Act of 1940
Liquidity
Long-term debt securities

Maloney Act
Margin
Market capitalization (large-cap, mid-cap, small-cap, microcap)
Market maker
Money market
Municipal securities
Nasdaq
Nasdaq Stock Market
National Association of Securities Dealers (NASD)
Negotiated market
Notes (debt)
Options
Original maturity (debt securities)
OTC Bulletin Board (OTCBB)
Over-the-counter (OTC)
Pink Sheets
Primary market
Private placement
Prospectus
Red herring
Registration
Secondary market
Secondary offering
Securities Act of 1933
Securities and Exchange Commission (SEC)
Securities Exchange Act of 1934
Securities Investor Protection Act of 1970
Securities Investor Protection Corporation (SIPC)
Self-regulatory organization (SRO)
Short-term debt securities
Stock exchange
Syndicate
Third market makers
Treasury bills
Underwriting

One of the major advantages of investing in securities, in contrast to investing in art or real estate, is that active markets exist where the current prices of securities are readily available online, and they can bought and sold quickly. This chapter examines two major topics: (1) the securities and commodity markets, and how they are changing as a result of technology; (2) the laws and organizations designed to protect investors. Because the markets are changing as a result of technology, globalization, and other factors, the laws and rules of the securities and commodity markets must change as well.

MONEY AND CAPITAL MARKETS

Business concerns and governments raise external funds in several different ways. They can borrow funds and incur debts, or they can sell stock that represents ownership or equity in their firms. They borrow from banks as well as in the money and capital markets. The difference between the money and capital markets is the maturity of the debt obligations traded in each. The **money market** is the market for short-term debt securities, and the **capital market** is for longer-term debt and equity securities. A **short-term debt** usually refers to securities with an original maturity of 1 year or less. **Treasury bills**, for example, have a maturity of 1 year or less. **Long-term debt** refers to securities with original maturity of greater than 1 year. The **original maturity** is the maturity at the time the security is issued. Debt securities have a date in the future when the borrowed amount must be repaid. As the debt securities mature over time, long-term debts become short-term.

Examples of money market instruments are presented in Table 2.1. Businesses, financial institutions, and governments hold most of the money market instruments, although some individuals do hold large CDs, Treasury bills, and municipal notes.

As previously noted, the capital market is where longer-term debt and equity securities are traded. Corporations and governments issue debt securities. The debt securities include intermediate-term **notes** with maturities ranging from less than 1 year to 10 years, and **bonds** with maturities of 10 years or more. There is no

Table 2.1 Money market instruments and issuers[1]

Instruments	Issuers
Federal funds	Banks
Negotiable certificates of deposit (large CDs for $100,000 or more)	Banks
Repurchase agreements	Securities dealers, banks, nonfinancial corporations
Treasury bills	US government
Municipal (state and local government) notes	State and local governments
Commercial paper	Businesses
Bankers acceptances	Businesses
Futures and options contracts	Dealers, banks
Swaps	Banks

universally accepted definition of intermediate-term and long-term. Most bonds have an original maturity of 15 years or more. The US Treasury has issued 30-year bonds. Some companies, such as Coca-Cola and Walt Disney, have issued bonds with an original maturity of 100 years. Most long-term debt instruments are held by financial institutions such as insurance companies, mutual funds, and retirement systems.

Government-sponsored enterprises issue asset-backed and other debt securities. **Government-sponsored enterprises (GSEs)** are privately owned corporations that receive some financial backing and direction from the federal government. They were established to provide funds to certain sectors of the economy, such as agriculture, real estate, and student loans. The GSEs include the Federal Home Loan Bank System, Federal Home Loan Mortgage Corporation (*Freddie Mac*), Federal National Mortgage Association (*Fannie Mae*), Farm Credit System, Federal Agricultural Mortgage Corporation (*Farmer Mac*), and the Student Loan Marketing Association (*Sallie Mae*). They issue long-term debt securities that are backed by mortgages, credit card loans, and student loans. Such securities are called **asset-backed securities**, and they will be discussed further in Chapter 5 along with capital market instruments. Individual investors may invest in bonds and asset-backed securities.

STOCK MARKETS

More than 80 million Americans own stocks, and the stock markets are where they can trade them. The stock market is divided into the primary market and the secondary market. These markets are analogous to the markets for automobiles. The primary market is where factory authorized dealers sell new cars to their original owners. However, no one keeps a car forever. Therefore, there is a need for a market to sell used cars. The secondary market is analogous to the market where used cars are bought and sold by dealers and individuals.

Primary market

The **primary market** refers to the initial issuance of securities by corporations and governments. Most companies raising equity capital hire investment bankers, such as Merrill Lynch or Lehman Brothers, to help them. **Investment bankers** underwrite securities and provide other services for the issuing company and for investors. The issuing firm may use one investment banker or a group of them, which is called a **syndicate**. The services provided by the investment bankers include helping with the Securities and Exchange Commission (SEC) registration and providing advice about the timing and pricing of the issue. Companies with large securities offerings must file with the SEC. More will be said about that shortly.

Underwriting means that the investment banker buys the securities from the issuing firm and then sells them to investors. The investment bankers act as market makers, or as dealers. **Market makers** are professional securities dealers who have an obligation to buy when there is an excess of sell orders and sell when there is an excess of buy orders.[2] They buy and sell at publicly quoted prices. Market makers in exchange listed stocks are called **third market makers. Dealers** buy and sell for their own accounts.

The first public sale of the stock is called an **initial public offering (IPO)**. In most cases, investment bankers offer the IPO to large institutions, such as mutual funds, and to their best customers. They may limit the amount each customer buys in order to spread the issue among a larger number of their clients.

Investment bankers also handle large blocks of outstanding securities that are referred to as a **secondary offering**. A **block** of stock is 10,000 shares or more. Suppose that a stockholder wants to sell 3 million shares of Microsoft. The sale of the stock in the usual way might depress the stock price because of the large volume being sold. In a secondary offering, the entire block is offered at a reduced price to induce investors to buy it.

The investment bankers' profits come from the fees they earn by helping the issuing firm with the registration process, and from the difference between the price at which they buy and sell the new securities.

Some issues of securities are **privately placed** with institutional investors rather than being sold to the public.

A few companies sell new issues of their shares directly to the public. In 1995, The Boston Beer Company, Inc. advertised for prospective investors in six-packs of its Samuel Adams Beer. The Boston Beer Company makes a variety of beers. The company offered a limited number of shares to its beer consumers at a price of $15 per share. In addition, there was a regular IPO at $20 per share, underwritten by Goldman Sachs & Co., Alex Brown & Sons, Hambracht & Quest, and Advest, Inc. Goldman Sachs was the lead underwriter; the other firms participated in the underwriting. The Boston Beer Company stock is traded on the New York Stock Exchange under the symbol SAM.[3]

Secondary market

The **secondary market** refers to markets where outstanding stocks, bonds, options, and other derivatives are traded.[4] It consists of (1) traditional brick and mortar stock exchanges, (2) the Nasdaq Stock Market, and (3) the over-the-counter (OTC) market which is where publicly held stocks and some other securities that are not listed on stock exchanges and the Nasdaq Stock Market are traded. It also includes electronic communications networks (ECNs), as well as futures exchanges where equity options are traded.[5]

INVESTOR INSIGHTS

ADVANTAGES OF CONTINUOUS MARKETS

A **continuous market** has frequent trading activity and continuous real-time executions. This means that investors can buy or sell securities when they wish to do so when the markets are open. In the past, trading hours were limited, but we are moving toward 24-7, being able to trade 24 hours per day, 7 days per week. A continuous market has the following attributes: high frequency of sales, narrow bid/ask spreads, small price changes between sales, prompt execution, low transaction costs, and liquidity.

Frequency of sales
Stocks can be traded anytime the market is open.

Narrow bid/ask spread
The **bid price** is the price at which a stock can be bought, and the **asked price** is the price at which it can be sold. A relatively small spread between the two is desirable. The average quotation spread on the New York Stock Exchange in 1998 was $0.20.[6]

Small price changes between transactions
When the spreads are small in actively traded securities, the price changes between transactions tend to be small. Securities that are not traded actively tend to have larger price changes between transactions.

Prompt execution
Orders to buy or sell at the current market price should be executed within minutes.

Low transaction costs
The cost of executing trades should be relatively low.

Liquidity
The term **liquidity** refers to the investor's ability to convert assets into cash on short notice with little or no loss in market value. Small price changes and prompt execution, and low transaction costs contribute to liquidity.

Stock exchanges The stock exchanges in the United States and the rest of the world are listed in Box 2.1.[7] Historically, stock exchanges were **auction markets** where securities are auctioned on the trading floor of the exchanges. However, an increasing number of orders are now being processed electronically on exchanges.

The New York Stock Exchange (NYSE) is the largest stock exchange in the US. The American Stock Exchange (Amex) is the second largest floor-based stock exchange, and it too is located in New York City. The remaining exchanges in the US are considered regional stock exchanges. The various stock exchanges and the Nasdaq Stock Market are linked together electronically though an electronic order-routing system called the **Intermarket Trading System (ITS)**. The Nasdaq Stock Market will be explained shortly.

Box 2.1 also lists foreign countries where there are stock exchanges. They are located in both mature and developing nations. The Tokyo Stock Exchange is the largest foreign stock exchange. There are many investment opportunities in foreign markets. The other side of that coin is that access to some of those markets is very difficult to obtain for individual investors, and there are more complications and risk in investing directly in those markets than investing in US markets. Accordingly, we are going to focus primarily on the US securities markets.[8] This still provides the opportunity to invest in foreign securities without the hassle and risks of direct investments. First, there are numerous mutual funds that specialize in investing in overseas markets. Second, many foreign securities are traded in US markets. Third, there are some linkages between US and foreign exchanges. The Nasdaq-Amex Market Group has formed partnerships with exchanges in Hong Kong, Europe, and elsewhere that may make foreign shares more readily available.[9] Within Europe, some new pan-European and virtual securities exchanges are emerging.[10] Such linkages will contribute to a global securities market and the problems of dealing in foreign markets may disappear.

The Nasdaq Stock Market The Nasdaq Stock Market was owned and operated by the **National Association of Securities Dealers (NASD)** until it became a for-profit exchange in 2000. **Nasdaq** (pronounced *naz dak*) stands for National Association of Securities Dealers Automated Quotation. More will be said about the NASD shortly in connection with the regulation of securities markets.

The Nasdaq Stock Market is the world's first electronic-based stock market. More than 5,000 companies are traded on it by more than 500 market makers who are members of the NASD. The market makers may deal with each other at wholesale (**inside market**) prices while selling to non-members at retail prices. The Securities and Exchange Commission does not classify the Nasdaq Stock Market as a *stock exchange*, therefore it is not listed in Box 2.1.

The Nasdaq Stock Market is divided into two segments: the *Nasdaq National Market* which handles the larger, well-capitalized companies, and the *Nasdaq Small-Cap Market* that handles smaller, emerging growth companies. The term "small-cap" refers to market capitalization, which is explained in the following "Investor Insights" box. Do not confuse small-cap with low stock prices. The minimum stock price for continued listing on the Nasdaq is $1.[11, 12]

In 1998, the NASD and the **American Stock Exchange (Amex)** merged and formed The Nasdaq-Amex Market Group, Inc. It oversees the operation of the Nasdaq Stock Market and the Amex. Both the Nasdaq Stock Market and Amex operate as two different markets under the NASD umbrella. Amex deals in equities and derivative securities. This was not a marriage made in heaven, and in 2001 they explored the possibility of splitting.[13]

Box 2.1   Stock exchanges of the world[14]

United States stock exchanges and websites
American Stock Exchange, www.amex.com
Boston Stock Exchange, www.bostonstock.com
Chicago Stock Exchange, www.chicagostockex.com
Cincinnati Stock Exchange, www.cincinnatistock.com
New York Stock Exchange, www.nyse.com
Pacific Stock Exchange, www.pacificex.com
Philadelphia Stock Exchange, www.phlx.com/index.stm

Stock exchanges elsewhere

Argentina	Iceland
Armenia	India
Australia	Indonesia
Austria	Iran
Bahrain	Ireland
Bangladesh	Israel
Barbados	Italy
Belgium	Ivory Coast
Bermuda	Jamaica
Bolivia	Japan
Botswana	Jordan
Brazil	Kenya
Bulgaria	Kuwait
Canada	Latvia
Chile	Lebanon
China	Lithuania
Colombia	Macedonia
Costa Rica	Malawi
Croatia	Malaysia
Cyprus	Malta
Czech Republic	Mauritius
Denmark	Mexico
Ecuador	Moldova
Egypt	Mongolia
El Salvador	Morocco
Estonia	Namibia
Fiji	Nepal
Finland	Netherlands
France	Nigeria
Germany	Norway
Ghana	Oman
Greece	Pakistan
Hong Kong	Palestine
Hungary	Panama

Box 2.1 Continued

Peru	Swaziland
Philippines	Sweden
Poland	Switzerland
Portugal	Taiwan
Qatar	Thailand
Romania	Trinidad & Tobago
Russia	Tunisia
Saudi Arabia	Turkey
Singapore	Ukraine
Slovakia	United Arab Emirates
Slovenia	United Kingdom
South Africa	Uzbekistan
South Korea	Venezuela
Spain	Zambia
Sri Lanka	Zimbabwe

In 1998, The Nasdaq-Amex Market Group added the Philadelphia Stock Exchange to its family. The Philadelphia Stock Exchange was founded in 1790, making it the first organized stock exchange in the United States. Today it trades stocks, options, and currencies. Nasdaq also has agreements with stock exchanges in Asia and Europe. These cross-border partnerships reveal that traditional brick and mortar exchanges and electronic exchanges are joining together, suggesting that additional relationships are likely to occur in both domestic and foreign markets, and that the role of electronic trading will grow.

INVESTOR INSIGHTS

MARKET CAPITALIZATION

Market capitalization is calculated by multiplying the number of shares outstanding by the market price per share. Because of the growth of stock prices over time, there is no universally accepted definition of what constitutes "large-cap," "mid-cap," and so on. Some mutual funds are advertised as large-cap or medium-cap. Morningstar ranks all of the common stocks in a fund's portfolio from highest to lowest based on market capitalization.[15] Their list is divided into fifths to determine which capitalization category they fall in (Giant, Large, Mid, Small, and Micro). The following sizes are approximations that can change over time.

- Large-cap: $10 billion or more
- Mid-cap: $1.5 billion to $9.9 billion

- Small-cap: $500 million to $1.4 billion

- Microcap: Less than $500 million.

According to the SEC, microcaps refers to low-priced stock issued by the smallest companies. These companies may not be required to file reports with the SEC, and there is a lack of public information about them. The SEC said, "While all investments involve risk, microcap stocks are among the most risky. Many microcap companies tend to be new and have no proven track record. Some of these companies have no assets or operations. Others have products and services that are still in development or have yet to be tested in the market."[16]

In 2001, the Nasdaq Stock Market announced that it was going to become the first US stock market to sell stock to the public.[17] The funds will be used for expanding overseas and for a new trading system.

Over-the-counter (OTC) market Today, the OTC market is a distinctly different market than the Nasdaq Stock Market. In 1971, Nasdaq was created to automate and trade OTC stocks. Over the years, it evolved into the Nasdaq Stock Market, and it is no longer associated with the OTC market.

The OTC market covers more than 6,000 stocks and bonds that are actively traded and about 30,000 securities that are traded infrequently. The OTC markets are **negotiated markets**, where dealers at different locations negotiate the price of the trade. OTC stock prices are quoted on the OTC Bulletin Board and in the Pink Sheets. The **OTC Bulletin Board (OTCBB)** is an electronic quotation system that displays pricing information for companies that are *not traded on the Nasdaq Stock Market, the Amex, or other national stock markets.*[18]

The **Pink Sheets**®, named for the color of paper that they are printed on, contain price and dealer information on OTC stocks and bonds.[19] They are also available online (www.pinksheets.com).

Electronic communications networks (ECNs) The development of the Internet and computer technology is changing the concept of stock exchanges and stock markets as an increasing volume of trades are being handled electronically, more efficiently, and with greater transparency than existed in the past. Some dealers have formed **electronic communications networks** where orders to buy and sell securities at specified prices are filled electronically and at very low cost. In addition, the ECNs operate before- and after-hours trading of securities. The NYSE and Nasdaq Stock Market traditionally opened at 9.30 a.m. and closed at 4.00 p.m., Eastern Standard Time, on normal trading days, which excludes weekends and certain holidays. Interestingly, the Nasdaq Stock Market opened its own ECN (the SuperMontage trading system) in 2002. Other ECNs (such as Instinet and Archipelago) and Bloomberg also operate in the Nasdaq market. About one-fourth of Nasdaq's trading volume in 2000 was through ECNs.[20]

The ECNs offer fast executions and low cost because there is little or no human intervention. The cost of execution has been reduced from as much as 7 cents per share to as low as one-half cent per share.[21] On the other side of the coin, the prices at which executions are made may not be the best available since the buyers and sellers are not exposed to broader and more liquid markets.

Alternative trading systems (ATSs) Alternative trading systems are similar to ECNs, but there is no dealer involved. They are electronic systems for matching counterparties' orders, maintaining limited order books, and executing trades. The ATSs are private markets that are only available to chosen subscribers. Nevertheless, they handle a substantial share of the total stock and bond trading volume.

Exchanges redefined As a result of these new trading technologies, the concept of a stock exchange has changed. It has been expanded from just a physical location (New York, Cincinnati, etc.) to include some aspects of electronic trading. The new statutory definition of a **stock exchange** is a "market place or *facilities* for bringing together purchasers and sellers of securities or for otherwise performing with respect to securities the functions commonly performed by a stock exchange."[22] The inclusion of the term "facilities" broadens the definition to include electronic exchanges. The International Securities Exchange (ISE) applied to the SEC in 2000 to become the nation's first entirely electronic options exchange where stock options will be traded.[23] **Options** are instruments that give the holder the right to buy or to sell an asset, such as shares of stock or a commodity, at a predetermined price within a certain time period.

The SEC adopted rules in 1999 to allow ATSs and ECNs to register as national securities exchanges, and as broker-dealers depending on their activities and trading volume. The purpose of the rules is to integrate ATSs and ECNs into the national market system. Archipelago, an ECN, and the Pacific Stock Exchange have applied to the SEC to become the first fully electronic stock exchange. It is to be called the Archipelago Exchange.[24]

Competition causes changes Competition from the new trading technologies contributed to changes in the way the NYSE operates. Expanded access to certain NYSE stocks was granted at the turn of the 21st century. NYSE Rule 390 required that any stocks listed on the NYSE prior to 1979 trade only on an exchange. The NYSE Board rescinded that rule in late 1999, and now it allows non-NYSE member dealers to trade those stocks, which include General Electric, IBM, and other blue-chip stocks, through the Intermarket Trading System (ITS) mentioned earlier.

Another change is the way that exchanges and markets are organized. The NYSE and the Nasdaq Stock Market were organized as member-owned not-for-profit organizations. Because of the competition, they are converting to shareholder-owned for-profit corporations. The Nasdaq Stock Market converted in 2000.

Up to this point in time, the NYSE and the Nasdaq Stock Market have largely regulated themselves as **self-regulatory organizations (SROs)**, setting their own trading rules, dealing with customer complaints, and trying to deter manipulation of the markets. However, once they are for-profit corporations, there may be a conflict of interest between their profit orientation and their self-regulation. With respect to this issue, SEC Chairman Arthur Levitt said: "At the very least, I believe that the strict corporate separation of the self-regulatory role from the marketplace it regulates is a minimum for the protection of investors in a for-profit structure."[25]

Other changes in the structure of the securities markets were announced in 2000. Three large investment banking firms (Bear Stearns, Chase, and J.P. Morgan) formed a joint venture to create Market Axess, the first web-based multidealer platform to link institutional investors together with these dealers to provide research, and make primary and secondary markets in fixed-income securities, thereby bypassing traditional markets.[26] Next, five of Wall Street's largest firms (Merrill Lynch, Goldman Sachs Group, Inc., Morgan Stanley Dean Witter, Edward Jones, and ABN Amro Holdings) prepared a "white paper" for the SEC proposing a central order system, where all orders will be executed, and a single regulator for the securities market.[27] The firms argue that the concentration of the market would better serve the interest of customers than the fragmented market that currently exists. Other dealers argue that fragmentation is another word for competition that benefits customers. Finally, as a consequence of the joint ventures, market affiliations, and changes in technology, the two major market rivals, the NYSE and NASD, held merger talks.[28]

As previously noted, one possible outcome of the aforementioned changes that global trading will be 24-7 (24 hours per day, 7 days per week). The technology is available to do it. Equally important, the markets will be global in scope. However, before that becomes a reality, a common set of rules is needed for all of the participants in the market.[29]

COMMODITY MARKETS

Some investors trade commodity futures contracts to buy and sell agricultural, financial instruments, and natural resource commodities. Such contracts are actively traded on commodity exchanges. **Futures contracts** are binding commitments to buy and sell commodities at a specified time and price in the future. Futures contracts on agricultural commodities have been traded in the United States for more than 100 years. Futures contracts also are traded on financial instruments, such as Treasury notes and bonds, and natural resources such as oil and gold.

In addition, options on commodity futures such as metals, electricity, and foreign currencies are traded on commodity exchanges and some stock exchanges.[30] Box 2.2 lists the commodity exchanges and the Amex Commodities Corporation, and their websites where available. These options give the right to buy or sell a futures contract at a certain price within a specified time.

Box 2.2 Commodity exchanges

Amex Commodities Corporation (ACC)
86 Trinity Place
New York, NY 10006
(212) 306-1419

Cantor Financial Futures Exchange (CFFE or CX)
One World Trade Center
101st Floor
New York, NY 10048
(212) 938-3548
cx.cantor.com

Chicago Board of Trade (CBOT)
141 West Jackson Boulevard
Chicago, IL 60604
(312) 435-3500
comments@cbot.com
www.cbot.com

Chicago Mercantile Exchange (CME)
30 South Wacker Drive
Chicago, IL 60606
(312) 930-1000
info@cme.com
www.cme.com

Citrus Associates of the New York Cotton Exchange, Inc. (CACE)
Four World Trade Center
New York, NY 10048
(212) 742-5054

Coffee, Sugar & Cocoa Exchange, Inc. (CSCE)
Four World Trade Center
New York, NY 10048
(212) 742-6000
(800) 433-4348
www.nybot.com

Commodity Exchange, Inc. (CEI or Comex)
One North End Avenue
New York, NY 10282

(212) 299-2000
www.nymex.com

Commodity Futures Trading Commission (CFTC)
Three Lafayette Centre
1155 21st Street, NW
Washington DC 20581
(202) 418-5000
www.cftc.gov

Kansas City Board of Trade (KCBT)
4800 Main Street
Kansas City, MO 64112
(816) 753-7500
(800) 821-5228
kcbt@kcbt.com
www.kcbt.com

MidAmerica Commodity Exchange (MACE or MidAm)
141 West Jackson Boulevard
Chicago, IL 60604
(312) 341-3000
dbed50@cbot.com
www.midam.com

Minneapolis Grain Exchange (MGE)
130 Grain Exchange Building
400 South 4th Street
Minneapolis, MN 55415
(612) 338-6212
mgex@ix.netcom.com
www.mgex.com

National Futures Association (NFA)
200 West Madison Street
Suite 1600
Chicago, IL 60606
(800) 621-3570
(312) 781-1410
www.nfa.futures.org

New York Cotton Exchange (NYCE)
Four World Trade Center
New York, NY 10048
(212) 742-5054
www.nybot.com

Box 2.2   Continued

New York Futures Exchange (NYFE)
Four World Trade Center
New York, NY 10048
(212) 742-5054
www.nybot.com

**New York Mercantile Exchange
(NYME or NYMEX)**
One North End Avenue
New York, NY 10282-1101
(212) 299-2000

marketing@nymex.com
www.nymex.com

Philadelphia Board of Trade (PBOT)
1900 Market Street
Philadelphia, PA 19103
(215) 496-5000
(800) 843-7459
info@phlx.com
www.phlx.com

Source: National Futures Association, www.nfa.futures.org/basic/exchanges.asp

---

Technology also plays an important role on commodities exchanges. The Chicago Board of Trade allows members of the exchange and their customers to have electronic access to trading 20 hours per day (8 p.m.–4 p.m. CST), Sunday through Friday.

REGULATION OF THE SECURITIES INDUSTRY

Millions of Americans made their first investment by buying government bonds to support the war effort during World War I. This experience set the stage for them to invest in stocks and bonds in the years to come. Investing in stocks was a fun and popular thing to do, and Wall Street became New York's biggest tourist attraction. Passengers on Cunard ships could buy and sell shares by radio telegraphy as they crossed the Atlantic ocean.[31] The booming stock market of the 1920s went bust when the stock market crashed in the fall of 1929. Between September 3 and November 13, the price of American Telephone and Telegraph stock went from $304 to $197 per share, and General Electric went from $396 to $168 per share. The Great Crash, as it was called, ruined thousands of investors financially.

The financial excesses that occurred during this period led to the passage of legislation to protect investors. The principal legislation and the regulatory agencies are examined next.

Securities legislation

This section provides an overview of the major laws concerning the securities industry, and the government and self-regulatory agencies responsible for enforcing those laws.

Securities Act of 1933   The purpose of this Act is to provide for full and fair disclosure of the character of securities initially sold in interstate commerce, and to prevent fraud in their sale. The Act dealt with the **registration** of securities with the Securities and Exchange Commission. Registration does not mean that the SEC endorses the securities as a suitable investment. It does mean that a company provided the information called for by the Act.

Companies with large issues of securities must be registered with the SEC. Companies with small issues of securities (offering less than $5 million in 12 months; those sold to only 35 or fewer individuals; or to any number of high net-worth or high-income individuals) do not have the same requirements for registration as the large offerings, but they still have to file certain forms with the SEC.[32]

Part of the registration process is providing a document called a **prospectus** to investors. It must contain sufficient information so that investors can make an intelligent decision about buying the security.[33] Information contained in a prospectus includes:[34]

- A description of the issuing company's business and properties;

- Information about the company's management and financial condition;

- A description of the security being offered for sale, including names of the underwriters and the amount of the proceeds, commissions, and discounts to underwriters, and the proceeds to the issuer;

- How the proceeds are going to be used by the registrant;

- A list of the controlling interests of the registrant;

- Pending legal proceedings;

- Description of the type of security being registered and provisions relevant to the investors;

- List of directors, executive officers, and their remuneration;

- Information about options to purchase securities from the registrant or its subsidiaries;

- Principal holders of the type of securities being issued;

- Interests of management in certain transactions.

All US companies with more than 500 investors and $10 million in net assets, and all companies with securities listed on Nasdaq or major national exchanges, such as the New York Stock Exchange, must file periodic reports with the SEC. These include the annual report (Form 10-K), and others. They are available on **EDGAR**, which stands for the SEC's Electronic Data Gathering, Analysis, and Retrieval system, where most domestic publicly held companies make their filings of SEC documents electronically. There are about 15,000 publicly held companies that have disclosure requirements and must make periodic reports to their investors. This database is available to the public at the SEC's website and from other sources.[35]

Securities Exchange Act of 1934 and the Securities and Exchange Commission

This Act deals with the trading of outstanding securities and it created the Securities and Exchange Commission. The Act regulates the securities exchanges and the OTC markets operating in interstate commerce. The **Securities and Exchange Commission (SEC)** is the primary agency responsible for administering and enforcing federal securities laws.[36] The laws and regulations are aimed at promoting fairness, efficiency, and transparency in the securities markets.

The Exchange Act also gave the Board of Governors of the Federal Reserve System the right to limit the amount of credit (**margin**) that may be extended by brokers, banks, and other lenders on securities that are used as collateral for loans. The margin requirement is expressed as a percentage of the market value of the collateral at the time the credit is extended. A 50% margin requirement means that an investor can buy $10,000-worth of marginable stock by putting up $5,000 in cash or suitable collateral. The broker, bank, or other lender will put up the remainder. Securities traded on registered stock exchanges, and certain OTC stocks as determined by the Federal Reserve, are eligible for margin.

The SEC also oversees the National Association of Securities Dealers. The **National Association of Securities Dealers (NASD)** is a self-regulatory organization (SRO) consisting of all brokers and dealers who do business with the public. There are more than 5,500 securities firms that are members of the NASD.[37] It also coordinates its actions with other SROs in the securities industry (such as the stock exchanges) and government agencies to reduce regulatory duplication.

The NASD was created in 1939 in order to comply with 1938 **Maloney Act** amendments to the Securities Exchange Act of 1934. It was organized to (1) promote the investment banking and securities businesses, (2) standardize industry practices and principles, and (3) promote high standards among its members. The NASD's rules must be designed to prevent fraud and manipulation, to promote just and equitable rules of fair trade, and to protect investors and the public interests. It is responsible for overseeing the conduct of its members and the Nasdaq and the Amex markets.[38] The SEC must approve any changes in the rules affecting the trading or listing requirements.

Investment Company Act of 1940 and the Investment Advisor Act of 1940

These two acts gave the SEC authority over investment companies and investment advisors. Under the **Investment Company Act of 1940**, investment companies with 100 or more stockholders are required to register with the SEC. The purpose of the legislation is to ensure that investors have adequate information about the investment companies and their operations. It also placed limits on their investing activities. For example, for 75% of the fund's total portfolio, no more than 5% can be invested in any one company. This provides diversification. However, the remaining 25% of the portfolio can be non-diversified, or invested in a single security.[39]

The **Investment Advisor Act of 1940** requires that persons engaged for compensation in the business of advising others on buying and selling securities must be registered with the SEC. It also prohibits fraudulent, deceptive, and manipulative processes. In 1970, the Act was extended to include advisors to registered investment companies. Banks, brokers, accountants, and others whose advice is incidental to the performance of their business are not required to register with the SEC.

Securities Investor Protection Act of 1970

The **Securities Investor Protection Act of 1970** created the **Securities Investor Protection Corporation (SIPC)**, a nonprofit membership corporation that provides financial protection for customers of failing member brokers and dealers.[40] Each customer's claims are covered up to a maximum of $500,000, except for claims for cash, which are limited to $100,000. The SIPC does not protect customers from trading losses or losses in market value, nor does it cover commodity accounts.

Insider Trading and Fraud Act of 1988

An **insider** refers to an officer, director, or large shareholder of a publicly traded firm, and anyone else who possesses nonpublic information about that firm. A firm's attorneys and accountants are in this category. This law makes it illegal for insiders to use nonpublic information to profit from trading securities in that firm. Once information becomes public, they can trade like other investors. Nevertheless, insiders are required to report monthly their trading activity to the Securities and Exchange Commission. Insider trading activity is published monthly in the SEC's *Official Summary of Securities Transactions and Holdings*. Some investors believe that large volumes of buying or selling by insiders provides some information about the future prospects of the firm.

Commodity Futures Trading Commission (CFTC)

The **Commodity Futures Trading Commission** was created by Congress in 1974 to regulate commodity futures markets and related options markets in the United States. The CFTC and SEC have split jurisdiction over options.[41] The SEC has jurisdiction over options on securities, including debt and exempt securities and options on foreign currency traded on national stock exchanges. The CFTC has jurisdiction over stock index futures and options on stock indexes, as well as jurisdiction over options on agricultural, financial instruments, and natural resource commodities traded on a designated contract market – an exchange defined by the CFTC.

In 1974 Congress also authorized the creation of the **National Futures Association (NFA)**, under the oversight of the CFTC. The NFA is a self-regulatory organization that regulates all firms and individuals who conduct futures trading business with public customers.[42] The NFA began operation in 1982.

INVESTOR INSIGHTS

INVESTORS' BILL OF RIGHTS[43]

Making Informed Decisions
In many important ways, an investor is not simply a consumer but a party to a legal contract. Both the offeror and purchaser of an investment have rights and responsibilities. This "Bill of Rights" is designed to assist you the investor in making an informed decision before committing your funds. It is not intended to be exhaustive in its descriptions.

Honesty in advertising
Many individuals first learn of investment opportunities through advertising in a newspaper or magazine, on radio, television, the Internet, or by mail. Phone solicitations are also regarded as a form of advertising. In practically every area of investment activity, false or misleading advertising is against the law and subject to civil, criminal or regulatory penalties.

Bear in mind that advertising is able to convey only limited information, and the most attractive features are likely to be highlighted. Accordingly, it is never wise to invest solely on the basis of an advertisement. The only bona fide purposes of advertising are to call your attention to an offering and encourage you to obtain additional information.

Full and accurate information
Before you make an investment, you have the right to seek and obtain information about the investment. This includes information that accurately conveys all the material facts about the investment, including the major factors likely to affect its performance.

You also have the right to request information about the firm or the individuals with whom you would be doing business and whether they have a "track record." If so, you have the right to know what it has been and whether it is real or "hypothetical." If they have been in trouble with regulatory authorities, you have the right to know this. If a rate of return is advertised, you have the right to know how it is calculated and any assumptions it is based on. You also have the right to ask what financial interest the seller of the investment has in the sale.

Ask for all available literature about the investment. If there is a prospectus, obtain it and read it. This is where the bad as well as the good about the investment has to be discussed. If an investment involves a company whose stock is publicly traded, get a copy of its latest annual report. It can also be worth while to check out the Internet or visit your public library to find out what may have been written about the investment in recent business or financial periodicals.

Obtaining information isn't likely to tell you whether or not a given investment will be profitable, but what you are able to find out – or unable to find out – could help you decide if it's an appropriate investment for you at that time. No investment is right for everyone.

Disclosure of risks

Every investment involves some risk. You have the right to find out what these risks are prior to making an investment. Some, of course, are obvious: shares of stock may decline in price; a business venture may fail; an oil well may turn out to be a dry hole. Others may be less obvious. Many people do not fully understand that even a US Treasury bond may fluctuate in market value prior to maturity; or that with some investments it is possible to lose more than the amount initially invested. The point is that different investments involve different kinds of risk and these risks can differ in degree. A general rule of thumb is that the greater the potential reward, the greater the potential risk.

In some areas of investment, there is a legal obligation to disclose the risks in writing. If the investment doesn't require a prospectus or written risk disclosure statement, you might nonetheless want to ask for a written explanation of the risks. The bottom line: unless your understanding of the ways you can lose money is equal to your understanding of the ways you can make money, don't invest!

Explanation of obligations and costs

You have the right to know, in advance, what obligations and costs are involved in a given investment. For instance, does the investment involve a requirement that you must take some specific action by a particular time? Or is there a possibility that at some future time or under certain circumstances you may be obligated to come up with additional money?

Similarly, you have the right to a full disclosure of the costs that will be or may be incurred. In addition to commissions and sales charges or "loads" when you buy and/or sell, this includes any other transaction expenses, maintenance or service charges, profit-sharing arrangement, redemption fees or penalties and the like.

Time to consider

You earned the money and you have the right to decide for yourself how you want to invest it. That includes sufficient time to make an informed and well-considered decision. High-pressure sales tactics violate the spirit of the law, and most investment professionals will not push you into making uninformed decisions. Thus, any such efforts should be grounds for suspicion. An investment that "absolutely has to be made right now" probably shouldn't be made at all.

Responsible advice

Investors enjoy a wide range of different investments to choose from. Taking into consideration your financial situation, needs and investment objectives, some are likely to be suitable for you and others aren't, perhaps because of risks involved and perhaps for other reasons. If you rely on an investment professional for advice, you have the right to responsible advice.

In the securities industry, for example, "suitability" rules require that investment advice be appropriate for the particular customer. In the commodity futures industry a "know your customer" rule requires that firms and brokers obtain sufficient information to assure that investors are adequately informed of the risks involved. Beware of someone who insists that a particular investment is "right" for you although he or she knows nothing about you.

Best effort management

Every firm and individual that accepts investment funds from the public has the ethical and legal obligation to manage money responsibly. As an investor, you have the right to expect nothing less.

Unfortunately, in any area of investment, there are those few less-than-ethical persons who may lose sight of their obligations, and of your rights, by making investments you have not authorized, by making an excessive number of investments for the purpose of creating additional commission income for themselves or, at the extreme, by appropriating your funds for their personal use. If there is even a hint of such activities, insist on an immediate and full explanation. Unless you are completely satisfied with the answer, ask the appropriate regulatory or legal authorities to look into it. It's your right.

Complete and truthful accounting

Investing your money shouldn't mean losing touch with your money. It's your right to know where your money is and the current status and value of your account. If there have been profits or losses, you have the right to know the amount and how and when they were realized or incurred. This right includes knowing the amount and nature of any and all charges against your account.

Most firms prepare and mail periodic account statements, generally monthly. And you can usually obtain interim information on request. Whatever the method of accounting, you have both the right to obtain this information and the right to expect that it be timely and accurate.

Access to your funds

Some investments include restrictions as to whether, when, or how you can have access to your funds. You have the right to be clearly informed of any restrictions in advance of making the investment. Similarly, if the investment may be illiquid – difficult to quickly convert to cash – you have the right to know this beforehand. In the absence of restrictions or limitations, it's your money and you should be able to have access to it within a reasonable period of time.

You should also have access to the person or firm that has your funds. Investment scam artists are well versed in ways of finding you but, particularly once they have your money in hand, they can make it difficult or impossible for you to find them.

Recourse, if necessary

Your rights as an investor include the right to seek an appropriate remedy if you believe someone has dealt with you – or handled your investment – unfairly or dishonestly. Indeed, even in the case of reasonable misunderstandings, there should be some way to reconcile differences.

It is wise to determine before you invest what avenues of recourse are available to you if they should be needed. One means of exercising your right of recourse may be to file suit in a court of law. Or you may be able to initiate arbitration, mediation, or reparation proceedings through an exchange or a regulatory organization.

Municipal Securities Rulemaking Board (MSRB) The **Municipal Securities Rulemaking Board** is a self-regulatory organization established by Congress in 1975 to regulate brokers and dealers that underwrite, trade, and sell municipal securities to investors.[44] **Municipal securities** are bonds and notes issued by state and local governments. The MSRB's rules do not apply to investment trusts, bond funds, or similar programs issued by investment companies. The MSRB is under the oversight of the SEC.

State governments

Every state has laws requiring the registration of securities, brokers, and dealers. These state laws are commonly called **blue sky laws**. The term "blue sky" is believed to have originated when a judge ruled that a particular stock had about the same value as a patch of blue sky.[45]

State securities laws may differ from federal laws. You should contact your state securities regulator for information about the laws or rules in your state, or contact the North American Securities Administrators Association for more information.[46]

International regulatory cooperation

As financial markets become global, regulators throughout the world are working together in both formal and informal associations to promote the public interest in their respective countries and to establish best practices and agreed-upon standards among market participants. They also have to deal with the convergence of the securities, commodities, insurance, and banking industries as well as the implications of the Internet for regulators.[47]

CONCLUSION

The market for securities is divided into the money and capital markets. The money market is where short-term debt instruments are traded. The capital markets are where longer-term debt and equity instruments are traded. The capital market is further divided into the primary and secondary markets. The primary market is where new securities are sold to investors and the secondary market is where outstanding issues are traded. Securities can be sold on organized stock exchanges, in the Nasdaq Stock Market, in the OTC market, or in various electronic markets with little or no human intervention. Changes in technology are driving these markets closer together, both in the US and abroad. The changes may lead to trading being available 24 hours per day in most, if not all, securities.

In addition to the securities markets, commodities are traded on commodity exchanges. Commodities cover agricultural commodities, financial instruments, and natural resource commodities.

The securities and commodity markets are regulated to protect the investing public and to promote the efficient allocation of capital. Federal laws created the Securities and Exchange Commission and the Commodity Futures Trading Commission, and paved the way for self-regulatory organizations to be organized to protect the public and to maintain the integrity of the securities markets. As the markets change, the rules of the game must change too. Definitions of what constitutes exchanges and how they operate are changing with the times. Private exchanges and markets are going public as technological changes drive market forces.

SELF-TEST QUESTIONS

1. Explain how to buy Treasury bills from the US government. What are the recent auction rates? To answer these questions, see the website for the Bureau of Public Debt: www.publicdebt.treas.gov.
2. The New York Stock Exchange is both a primary and secondary market. What are the latest IPOs on the NYSE? To answer this question, go to the NYSE website, www.nyse.com, then click on "Listed Companies," and "IPO Showcase."
3. What are some of the advantages of owning stocks that are traded on stock exchanges or in the Nasdaq Stock Market?
4. The prices of equity securities traded in the secondary markets are affected by earnings announcements, expected changes in interest rates, and other factors.

What are the major factors affecting prices today? To answer this question visit CNNmoney, CNBC, or CBS Market Watch: <u>CNNmoney.com</u>; <u>www.cnbc.com</u>; <u>www.marketwatch.com</u>.

5. With respect to the previous question, suppose that AOL.com announced higher than expected earnings for the last quarter. How would you expect the stock price to react? Why?

6. While trading of stocks and bonds can be conducted on the Internet, trading of commodities is in the "pits." What does that mean? Read about the history of the Chicago Board of Trade to find the answer. See the MidAmerica Commodity Exchange's web page, <u>www.midam.com</u>, then click on "About MidAm," then on "The MidAm Yesterday and Today."

7. How can you determine if the broker or investment advisor who called you is legitimate? To find the answer to this question, visit the SEC website, <u>www.sec.gov</u>, then click on "Investor Assistance and Complaints," "Protect Your Money," and "Check Out."

8. Throughout the chapter the point was made that government regulations must change in response to changing technology, globalization, and so on. What changes in the rules are being proposed by the SEC? Use the SEC website, <u>www.sec.gov</u>, then click on "Current SEC Rule Making," "Proposed Rules" to find the answers.

9. According to the NASD, what are the major issues of concern to investors? How might these issues affect you? See the NASD website, <u>www.nasd.com</u>, then click on "Speeches."

10. The National Futures Association is an SRO for the US futures industry. It is committed to protecting the rights of investors in the futures market. How does it do that? To find the answer, visit the NFA website, <u>www.nfa.futures.org</u>, then click on "Investor Services."

NOTES

1   For additional details, see Timothy Q. Cook and Robert K. LaRoche, *Instruments of the Money Market*, 7th edn (Federal Reserve Bank of Richmond, 1993).

2   The definition of market makers is from the Commodities Futures Trading Commission, "Glossary of Futures Trading," <u>www.cftc.gov</u>. It is similar to the definition used by the SEC. See <u>www.sec.gov/consumer/keyword/market/html</u>.

3   For additional information about The Boston Beer Company, see <u>www.samadams.com</u>.

4   Standard & Poor's Depository Receipts (SPDRs) and World Equity Benchmark Shares (WEBS) are examples of derivatives (unit investment trusts) that track the performance of stock indexes. SPDRs and WEBS are traded on the Amex.

5   See the Chicago Board of Trade website: <u>www.cbot.com</u>.

6   *New York Stock Exchange Fact Book: 1998* (New York: New York Stock Exchange, 1999), 20.

7   The listing is based on the "Year-End Review of Global Stock Markets," *Wall Street Journal*, January 3, 2000, R21.

8   For more information about stock markets overseas, see the Brain Bank at www.cftech.com/BrainBank/FINANCE/WorldStockExchange.html.

9   For more information about this partnership, see www.nasdaq-amex.com.

10 "Exchanging Places," *The Economist*, November 20, 1999, 89–91; "Hunting Where There Are Duck," *The Economist*, June 30, 2001, 68.

11 Both Nasdaq and the NYSE have rules concerning the minimum price and/or market capitalization at which continued listing is permitted; Ruth Simon, "More Companies are Learning Harsh Lessons on Delisting," *Wall Street Journal*, March 20, 2001, C1, C2.

12 For up-to-date information about Nasdaq, stock prices, and more, see www.nasdaq.com.

13 Kate Kelly, "Nasdaq and the Amex May Be Soon Calling it Splits," *Wall Street Journal*, April 18, 2001, C1, C17.

14 For links to foreign stock market websites, see the New York Stock Exchange site (www.nyse.com). Click on "International" and then "Global Market Place."

15 See www.morningstar.com.

16 "Microcap Stock: A Guide for Investors," Securities and Exchange Commission, February 1999. See www.sec.gov/consumer/microbro.htm (visited 12/21/99).

17 Carol Vinzant, "Nasdaq to Go Public, Global," *Washington Post*, April 27, 2001, E01. See www.washingtonpost.com (visited 4/30/01).

18 The OTCBB is regulated by the NASD, but the OTCBB is not part of the Nasdaq Stock Market.

19 The Pink Sheets are published by Pink Sheets LLC, the new name for the National Quotation Bureau as of June 2000.

20 James J. Angel, *Market Mechanics: An Educator's Guide to U.S. Stock Markets* (Washington, DC: The Nasdaq Stock Market University Outreach, 2001).

21 Pallavi Gogoi, "Behind NASDAQ's Hissy Fit," *Business Week*, March 5, 2001, 105.

22 SEC Rules, "Regulation of Exchanges and Alternative Trading Systems," www.sec.gov/rules/final34-40760.txt (visited 12/29/99). Also see 17 CFR (Chapter 17 of the Code of Federal Regulations) Parts 202, 240, 242, 249. The details of the legal definitions of exchanges, ECNs, and ATSs are beyond the scope of this text. The intent here is to give a broad overview of the markets.

23 See www.iseoptions.com for details.

24 See www.tradearca.com, press release, March 14, 2000; July 13, 2000.

25 "Dynamic Market, Timeless Principles," remarks of Arthur Levitt, US Securities and Exchange Commission Chairman, made at Columbia Law School, New York, September 23, 1999. See www.sec.gov/news/speeches/spch295.htm. Also, the "Report Pursuant to Section 21(a) of the Securities Exchange Act of 1934 Regarding the NASD and the Nasdaq Market" identified a number of problems associated with the NASD's oversight duties. See www.sec.gov/news/extra/21a.txt (visited 12/21/99).

26 For additional information, see www.marketaxess.com. Operations of Market Access began in 2000.

27 Michael Schroeder, Randall Smith, and Greg Ip, "Sweeping Change in Market Structure Sought," *Wall Street Journal*, February 29, 2000, C1, C22.

28 Michael Schroeder, "NASD, NYSE Discussed Merging to Keep Up With Market Changes," *Wall Street Journal*, March 3, 2000, C1, C17.

29   For further information on this topic, see "Implications of Electronic Trading in Financial Markets," Committee on the Global Financial System, Bank for International Settlements, Basel, Switzerland, January 2001 (www.bis.org).

30   The American Stock Exchange trades options on broad-based and sector indexes and domestic and foreign stocks, including Long-term Equity AnticiPation Securities® (LEAPS®), with expirations up to 3 years, and FLEX Options – otherwise conventional options that allow the investor to set strike, expiration, and other key contract terms on a number of equities and indexes. For more details, see www.amextrader.com.

31   "The Key to Industrial Capitalism: Limited Liability," *The Economist*, December 31, 1999, 89.

32   For additional details on exempt offerings, see SEC Regulations A and D.

33   A preliminary prospectus is called a **red herring** because some of the statements on the front page are in red to warn investors that the statement is incomplete. The price, for example, is missing. It is determined shortly before the securities are issued.

34   Details about registration can be found at the SEC's website (www.sec.gov). The prospectus is part of the registration process. The forms (S-1, or SB-2) can be found under "Small Business Forms and Related Regulations." See Regulations S-K and Regulation C for nonfinancial requirements and Regulation S-X for financial statement requirements.

35   See www.sec.gov; also see www.freeedgar.com.

36   For more information about the SEC, see www.sec.gov.

37   For more information about the NASD, see www.nasd.com.

38   The "Report Pursuant to Section 21(a) of the Securities Exchange Act of 1934 Regarding the NASD and the Nasdaq Market" identified a number of problems associated with the NASD's oversight duties. See www.sec.gov/news/extra/21a.txt (visited 12/21/99).

39   See Section 5 B 1 of the Investment Company Act for details.

40   See www.sipc.org for more details.

41   See the CFTC website: www.cftc.gov. In 1982 the CFTC/SEC Accord codified the jurisdiction of each agency by adding Section 2 (a)(1)(A) and (B) to the Commodity Exchange Act – 7 US Code.

42   See www.nfa.futures.org for more details.

43   Source: www.nfa.futures.org/investor/bor.html (visited 1/21/00). The Investors' Bill of Rights was prepared as a service to the investing public by the National Futures Association, American Association of Individual Investors, Commodity Futures Trading Commission, Council of Better Business Bureaus, National Consumers League, North American Securities Administrators Association, and US Postal Service. Contact these organizations to register complaints.

44   See www.msrb.org for more details.

45   See *Hall v. Geiger-Jones Co.*, 242 US 539 (1917).

46   North American Securities Administrators Association, One Massachusetts Ave NW, Washington, DC, 20001 (tel: (202) 737 0900). Also see www.nasd.com for links to state administrators.

47   These and related issues are discussed in "Vision and Strategies for the Future: Facing the Challenges of 1997 through 2002" (CFTC, September 1997), www.cftc.gov/strplan97/home.html (visited 1/4/00).

3 Dealing with Brokers and Dealers Online

Key Concepts

Asset management
Beneficial owner
Best execution
Block trade
Buying power
Covering the short
Credit balance
Day orders
Day trading
Debit balance
Decimal pricing
Down-ticks
Equity
Fill or kill order
Freeriding
Goods 'till cancelled (GTC) orders
Limited liability company (LLC)
Long
Lot (round and odd)
Margin
Margin call
Margin requirements
Orders (limit and market)
Payment for order flow
Restricted account
Settlement date
Short

Short sale
Stop orders
Street-name ownership
Undermargined
Up-ticks
Wrap accounts

The first Internet-based trading system was introduced in 1995. By 2001, there were more than 200 broker-dealer firms providing online trading services to about 7.8 million retail investors out of the 80 million that own stock. The types of services and products offered online, and their quality, varied widely.[1]

ONLINE PRODUCTS AND SERVICES

Full-service brokerage firms

In a traditional full-service brokerage firm there is a personal relationship between a broker and the customer. Brokers are called *account executives*, *financial advisors*, and *registered representatives* in the various firms. The customer talks to a broker who provides advice and information, takes transactions orders, executes transactions, and offers other services. The broker is required to know his or her customers' investment objectives. Their conversations are face to face, or by phone. The broker then uses his or her firm's order routing system to execute the transaction orders. Traditional full-service brokerage firms also offer online products and services. For example, over 80% of Charles Schwab's trades are done online.[2]

Box 3.1 illustrates some of the services and products offered by both full-service and online brokerage firms. The extent to which these services are offered varies from firm to firm, as well as with the dollar value of the clients' accounts. High net-worth individuals get more and better services than small account holders.

Online brokerage firms

The relationship between exclusively online brokerage firms and their customers is different than that of full-service brokerage firms. In an exclusively online brokerage account, there are no personal relationships. The customer deals with the firm though its web pages. The transaction begins at the customer's computer and modem. A message is sent over the customer's Internet service provider (ISP), such as America Online (AOL), through the Internet to the broker's ISP. The message then goes to the broker's web server, and finally to the broker's order routing system. With customers scattered throughout the world, many using different systems, it is easy to understand how the lines of communication may not always function as

---

Box 3.1   Selected services offered by brokerage firms
- After-hours trading
- Alerts for earnings, new issues, news affecting your portfolio, etc.
- Banking services and products offered by affiliated banks
- Bill payment services
- Cash management services such as money market funds, checking accounts, credit cards, debit cards, bill payment, direct deposit, etc.
- Chat rooms
- Comprehensive statements of all accounts
- Direct access trading
- Dividend reinvestment plans
- Extra insurance on accounts
- Mutual funds
- Professional training online and seminars for traders and investors
- Real-time and delayed quotes
- Real-time charts and news
- Registered representatives to answer questions, provide advice, and handle orders
- Research reports – customized and standard for stocks, bonds, and mutual funds – online, faxed, or mailed
- Stock screener to help select stocks
- Tax information
- Tax sheltered investments, including oil and gas, cattle, equipment leasing, and real estate
- Trust services

---

desired. System delays and outages can and do occur from time to time. However, they are no worse than busy telephone lines at full-service brokerage firms. The delays, outages, and other factors may make it difficult to cancel orders at prices that are significantly different than those that were quoted when the order was entered, or to enter orders.

Nevertheless, online brokers can "personalize" services to meet the needs of their customers. Online brokers offer trading in securities, listed options, and mutual funds. Some have pre-opening and after-hours trading. To help investors make decisions about what to trade, market data, analysis, and charts are commonly available at no extra cost. Also available are screens listing securities by certain specified characteristics to facilitate the selection of stocks and mutual funds, asset allocation tools, and calculators for determining the stock values and the cost of owning mutual funds. Finally, customers can determine the type of information they want to receive from their brokers. Such personalized information includes breaking news about securities they own, portfolio information, and more. The amount and quality of the information, as well as the degree of personalization, usually depends on the asset size of the account. As previously noted, high net-worth customers get more and better services than those with smaller accounts.

Many online brokerage firms are not *exclusively* online. Equally important, they offer a variety of services targeted at different types of investors. By way of illustration, the following list of firms was taken from the Netscape search engine, searching Investing/Brokerages/Online_Brokers.[3]

- *5th Market Alternative Trading Hub* Broker-dealer specializing in convertible bond securities and risk-arbitrage trading.

- *AbnAmro Inc.* Prime brokerage services from online trading to hedge funds.

- *Active Trading Network* Customers trade directly with experienced traders on their trading floor. The traders have access to all ECNs, including island and Instinet.

- *Brown and Company Online* Discount broker for experienced investors who are able to manage their own accounts. $5 market orders, $10 limit orders.

- *ComdirectUK* Online broker for UK residents. Free information, including company profiles, detailed quotes, and news.

- *Eurotrade* Transparent and direct-to-market trading in global financial markets via the Internet.

- *InvestorLine* This is an online discount brokerage firm owned by the Bank of Montreal.

- *Swiss e Trade* Located in Switzerland, this offers online currency trading and discount stock trading on the Nasdaq and NYSE exchanges.

- *VMS Keytrade* European firm offering the opportunity to place trades on the three major American stock exchanges, Nasdaq, Paris and Brussels.

- *Wachovia Online* Offers online trading brokerage though their investment center as well as other personal and corporate financial services.

Initially, online brokerage firms had a competitive advantage over full-service brokers who charged higher commissions. That advantage disappeared when the full-service firms began offering online services, and cut their commission rates. The advantage went back to the online full-service firms that offer advice and other services. The net result is that there has been consolidation of the online brokerage firms as some have merged or gone out of business. Other online firms are expanding their offerings so that they can compete with full-service brokers.

Under the Gramm-Leach-Bliley Act of 1999, brokers, banks, and insurance companies can be owned by Financial Holding Companies. Consequently, brokers can offer banking services and vice versa. For example, E*Trade, an online broker, owns E*Trade Bank that offers a full banking service.[4] Mellon Bank Corp. owns Dreyfus Corp., which is known for its mutual funds. Regions Bank acquired Morgan Keegan, a brokerage firm. Before the acquisition, Regions Investment Company, Inc. offered a wide variety of investment services including discount brokerage. Citigroup owns Salomon Smith Barney Private Client Group that provides investment services to high net-worth individuals. The result of the change in the law is that the distinction between the different types of financial service providers is becoming blurred as we move toward financial supermarkets where you can have one-stop shopping to meet all of your financial needs.

Day-trading firms

Day trading means buying and selling the security the same day. Day-traders try to profit from small price changes rather than buying and holding securities for longer periods.[5] In other words, they speculate on short-term price changes. Day-trading firms advertise themselves as such and solicit full-time day-traders. The firms teach their customers how to do day trading and trading strategies. In addition, the firms provide their customers with on-site real-time data (no delayed quotes) and proprietary software to analyze stocks, after-hours trading, and other services. In contrast to full-service and discount online brokers, day-trading firms promote and facilitate a particular type of trading.

Most day-trading firms are brokers and dealers that are registered with the SEC and the NASD who have regular customer accounts. However, some are **limited liability companies (LLCs)** that sell interests in the firm to the day-traders. In this case, the day-traders who are part-owners (associated persons) of the LLCs are not considered customers. Therefore, the LLC has no duty to supervise the behavior of these associated persons. Although the LLCs are registered with the SEC, they are not required to register with the NASD because they do not have customer accounts and they are members of a national stock exchange, such as the Philadelphia Stock Exchange.[6] In addition, the day-traders in the LLCs can leverage their funds up to 10 to 1 – more than is permitted under usual margin requirements, which is 2 to 1. More will be said about margin requirements shortly.

A study of day-trading firms by the North American Securities Administrators Association found that "70% of public traders will not only lose, but will almost certainly lose everything they invest."[7] Day-traders face the risk of losing more than they invest because of two factors. First, the market value of the securities they buy on margin may decline to a point where the amount owed exceeds the equity in the account. Second, short sellers may face unlimited losses when stock prices rise. Only 11.5% of all accounts the study examined conducted profitable short-term trading.

BROKER COMPENSATION

Brokerage firms are in business to make a profit, and they do so by selling securities and related services. As a result of intense competition between online brokers, the average commission charged by the top ten firms declined from about $50 in 1996 to $15.75 in 1999. For example, Merrill Lynch offered online customers a commission of $29.95 per stock trade, compared with $100–400 for full-service brokerage.[8]

Brokers' income depends on the types of securities they sell and other factors that are described below. For example, brokers generally earn more by selling mutual funds than they do by selling stocks. Moreover, they may get higher fees for selling in-house mutual funds than for selling other funds.[9]

Commissions also depend on the type of trade, the number of trades, and where the shares are traded. For example, Ameritrade advertised their online Express Account as having commissions of $8 for Internet stock market trades, $18 for broker-assisted trades, and $12 for using the automated telephone trading system.[10] Special types of orders (limit and stop orders) cost $5 more. In terms of number of trades, Schwab's Active Trader commission discounts for equity trades of 1,000 shares or less – $29.95 for up to 30 qualifying trades, $19.95 for 31–60 trades, and $14.95 for 61 or more trades.[11]

Some brokerage firms charge a flat fee instead of charging for each transaction. For example, Charles Schwab charges a flat rate of $29.95 for option trades placed through their automated channels, or $54.95 if the option trade is placed with a Schwab representative. In addition, some firms also charge account maintenance fees. The amount of the fees usually varies depending on the level of the account balance and the number of commissionable trade orders made.

Payment for order flow

Payment for order flow is the fee that exchanges or market makers pay to brokers to send your order to them. The fees are small, such as 1 cent per 1,000 share order. However, because of the volume of trading, the fees add up to substantial income for the brokers. Equally important, the fact that a broker is receiving a fee from one market rather than another may influence how orders are routed and the best execution (discussed below). The SEC requires brokers to disclose payment for order flow to their customers.

Best execution

Brokers have a duty of **best execution**.[12] It comes from the common law duty of loyalty, which obligates an agent to act exclusively in the principal's best interest. The best execution for retail customers means obtaining the best price or terms available under prevailing market conditions. Prices do vary in different market centers. Some market centers have immediate automated execution of trades, while others offer delayed trading with the possibility of price improvement.

There are no SEC regulations requiring that a trade must be executed within a specified period of time. Some brokerage firms match buy and sell orders in-house instead of using market centers. Therefore, best execution depends on the brokers and on the efficiency of the market centers. An SEC report that compared trading cost on the NYSE and Nasdaq found that except for all but the very largest company securities, the NYSE spreads between bid and asked prices were narrower than those on Nasdaq.[13] However, there are SEC regulations that require the broker to reveal to their customers the market centers where they route most of their orders, and the extent to which they provide prices better than the public quotes to investors.

While price has been the principal factor in determining if a broker-dealer has satisfied its obligation for best execution, the SEC has stated that six other factors should be considered: (1) order size, (2) speed of execution in competing markets, (3) trading characteristics of the security, (4) availability of information comparing markets and the technology to do it, (5) access to competing markets, and (6) the cost of such access.[14]

Institutional investors, with large block trades of securities to be traded, may consider anonymity and liquidity to be just as important as the best price. A **block trade** is generally 10,000 shares or more.

The issues of payment for order flow and best execution become intertwined when a broker sends a transaction order to a market maker in order to receive a commission, and that market may not have the best execution. For example, suppose that a transaction is for 1,000 shares, and the broker receives 1 cent per share from the market maker. The broker earns an extra $10 (1,000 × $0.01 = $10.00). Further suppose that it was not the best execution, and the execution cost the customer 2 cents more than it would have elsewhere. The hidden cost to the customer is $20 ($0.02 × 1,000 = $20.00). The move to **decimal pricing** (prices in dollars and cents rather than fractions of a dollar) in 2000 reduced the opportunities to improve prices between market centers.

Asset management and wrap accounts

Transactions fees per trade have declined sharply because of competition. Some brokerage firms recognized that while having competitive transactions fees was good for customers, it was bad for the broker's income. Consequently, they are emphasizing **asset management** services catering to high net-worth individuals. Asset management includes trust services as well as providing advice on asset allocation – how investment funds should be invested in various types of assets – trading, and other services. Such services are available in **wrap accounts** where the brokerage and money management fees are wrapped into one all-inclusive flat fee. The minimum value of account sizes at firms varies widely. The basic wrap fee may be from 2–3% of the value of their portfolios for asset management services. Three percent of a $1 million portfolio is $30,000 per year. The funds that are not invested in stocks and bonds are frequently invested in a money-market fund, which has management fees of about three-quarters of a percentage point per year. Thus, investors must decide if such advice and services are worth the cost.

INVESTOR INSIGHTS

COMPLAINTS ABOUT BROKERS AND HELPFUL INFORMATION

In 1999, the SEC received almost 74,000 complaints.[15] Most complaints about broker-dealers involve difficulty in transferring accounts, problems with the execution and processing of orders online, unauthorized transactions, and misrepresentations. In fiscal 2000 (October 1–September 30) the SEC received 4,200 online trading complaints. In addition to the problems mentioned above, these complaints involved difficulty accessing the account, margin position sellouts, errors in processing orders, and best execution problems.

If you have a problem, first contact your firm's compliance officer and try to resolve the issue. If that does not work, then inquires and complaints can be sent by e-mail to the SEC's Office of Investor Education and Assistance at help@sec.gov, or use their complaint form at www.sec.gov/compform.htm. The SEC will send a letter to the broker asking them to respond to you within 30 days. However, the SEC staff does not resolve individual disputes between brokers and their customers.

Most brokers require their customers to sign predispute arbitration agreements requiring that the dispute be resolved through self-regulatory organization (SRO) sponsored arbitration rather than suing in court. The New York Stock Exchange (NYSE) and the National Association of Securities Dealers (NASD) are examples of SROs. The NASD, for example, operates a dispute resolution forum to assist in the resolution of monetary and business disputes between investors and securities firms. They may assist in both mediation and arbitration of the issues.[16] Despite SRO involvement, about half of the investors who won financial settlements in arbitrations were never paid.[17] Most of the unpaid awards are from brokers that are no longer in business.

For additional information about investor education concerning online trading, see www.sec.gov. This site also contains calculators for estimating how much should be saved for retirement and comparing the costs of mutual funds, tips for investing, and other information.

Finally, www.consumer.gov is the federal government's resource to help consumers. The "Money" section of the web page provides information about investments and other financial issues.

Kinds of orders

The best execution and the prices that customers pay or receive depends, in part, on the kinds of orders that they use. Orders to buy or sell stock can be classified by size, price limits, time limits, and special features.

Size The size of an order refers to the number of shares traded. The normal unit of trading is 100 shares, commonly referred to as a **round lot**. Some preferred stocks and inactive stocks have round lots of 10 shares. An **odd lot** is anything less than the normal unit of trading. Thus, 1–99 shares is an odd lot for the normal unit of trading. Some brokers charge an odd lot differential for dealing in odd lots.

Types of transactions Orders are either to buy or sell stock. Orders to sell stock have to be marked long or short. The term **long** means that the customer owns the stock being sold. The term **short** means that the customer may not own the stock being sold. A **short sale** is defined as the sale of a security at a high price in anticipation of buying that security back at a lower price. For example, a customer sells stock at $40 per share and hopes to buy it back at $30 per share, thereby making a profit of $10 per share. Short sales are used by speculators as well as those who want to lock in a profit in order to carry it over from one tax year until the next calendar year.

When a short sale occurs, the broker lends the stock to the customer to deliver to the buyer. At some point in time in the future, the customer must replace the borrowed stock and any dividends paid during that period. This is called **covering the short** position.

Price of orders Orders must specify if the stock is to be bought or sold at the market price or at a limited price. **Market orders** are filled at the current trading price at that time. **Limit orders** are filled at a specified price or a better price. For example, an order is given to the broker to buy 100 shares of XYZ at $25 or less. The maximum price that will be paid is $25 per share, but it is also possible that the stock may be bought for $24.75. Likewise, an order to sell 100 shares of ABC at $52 per share may be executed at $52 or at a higher price if it is available at that time.

Price changes are referred to as **up-ticks** if the last price is higher than the previous regular trade, and **down-ticks** if it is lower than the previous one. The rules for short selling exchange listed stocks require that a stock cannot be sold short unless there is an up-tick. The NASD also has pricing rules concerning the short selling of Nasdaq stocks.[18]

Time limits Orders that are entered for just one day are called **day orders**. If the day orders are not filled at the end of the trading day they are cancelled. **Fill or kill orders** are either filled immediately, or they are killed. **Good 'till cancelled (GTC) orders** are orders that remain in place until they are cancelled, or they reach the time limit set by the brokerage firm, which is usually 30–60 days.

Stop orders Stop orders are used to protect a profit or minimize a loss. They are placed on opposite sides of the market from limit orders. By way of illustration, assume that an investor bought a stock at $20 per share and that it is currently selling at $44 per share. If the stock continues to advance, the investor does not want to sell it. However, if it declines he wants to lock in the profit. Therefore, he uses a "sell" stop order at $40 per share. If the price declines to $40, the order will be executed as a market order.

Similarly, a "buy" stop order can be used to minimize the loss from a short sale. If a stock was sold sort at $50 per share, a buy stop order could be placed at $55 to cover the short in the event the stock went up instead of going down.

TYPES OF ACCOUNTS

Cash and margin accounts are the two basic types of brokerage accounts that are used to trade securities. Cash management accounts, that combine all of the customer's assets into one master account, are becoming increasingly popular. Such accounts also may have checking accounts and debit cards as part of the package. Special accounts may be required to deal in commodities.

The rules concerning the cash and margin accounts discussed below are those of the New York Stock Exchange[19] and the National Association of Securities Dealers. The illustrations do not cover the full extent of their rules. For simplicity, the discussion that follows is limited to stocks. Different rules may apply when dealing in other types of securities and commodities.

Cash accounts

No credit is extended with a cash account. The customer pays in full for the purchase of securities on or before the settlement date. The **settlement date** is the date on which payment for securities bought or delivery of securities sold is due. The settlement date for stocks, bonds, municipal securities, mutual funds traded through a broker, and limited partnerships that trade on an exchange is three business days after the trade date. This is commonly referred to as $T+3$ trade settlement. Federal government securities and options settle one business day after the trade date. Business days do not include Saturdays, Sundays, or holidays. Thus, a stock bought on Monday of a normal business week would settle on Thursday of that week. Most brokers will not make payment of the funds realized from the sale of securities before the settlement date. Equally important, they may charge interest or fees for late payment.

Finally, customers must pay for the securities they buy on or before the three-day settlement date before they sell them. Buying and selling securities before payment is called **freeriding**. Freeriding is against the rules of the Federal Reserve Board. Brokers are required to freeze the accounts of freeriders for 90 days. Customers can still trade in that account provided that they fully pay for purchased securities on the transaction date.

Customers can take delivery of stock certificates or bonds that they purchased, or they can ask the broker to keep the securities for them in **street-name ownership**. The company registers the brokerage firm as the shareholder. However, the brokerage firm has records showing the customer is the **beneficial owner** – one who does not have title to the property but has the rights of ownership. The broker holding the stock has a fiduciary responsibility to the customer. More will be said about this in the next chapter.

The advantages of keeping securities in street-name are that it is safe, and readily available for sale. Margin accounts are required to keep the securities in street-name. The disadvantages are that some brokers charge an inactivity fee, and if you want to sell the securities through a different broker, it may take several weeks to transfer them. In addition, some brokers only pass along dividends and interest payments to investors on a weekly, biweekly, or monthly basis. Finally, since your name is not on the books of the company, you may not receive certain corporate communications.

Customers who take delivery of the stock certificate can have it registered in their individual name, or joint tenants if there are two or more names. For example, a husband and wife may have the stock registered in both of their names followed by the phrase *joint tenants with rights of survivorship and not as tenants in common* or as *tenants by the entireties.* If one spouse dies, the stock goes to the other. Two business partners might register the stock as *joint tenants with rights of survivorship as tenants in common* so that each is entitled to his or her share upon death of the other. Get proper counseling before registering the stock.

Margin accounts

Customers use margin accounts to buy securities on credit extended by their brokers and banks. When a customer opens a margin account, he or she signs an agreement promising to observe the regulations of the Federal Reserve Board, the stock exchange, and the firm. To open a margin account, most firms require either $2,000 or more in equity, or 100% of the purchase price, whichever is less. They also require the customer to give them the right to borrow their securities. More will be said about this in connection with short sales.

The Federal Reserve Regulation T governs **margin requirements** extended by brokers. The "initial margin" requirement to buy stocks is 50%. This means that the customer must deposit 50% of the value of the stocks purchased with the broker, and the broker will lend the other 50% to the customer, and charge interest on the amount loaned. The initial margin deposit may be paid in cash, or by using other securities for collateral. For example, suppose that a customer wants to buy stock costing $10,000. The customer may deposit $5,000 with the broker, or $10,000 in collateral securities.

Because stocks can decline in value, the Federal Reserve has established minimum "maintenance margin" requirements. The dollar amount of the minimum maintenance margin must be at least equal to:

1. 25% of the market value of all securities held in the account (**long** means stocks held in the account);

2. $2.50 per share or 100% of the current market value, whichever is greater, for each stock short in the account selling at less than $5 per share (**short** refers to stocks that have been sold);

3. $5.00 per share or 30% of the current market value, whichever amount is greater, of each stock short in the account selling at $5 or more.

Many brokerage firms have a 30–40% maintenance margin requirement. If a customer's account is below the initial or the firm's maintenance margin minimums, the broker may ask the customer for additional cash or securities to make up the deficiency. The request for additional margin is known as a **margin call**. Regular margin customers must comply within a specified number of days (e.g. 15 days). Day-traders are given less time (e.g. 7 days) to comply. However, brokers are not *required* to issue a margin call, and they can sell securities without notification to meet the maintenance margin.

Some firms do not make clear some of the risks involved in margin trading. These risks include:[20]

- The customer may lose more funds than he/she deposits in the margin account if the securities decline in value. In addition, interest must be paid on the borrowed funds.

- A customer may be required to put up more funds (a margin call) if the securities in the account decline in value.

- Under some circumstances, the firm has the right to sell securities in the margin account without contacting the customer.

Margin

When a customer buys stock on margin, the amount owed the brokerage firm is called the **debit balance**. The debit balance also includes the broker's interest charges and cash withdrawals made by the customer. The **credit balance** is the amount of money that the broker owes the customer. Credit balances arise when cash is deposited in the account, dividends or interest payments are received on securities that are held, and when securities are sold. The **equity** (E) in an account is the difference between the market value (V) of the securities being held as collateral less the debit balance (D):

$$\text{Equity } (E) = \text{Market value of collateral } (V) - \text{Debit balance } (D) \qquad (3.1)$$

As previously noted, the minimum equity value is $2,000 or more.

The margin for stock that is being held (long) in the account is equity divided by the value of the collateral:

$$\text{Margin} = E/V = \frac{\text{Market value of collateral } (V) - \text{Debit balance } (D)}{\text{Market value of collateral } (V)} \qquad (3.2)$$

By way of illustration, assume that a customer bought 100 shares of stock at $60 per share, and that the initial margin requirement is 50%. The customer deposits $3,000 and borrows the remainder from the broker. For simplicity, commissions and taxes are excluded from the calculations. The margin in this example is 50%.

$$\text{Margin} = \frac{6{,}000\ (V) - 3{,}000\ (D)}{6{,}000\ (V)} = 50\%$$

What happens if the stock appreciates to $90 per share? Now the value of the collateral is $9,000. The debit balance of $3,000 remains the same. Thus, the margin is now:

$$\text{Margin} = \frac{9{,}000\ (V) - 3{,}000\ (D)}{9{,}000\ (V)} = 66.67\%$$

At this point, the customer can withdraw in cash up to 50% of the unrealized paper profit. This is possible because the initial margin requirement is 50%. The dollar amount that can be withdrawn is known as the "excess." In this example, the excess is $1,500. If the initial margin requirement had been 80%, then 20% of the excess amount could have been withdrawn.

Buying power

Alternatively, the customer could buy additional securities without depositing any more funds. The dollar amount of securities that can be bought is known as **buying power**. Buying power is determined by multiplying the excess by 100% divided by the initial margin requirement. Using the dollar amounts from the previous example, the excess is $1,500, the initial margin requirement is 50%, and the buying power will be $3,000.

$$\text{Buying power} = \frac{\text{Excess} \times 100\%}{\text{Initial margin requirement}}$$

$$= \frac{1{,}500 \times 100\%}{50\%} = \$3{,}000. \tag{3.3}$$

Minimum margin requirement

When the margin in the account falls below the Federal Reserve's maintenance margin or the firm's lower limit, the account is said to be a **restricted account**, and the customer cannot withdraw cash unless additional collateral securities are deposited. However, the customer can sell a security and buy another of equal value the same day without putting up additional funds. For example, suppose that the market value of the securities declined to $5,000. Then the margin in the account would be 40%, well below the 50% initial margin requirement.

$$\text{Margin} = \frac{5000\ (V) - 3000\ (D)}{5000\ (V)} = 40\%$$

As noted previously, the minimum margin requirement is 25%. The collateral value that will result in the 25% minimum margin may be determined by multiplying the debit balance (D) by $\frac{4}{3}$ or 1.3333. Based on the previous example, the debit balance is $3,000, and the minimum value of the collateral is $3,999.

$$\text{Minimum value of collateral} = \text{Debit balance}\ (D) \times 1.3333 \qquad (3.4)$$

$$\$3,999 = \$3000\ (D) \times 1.3333$$

$$\text{Margin} = \frac{3,999.90\ (V) - 3,000\ (D)}{3,999.90\ (V)} = 25\%$$

Accounts that are below 25% are **undermargined**. Before the margin falls that low, the broker usually will notify the customer with a margin call to deposit additional cash or securities. As noted previously, failure to comply can result in the forced sale of securities by the broker.

COMMON MISTAKES WHEN TRADING ONLINE

Trading stocks online may not be instantaneous. Sometimes there are delays because the Internet service provider (ISP) is slow; the broker may have inadequate hardware/software to deal with a huge inflow of orders; or the problem might be that the stocks are not quoted correctly (a decimal point was left off the stock price[21]); or for some other reason. In the US, for example, less than 1% fail to complete on schedule.[22] However, in Europe the failure rate is 20%. Because of such delays, some investors mistakenly assume their orders were not executed, and they submit them again. The end result is that they might have bought or sold twice as much stock as they intended to. Similarly, customers who want to cancel an order should first determine if the trade has been executed. You cannot cancel executed trades.

In a volatile market, stock prices can vary widely. To avoid paying too much or selling too low, investors should use limit orders that place a price limit on the security to be bought or sold. The alternative is to use market orders where securities are traded at the current market price.

INVESTOR INSIGHTS

CHAT ROOMS AND MESSAGE BOARDS: DON'T BELIEVE EVERYTHING YOU READ OR ARE TOLD BY STOCK-PICKERS

Some brokerage firms sponsor Internet chat rooms and bulletin boards for their customers or anyone else who wants to participate in these "forums." The opinions expressed in these forums are those of the participants, but they are not those of the sponsoring firms. While some of the messages on bulletin boards contain true information, many are bogus.

Yun Soo Oh Park IV, or "Tokyo Joe" as he was known, was a burrito vendor with the dream of becoming rich, and he did. He began by posting stock recommendations on message boards. Tokyo Joe had a flair for picking technology stocks, and he was willing to share that information with others – for a fee. However, he was not a registered investment advisor. The Securities and Exchange Commission (SEC) alleges that he and his company, Society Anonyme Corp., collected more than $1.1 million in fees from investors. Part of his profits came from the "pick of the day" stocks that he bought, and then sold at a profit when they were recommended to the paying investors who bid up the price. However, he did not tell them that he owned those stocks, or that he had placed orders to sell them, or that he was paid by one of the companies to recommend their stock. Moreover, he charged investors up to $200 per month for his stock picks and investment advice. The SEC alleges that he posted on his website false and misleading performance results in order to recruit new members for the Society Anonyme. The SEC brought fraud charges against Tokyo Joe, alleging that he manipulated stock prices and defrauded investors. They settled the case in 2001. Part of the settlement was that he was to repay $324,934 and received a fine of $429,696 for a total $750,000. In addition, he had to post a hyperlink on his website for 30 days to the SEC settlement. Tokyo Joe neither admitted nor denied wrongdoing. The bottom line is: *don't believe everything that you read or are told by stock-pickers.*

Matthew Bowen recruited investors over the Internet to buy stock in his company, Interactive Products and Services. He raised $190,000 from 150 investors. Instead of using the funds for the company, he used them for his personal profit. Matthew was convicted of 54 felony counts and was sentenced to 10 years in jail.

Sources: Aaron Elstein, " 'Tokyo Joe' Reaches a Deal With the SEC in Fraud Case," *Wall Street Journal*, February 7, 2001, C1, C17; "SEC Sues Internet Stock Picker 'Tokyo Joe' for Securities Fraud," Securities and Exchange Commission, January 5, 2000, www.sec.gov/news/tokyojoe.htm; "Tokyo Joe Settles," *CNNmoney*, March 8, 2001, CNNmoney.com (visited 3/8/01); "Internet Fraud: How to Avoid Internet Investment Scams," Securities and Exchange Commission, October 1998, www.sec.gov/consumer/cyberfr.htm.

Securities Investor Protection Corporation (SIPC)

The SIPC is a nonprofit membership corporation funded by member securities brokers and dealers who are registered with the SEC.[23] The SIPC protects the customers of its member firms. Some firms are excluded from membership in the SIPC. These include brokers and dealers who deal exclusively in mutual funds, the sale of variable annuities, the business of insurance, or whose principal business is outside the US and its territories.

If a SIPC member firm goes bankrupt, customers' securities that are registered with the SEC and cash are protected up to $500,000, including a $100,000 limit in cash. Many limited partnerships that invest in real estate and oil, as well as commodity contracts and options, are not registered with the SEC, and they are not covered by the SIPC.

After the firm is liquidated, customers with additional claims may receive additional funds on a prorate basis with other creditors. The SIPC does not protect investors from trading losses.

Privacy

A survey by American Express covering 10 countries found that 79% of financial service company clients considered privacy and security major issues in dealing online.[24] The SEC has rules for financial institutions under their jurisdiction (brokers, dealers, investment companies, and investment advisers registered with the SEC) concerning the safeguards and protection of customer records.[25] Because e-mail transmissions sent through the Internet are not secure, many brokers use some form of encryption technology. Confidential information should not be sent by e-mail. All brokers require the use of passwords to access accounts. Nevertheless, there is a risk that the passwords may be appropriated by a third party.

Under the SEC "Privacy of Consumer Financial Information (Regulation S-P)" rules, financial institutions under their jurisdiction must provide customers the option to "opt out" of having their nonpublic personal information disclosed to nonaffiliated third parties.[26] Such information includes account balance information, whether the individual is or has been a customer, information collected through an Internet "cookie," information from applications, consumer reports, and so on.

The financial institutions must make the "opt out" option available to consumers at the time the relationship is established, and annually thereafter. Posting of such notices can be in writing or electronically if the consumer agrees.

Conclusion

In the beginning, investors talked to brokers who provided investment advice and executed orders. Then came the Internet and online brokerage accounts where no human contact was necessary to execute orders. As a result of competition between firms for online business, commissions for trades were driven down. One consequence of this was that the brokerage firms turned to offering more personal services, such as local offices and talking to their customers. Personal services generate more income than just ordinary stock transactions. Consider the following advertisements that appeared in the *Wall Street Journal*. UBS Paine Webber Inc. stated "Why the most valuable conversation you could have today is with your UBS Paine Webber Financial Advisor."[27] Merrill Lynch explained how a financial advisor helped a customer develop a customized plan to deal with her retirement account.[28] And Credit Suisse/First Boston (CSFB) advertised how their 28,000 employees and their research "empowered change."[29]

The end result is that investors have a wider variety of choices of the brokerage services available to them, online and with or without contact with brokers. The services presented in this chapter covered the types of orders (market, limit, long, short, etc.) and the types of accounts (cash and margin) that are available. Finally, the SIPC and privacy issues were discussed.

SELF-TEST QUESTIONS

1. What services do brokerage firms offer? To answer that question, check the websites for several brokerage firms of your own choosing, or the following: Charles Schwab (www.schwab.com), Merrill Lynch (www.ml.com), Credit Suisse/First Boston (www.csfb.com), UBS Paine Webber (www.ubspainewebber.com).
2. How much does it cost to trade 100 shares of stock @ $50 per share at these firms?
3. What is the minimum dollar amount required to open a margin account at these firms?
4. How much is a "wrap account" at these firms?
5. What do these firms have to say about "privacy"?
6. What brokerage services do banks offer? To answer this question, check the websites for several banks of your own choosing, or the following: Citibank (www.citibank.com), Bank of America (www.bankofamerica.com), AmSouth Bank (www.amsouth.com).
7. How can you settle a dispute that you may have with your broker?
8. Suppose that you bought $10,000-worth of stock on margin, and you put up $5,000. If the stock price increases 25%, what is your percentage gain? The SEC website (www.sec.gov) has interactive tools, including a margin calculator, that will help answer this question.
9. What do the SEC (www.sec.gov), NASD (www.nasd.com), and NYSE (www.nyse.com) have to say about investors' complaints?
10. What types of investment are covered by SIPC insurance? To answer this question, see www.sipc.org.

NOTES

1 US Securities and Exchange Commission, "Examinations of Broker-Dealers Offering Online Trading: Summary of Findings and Recommendations," January 25, 2001; "Testimony of Arthur Levitt, Chairman of the SEC, before the Senate Permanent Subcommittee on Investigations, Committee on Governmental Affairs, Concerning Day Trading," September 16, 1999. See www.sec.gov/new/testimony/tsty2199.htm (visited 12/27/99).

2 "Online-Broker Sector Could Consolidate as Some Firms' Stock Prices Stay Weak," *Wall Street Journal*, February 13, 2001, C1, C4.

3 Visited 2/16/01. The listing of firms is not complete.

4 See www.etrade.com.

5 The information on day trading firms draws on "Testimony of Arthur Levitt, Chairman of the SEC, before the Senate Permanent Subcommittee on Investigations Committee on Governmental Affairs, Concerning Day Trading," September 16, 1999. See www.sec.gov/new/testimony/tsty2199.htm (visited 12/27/99).

6 The Philadelphia Stock Exchange requires persons associated with member firms to take the Series 7 Exam to qualify them as general securities representatives.

7 "Report of the Day Trading Project Group, Findings and Recommendations," Washington, DC, North American Securities Administrators Association, August 9, 1999.

8 "Going for Brokers," Online Finance Survey, *The Economist*, May 20, 2000, 9.

9 Arthur Levitt, "Common Sense Investing in the 21st Century Marketplace," US Securities and Exchange Commission, November 20, 1999. See www.sec.gov/news/speeches/spch324.htm (visited 12/20/99).

10 www.ameritrade.com; special offer sent by mail to the author, January 2001.

11 *The Schwab Investor*, February 2000.

12 Arthur Levitt, "Best Execution: Promise of Integrity, Guardian of Competition," US Securities and Exchange Commission, November 4, 1999. See www.sec.gov/news/speeches/spch315.htm (visited 12/20/99).

13 "Report on the Comparison of Order Executions Across Equity Market Structures," Securities and Exchange Commission, January 8, 2001. See www.sec.gov/rules/othern/ordxmkt.htm.

14 Laura S. Unger, "On-Line Brokerage: Keeping Apace of Cyberspace," US Securities and Exchange Commission, November 22, 1999. See www.sec.gov/news/studies/cybexsum.htm (visited 11/23/99).

15 "Dramatic Rise in Volume of Investor Requests for Help," SEC News Desk. See www.sec.gov/consumer/jdatacom.htm (visited 2/13/01).

16 For more about what the NASD Dispute Resolution does, see www.nasd.com. For NYSE dispute resolution, see www.nyse.com.

17 Robert Kowalski, "NASD Plan Would Let Investors Take Brokerages to Court Over Unpaid Arbitration Awards," *TheStreet.com*, www.thestreet.com, February 6, 2001 (visited 2/9/01). US General Accounting Office, "Securities Arbitration: Actions needed to Address Problem of Unpaid Awards," GAO/GGD-00-115, June 15, 2000.

18 See NASD Rule 3350.

19   For detail on NYSE rules, see *New York Stock Exchange, Inc., Constitution and Rules*, September 1999 (Chicago, IL: Commerce Clearing House, Inc., 1999).

20   US Securities and Exchange Commission, "Examinations of Broker-Dealers Offering Online Trading: Summary of Findings and Recommendations," January 25, 2001.

21   Comstock, a service of Standard & Poor's that provides stock quotes to brokers, investors, news services, and so on, left the decimal points out of their stock quotes. "Glitch Hits Online Trade," *CNNmoney*, February 5, 2001 (CNNmoney.com, visited 2/5/01).

22   Jeffrey E. Garten, "Global Stock Trading Needs Fixing – and Fast," *BusinessWeek*, January 29, 2001.

23   For additional details see www.sipc.org.

24   Ben Vickers, "Europe Lags Behind U.S. on Web Privacy," *Wall Street Journal*, February 20, 2001, B11.

25   Regulation S-P, Securities Exchange Act Release No. 42974 (June 22, 2000), 65FR 40333; also see the Gramm-Leach-Bliley Act of 1999, Public Law 106-102, Section 501.

26   See 12 CFR 40, Privacy of Consumer Financial Information; 17 CFR 248, SEC Privacy of Consumer Financial Information (Regulation S-P).

27   *Wall Street Journal*, June 19, 2001, A5.

28   *Wall Street Journal*, June 19, 2001, A9.

29   *Wall Street Journal*, June 19, 2001, A11.

PART TWO

Types of Securities

4. Stocks   65
5. Debt Securities   81
6. Investment Companies and Mutual Funds   96

4 Stocks

Key Concepts

American Depository Receipts (ADRs)
Ask (price)
Beneficial share owner
Bid (price)
Blue-chip
Book-entry ownership
Business corporation
Common stock
Date declared (dividend)
Date of record (dividend)
Date payable (dividend)
Decimalization
Depository Trust and Clearing Corporation (DTCC)
Direct ownership
Dividend dates (declared, record, and ex-dividend)
Dividend reinvestment plans (DRIPs)
Dividends (cash and stock)
Dividend valuation model
Dividend yield
Dow Jones Composite Average
Dow Jones Industrial Average (DJIA)
Dow Jones Public Utility Average
Dow Jones Transportation Average
Ex-dividend date
Guilder shares
Indirect ownership
Intrinsic value

Joint stock company
Limited liability
Liquidity
Marketable
Nasdaq Composite Index
New York Stock Exchange Composite Index
Ownership of stock (direct and indirect)
Participating preferreds
Par value
Preemptive rights
Preferred stock
Proxy
Residual claimant
Rights (stock)
SEC Reg FD
Settlement date
Spread (price)
Standard & Poor's Stock Price Indexes
Stock split
Street-name (stock)
Tracking stock
Unlimited liability
Warrants (stock)

A Brief History of Stocks

The first shares of stock were issued in London in 1553 by the Muscovy Company, a joint stock company that was established to trade with Russia.[1] A **joint stock company** is an unincorporated form of business organization where the ownership is represented by shares of stock that are transferable. The shareholders of these companies have unlimited liability. **Unlimited liability** means that the shareholders are financially responsible for the debts of the organization. If a joint stock company is unable to pay its debts, creditors look to the shareholders to satisfy their claims. Because of this risk, few investors would buy stocks. Those that did buy them had to closely monitor the firm in order to protect their investments. The monitoring was costly and inconvenient, which did not add to the appeal for buying stocks. Consequently, they were not suitable for many potential investors.

In addition to unlimited liability, the early shareholders of joint stock companies faced two other types of risk. First, the prices of their shares could decline. That risk is still with us today. Second, their shares were marketable, but not liquid. In terms of securities, **marketable** means that shares of stock can be sold, but it may take a long time to do so, and **liquidity** means that a security can quickly be sold or converted into cash with little or no loss from current value. In other words, the early joint stock shareholders held shares that were difficult to sell because there were no organized securities markets at that time. That is no longer the case today because there are organized stock markets throughout the world.

It was not until 1811 that a limited liability law was enacted in New York, and it was soon followed in the other states. Today, **limited liability** means that the shareholders of a business corporation are not financially responsible for the debts of the firm that they own. A public **business corporation** is a legal entity formed for the purpose of transacting business for profit.[2] The extent of a shareholder's loss in a business corporation is limited to the cost of their shares. Therefore, most investors are passive or they take a less active role in monitoring the firm. The limited liability opened the door for firms to raise large sums from both equity and debt investors.

One disadvantage of being a publicly held company is the SEC requirement to disclose financial data and other information on a periodic basis to shareholders, analysts, and competitors. In addition **SEC Reg FD**, which stands for Regulation Fair Disclosure, requires that companies disclosing material nonpublic information must disseminate it broadly so that all market participants can take advantage of the information instead of a few insiders.[3] Most, but not all, companies comply with regulations. Enron, the seventh largest company in the US, and the largest ever bankruptcy when it failed in 2001, did not comply with Reg FD or other rules.

It is the combination of limited liability of corporations and active capital markets that provide liquidity and make stocks an attractive investment. In 1995, an estimated 69.3 million investors owned stocks directly, or indirectly through mutual funds and retirement plans.[4] About one-quarter of the shareholders were under the age of 35, and about 86% had incomes of less than $100,000. Most had a high school degree and half had completed college. However, there is a direct relationship between stock ownership and wealth. The higher the income level, the more likely it is that the individual will own stocks.[5]

TYPES OF STOCKS

Common stock

Ownership Common stock represents ownership in a corporation. But what does ownership mean? It means that common stockholders have the right to *vote* on important issues such as electing the board of directors and mergers. The board of directors, in turn, establishes general operating policies for the company and selects the management that runs it; they determine the payment of dividends, and they deal with other corporate issues. Stockholders also vote on appointing the independent auditors, compensation for executive officers, and other issues.

Stockholders can vote by attending the corporation's annual meeting. However, most vote using the proxy statements that they receive in the mail from the companies or their broker. A **proxy** is a legal designation of another person, such as the company directors, to vote the shares that you own. Some companies allow voting by phone and the Internet.

Most stockholders have little interest in actively participating in corporate governance, and they vote for the directors' recommendations. Other stockholders are activists, and if they don't like the performance of the company, they may try to vote out management or make other changes. For example, individual shareholders of The Coca-Cola Company introduced proposals concerning genetic engineering, recycling of soft drink containers, and a proposal on stock options for the 2001 annual meeting. Some institutional investors, such as TIAA-CREFF and CALPERS, take an activist role on behalf of all stockholders.

INVESTOR INSIGHTS

PRIMARY RESPONSIBILITIES OF THE BOARD OF DIRECTORS

The "Notice of the McDonald's Corporation 2001 Annual Shareholders' Meeting and Proxy Statement" listed the primary responsibilities of their board of directors.

- "Evaluating the performance of the Company and its executive management;

- "Reviewing and, where appropriate, approving fundamental operating, financial and other corporate strategies, as well as major plans and objectives;

- "Providing advice to the Chief Executive Officer and executive management;

- "Overseeing management to ensure that the Company's assets are safeguarded and business is conducted in compliance with laws and regulations; and

- "Evaluating the overall effectiveness of the Board, as well as selecting and recommending to the shareholders an appropriate slate of candidates for election to the Board."

Par value All stocks are issued with a par value, no-par value, or some nominal value. One purpose of the **par value** is to determine the proportionate share of ownership that each share represents. The total par value represents the amount of capital subscribed by the stockholders. Taxes are another factor affecting par value. Some states charge excise taxes and franchise fees based on the par value. Such laws encourage firms to issue stocks with low par values.

Dividends Dividends are the only return that stockholders receive from the company until they sell their stock. **Dividends** can be paid in cash, stock, property, or some combination of the three.

The board of directors decides the dividend policy based on the financial needs of the firm and the expectations of stockholders. In general terms, firms that are growing rapidly and require funds to support that growth pay little or no cash dividends. As their growth rate slows the firm may begin to pay cash dividends. Mature firms pay up to 65% of their after-tax profits as cash dividends.[6] The average **dividend yield** (cash dividend/stock price) of the Standard & Poor's composite index over the 1927–99 period was 5.19%.[7] However, in December 2001 it was only 1.36%.

Expected cash dividends are an important determinant of value. One method for determining the intrinsic value of stock prices is the dividend valuation model. The **intrinsic value** is the theoretical value of the stock, and it may differ from the market price. The theory behind the **dividend valuation model** is that the price of a stock today is equal to the present value of expected cash dividends. A simplified version of this model is used here to demonstrate some of the factors affecting stock prices. These factors include the *dollar amount*, and *growth rate* of cash dividends, as well as the *rate of return required by investors*. This simplified model does not apply if a company does not pay cash dividends. Nevertheless, it provides great insights about stock prices. Accordingly, the model states that the stock price today (P_0) is determined by dividing the cash dividend that is expected to be paid in time period 1 (D_1) by the rate of return required by equity investors (k), less the growth rate of cash dividends (g).

$$P_0 = \frac{D_1}{k-g} \qquad\qquad (4.1)$$

where

P_0 = current price (at time 0)
D_1 = cash dividend in time period 1
k = the rate of return required by equity investors
g = growth rate of cash dividends

By way of illustration, suppose that MedTech is expected to pay a $2 cash dividend; dividends are expected to increase 5% per year; and investors require a 10% rate of return. The theoretical value of the stock is $40 per share.

$$P_0 = \frac{2}{0.10-0.05} = \$40$$

If the profit outlook for the company improves, and the growth rate of dividends is expected to increase to 8%, the theoretical value of the stock will be $100 per share.

$$P_0 = \frac{2}{0.10-0.08} = \$100$$

More will be said about the dividend valuation model and other valuation models in Chapter 9.

Stock **dividends** and **stock splits** represent additional shares given to the share-holders. Stock dividends are usually expressed as a percentage, such as 10%, while stock splits are expressed as 2-for-1 or 3-for-1. By way of illustration, suppose that you hold 100 shares of stock priced at $10/share (i.e. therefore worth 100 shares × $10/share = $1,000) and the company declares a 10% stock dividend. If nothing else changes, you now hold 110 shares of stock worth $1,000, but now the value of each share is $9.091 ($1,000/110). Similarly, if the company announced a 2-for-1 split, you would hold 200 shares worth $5 each. Thus, stock dividends and splits *per se* do not affect the total value of the shares. However, they are a signal to investors about the future performance of the company which may affect share prices.

Three dates are important in connection with dividends. The **date declared** is the date on which the board of directors declares that the company is going to pay a dividend in the future. At the same time, they announce the **date of record**. Only those stockholders who are recorded on the transfer agent's books on the date of record are entitled to receive the dividend. It takes several days from the time people buy stock until their name is recorded on the transfer agent's books. So a date has to be established to let buyers know whether they are entitled to receive the dividend. That date is called the **ex-dividend date**, and on the NYSE it is usually the second business day preceding the record date.[8] Investors who buy stock before the ex-dividend date are entitled to receive cash dividends. Those buying stock on or after the ex-dividend date are not entitled to receive dividends. The date on which the dividend is paid is called the **date payable**.

Risk Common stock is the riskiest form of ownership. Common stockholders are called the **residual claimants** because they are entitled to what remains of earnings and assets after all prior claims have been satisfied. They may receive cash dividends if the firm is profitable, or they may lose their entire investment if the firm goes bankrupt. Nevertheless, common stock also offers the greatest opportunities for rewards in the form of dividends and share price appreciation. From 1926–99, the average return was 13.3% on large company stocks and 17.6% on small company stocks.[9] In contrast the average returns on long-term corporate and government bonds were 5.9% and 5.5% respectively. However, returns on stocks are more volatile than those on bonds. The standard deviations of annual returns were 20.2% for large company stocks and 33.6% for small company stocks. In contrast, the standard deviations were 8.7% for corporate bonds and 9.3% for the government bonds. These numbers suggest that high returns are associated with high risk. The sharp price declines in dot.com and tech stocks in 2000 and 2001 is one illustration of high risk.

Tracking stock

Selected companies have issued special classes of stock that may have different stockholder rights. Such stocks are called **tracking stocks** – which are also known as lettered stocks (i.e. Class B stock) – to "track" the performance of a high-growth business unit within the firm. General Motors created the first tracking stock in 1984 in connection with the acquisition of Electronic Data Systems (EDS). GM issued GM-E stock to track that division's performance. Tracking stocks also have been issued by AT&T, Disney, Pittston Co., and Sprint to name a few. Holders of tracking stocks may or may not have voting rights or claims to any assets.

The tracking stocks discussed here should not be confused with mutual funds (index funds) that use the term "tracking stock" in their names, such as the "Nasdaq-100 Index Tracking Stock." Mutual funds are explained in Chapter 6.

Preferred stocks

Preferred stockholders have a "preference" over common stockholders. The preference is that they generally have a fixed cash dividend, such as $5 per share, which must be paid before common stockholders receive any cash dividends. In addition, preferred stockholders have a priority over common stockholders if the company has to be liquidated.

Because most preferred stock dividends are fixed, preferred stockholders generally do not benefit from increased corporate earnings to the same extent as common stockholders. Those preferred stocks with increasing dividends are called **participating preferreds**. Some preferred stocks are convertible into common stocks, or they may be "called" (redeemed) by the issuing corporation.

Rights and warrants

When a corporation sells additional shares of common stock to the public, it may give its existing stockholders **preemptive rights** that permit them to buy additional shares of stock in order to maintain their proportionate share of ownership. Thus, a **right** is an option to buy stock at a specified price for a short period of time, usually 90 days or less. **Warrants** are options to buy the stock at a specified price for a longer period of time. Many warrants have a life of 5 or 10 years, and some are perpetual.

DIRECT AND INDIRECT OWNERSHIP

The stockholders of a company are the owners, but there is a difference between direct and indirect ownership. In **direct ownership**, the stockholder's name is registered on the books of the issuing corporation. In addition, the stockholder receives a stock certificate that is issued in his or her name reflecting the ownership. Dividend payments are sent to the stockholder, and some companies permit the dividend payments to be used to buy additional shares through dividend reinvestment plans, which will be explained shortly. Annual reports, proxy statements, and other corporate information are sent directly to the registered owner. When the stock is sold, the owner must deliver the stock certificate to the broker within *three business days* after the trade. This is called the **settlement date**. Traders refer to it as T+3, or trade date plus 3 business days. The investment community is working toward T+1, where trades will settle the next business day. Some firms do not execute trades until they receive the certificates in advance.

Indirect ownership occurs when customers have a security interest in an account at a brokerage firm. The customers may be required to hold stock in the broker's name if they buy stocks on borrowed funds (margin), or they may elect to do so for convenience. Holding stock in the broker's name is usually called holding stock in **street-name** or **book-entry ownership**. The stock is actually held in a broker's account at the **Depository Trust and Clearing Corporation (DTCC)**. The DTCC is a financial institution headquartered in New York City. It is a depository and clearinghouse for the settlement of securities trading of stocks and bonds in the US.[10] When stock is held in street-name, the customer is the **beneficial share owner**, while the stock is registered in the name of the broker or its designee. The broker has a fiduciary responsibility to pass on dividends. In addition, the broker also may forward annual reports, proxy statements, and other corporate information. Some brokers can send shareholder documents to their customers electronically via the Internet, thereby saving paper, time, and postage. Brokers may charge a fee for handling dividend reinvestment plans. Brokers inform customers about the status of their stocks and accounts through monthly or quarterly statements, and online customers can access their accounts at any time.

Holding stock in street-name facilitates trading because the stock is already on account, and the stock certificates do not have to be delivered to the broker. Also, dividends and interest paid on debt securities held can be swept into interest-bearing accounts. Finally, the stock certificates cannot get lost or stolen. The major disadvantage of holding stock in street-name is that it may take several weeks to move the stock to another brokerage firm, and the customer may not receive all of the communications from the company.

STOCK PRICES AND DECIMALIZATION

Decimalization is the process of converting from fractions to decimals the prices of all listed stocks and their associated options. Historically, stock prices in the US were quoted in dollar amounts and fractions thereof (e.g. 60\frac{5}{16}$). The use of fractions in stock prices dates back to the 1700s, when the Spanish silver coin, the *real*, was widely used as currency because it could be cut into fractional pieces.[11] With decimalization, stock prices are quoted in dollars and cents (e.g. $60.31).

One reason for the change in pricing is that most foreign stock exchanges use decimals. The problem was that the smallest price change for foreign stocks traded on US stock exchanges, such as Royal Dutch Petroleum, was $\frac{1}{16}$ or \$0.0625, whereas the smallest increment for the same stock traded in foreign markets that used decimals was less. The difference resulted in price disparities between various markets. The SEC also believed that decimal pricing would make it easier for investors to understand prices, reduce transaction costs, and facilitate globalization of our markets.[12] Accordingly, the SEC ordered the change in pricing. The conversion process to the decimal system on stock exchanges and Nasdaq began in 2000.

One consequence of decimalization is that **spreads** (differences between the bid and asked prices) are narrower, with some increments as small as 1 cent. The **bid** is the highest price that a buyer is willing to pay, and the **ask** is the lowest price that a seller is willing to accept. With fractions, a professional trader could profit from a small fractional change of $\frac{1}{16}$ in stock prices. With decimalization, the potential profit shrank to 1 cent.

AMERICAN DEPOSITORY RECEIPTS

American Depository Receipts (ADRs) are negotiable receipts of a domestic bank representing title to a specified number of non-US shares held in safekeeping in the firm's home country. Banks, such as Bank of New York and Citibank, register the securities with the SEC and get paid a fee for their services, which include distributing the foreign firm's dividends (less foreign taxes) to the holders of the ADRs. The advantages of ADRs are that they are traded like stocks in the US, thereby eliminating the problems of dealing with foreign securities. These problems include lack of liquidity, delays in delivery and settlement with a US custodian, different transactions costs, foreign currency risks, and others. The disadvantage is that holders of ADRs may not have the same rights as ordinary stockholders. For example, the holders of ADRs may have different rights regarding the sponsoring of corporate resolutions or voting.[13] Many ADRs are actively traded. These firms include Sony (Japan), BP Amoco (UK), De Beers Consolidated Mines (South Africa), and others.

Some foreign stocks that are not ADRs are traded in the US. Shares of Daimler/Chrysler common stock are traded on the NYSE, and on 20 other foreign stock exchanges.[14] They are the first true global equity shares that trade in whatever currency the stock exchange chooses. KLM Royal Dutch Airlines and Shell Transport and Trading are two more examples of foreign stocks that do not use ADRs. Dutch regulations do not permit their companies to issue ADRs. Instead, they issue shares registered in New York (called **guilder shares**), and then cancel an equivalent amount of home-country shares.

INVESTOR INSIGHTS

INVESTING IN FOREIGN STOCKS

BP Amoco, Nokia, Sony, and Volvo are foreign companies whose products are widely used in the US. The stocks and bonds of these and other foreign companies are actively traded in US stock markets. During the 1994–2000 period, trading of non-US stocks accounted for 8–12% of the volume of shares traded on the New York Stock Exchange. In 1999, 394 non-US companies were listed on the NYSE. Many US investors acquired foreign stocks though mergers that involve stock swaps. Most of the mergers involved European and Japanese companies.

The prices of selected foreign stocks can be found on CNNMoney (CNNmoney.com). First click on "Markets and Stocks" and then on "ADRs." The Bank of New York provides a complete listing of ADRs as well as other information about them. See www.bankofny.com/adr.

Sources: NYSE Fact Book 1999, www.nyse.com; *Treasury Bulletin*, December 2000, 91–8.

DIVIDEND REINVESTMENT PLANS (DRIPs) AND DIRECT STOCK PURCHASE PLANS

Some companies have dividend reinvestment plans (DRIPs) that allow direct registration with the company. Such plans allow investors to avoid paying commissions or fees to a broker, and the securities are registered with the issuing company.[15] In addition, the company can provide stock certificates that can be sold through any broker.

There are disadvantages to such plans as well. The price at which you buy the stock is based on the average price of the stock over a period of time. That period could be a day, week, or month depending on the company. And the price paid to buy the stock determines the number of shares that can be bought by reinvesting the dividends. Thus, the investor has no control over the price of the amount of stock they buy. Finally, keeping track of what is bought and when it was bought for tax purposes is cumbersome.

Some companies permit investors to buy stock directly from them rather than going through a stockbroker. For example, McDonald's Corporation offers *MCDirect Shares*, a direct stock purchase plan that provides investors with a convenient way to buy their stock and reinvest dividends.[16] The Coca-Cola Company has a

Dividend and Cash Investment Plan that allows existing investors to buy up to $125,000 per year of their stock.

"What's the Market Doing?"

Is the stock market up or down today? To answer that question most investors refer to major stock market averages and indexes, and we shall do the same. There are dozens of stock market averages and indexes that are used in the various stock markets throughout the world. Nevertheless, we will focus primarily on the Dow Jones Averages, Nasdaq, and the Standard & Poor's Stock Price Indexes that are widely used in the US, and mention several of the leading foreign indexes. Current domestic and world stock market averages, as well as explanations of what the market is doing, are available on a variety of websites. For example, see CNNmoney.com, www.bloomberg.com, and finance.yahoo.com. Additional sites where such information is available are listed in the "Directory of Websites" at the back of this book.

Dow Jones Stock Averages

Charles Henry Dow – co-founder of the Dow Jones, which publishes the *Wall Street Journal* – began publishing his average of representative stocks in 1884 in the *Customer's Afternoon Letter*. The *Afternoon Letter* ultimately became part of the *Wall Street Journal*, which began publication in 1889. Today there are four Dow Jones Averages: the 30 stocks Dow Jones Industrial Average, the 20 stocks Transportation Average, the 15 stocks Utilities Average, and the 65 stocks Composite Average.

The **Dow Jones Industrial Average (DJIA)** is the best known of the various Dow Jones stock averages. The DJIA was first published in 1896, and it included 12 industrial stocks. General Electric is the only one of the original industrial stocks still listed in the average. The number of stocks in the DJIA was gradually increased to 30, and it represents the large blue-chip stocks. **Blue-chip** refers to successful companies that have a reputation for quality goods, services, and financial stability. Today the DJIA is no longer limited to industrial stocks. As shown in Box 4.1, the DJIA includes some of the largest and best-known companies in the US. The companies used in the DJIA are subject to change. While representing blue-chips is a strength of this average, it is also a weakness because it does not represent a large number of medium and relatively small companies that are actively traded. No average is perfect.

The **Dow Jones Transportation Average** originally consisted of 20 railroad stocks and was referred to as the "Rail Average." Over time, the companies in it changed to

Box 4.1   DJIA stocks (February 2002)

AT&T	ExxonMobil	J.P. Morgan Chase
Alcoa	General Electric	McDonald's
American Express	General Motors	Merck
Boeing	Hewlett Packard	Microsoft
Caterpillar	Home Depot	Minnesota Mining and
Citigroup	Honeywell	Manufacturing
Coca-Cola	IBM	Philip Morris
Disney	Intel	Procter & Gamble
DuPont	International Paper	SBC Communications
Eastman Kodak	Johnson & Johnson	United Technologies
		Walmart

Source: *Wall Street Journal*. Companies in the DJIA are published daily.

include airlines, freight forwarders, companies engaged in mixed modes of trans-portation, as well as railroads. Similarly, the **Dow Jones Public Utility Average** expanded to include selected companies involved in energy, such as the Williams Company, which is best known for its pipelines. The **Dow Jones Composite Average** combines the industrial, transportation, and utility averages. Thus, the composition of stock indexes changes over time to reflect changes in the areas they attempt to track.

   The Dow averages have significance beyond their function as indicators of stock market prices. First, they are the oldest averages. Second, they are published by the *Wall Street Journal* – this is the most widely read financial newspaper and more space is given to the Dow averages than to the others. Third, they are widely used by stock market analysts who chart stock prices. Finally, the DJIA includes some of the largest companies in the world, and to paraphrase an old saying: what happens to General Motors affects the rest of the market.

Nasdaq

The **Nasdaq Composite® Index** includes more than 5,000 stocks that are traded in the Nasdaq Stock Market, the world's first electronic-based stock market. This average includes firms of all sizes and industries. Nevertheless, the Nasdaq Composite is con-sidered "tech heavy" because of the weighting given to very large hi-tech companies.

New York Stock Exchange Indexes

The **New York Stock Exchange Composite Index** covers all of the stocks listed on the New York Stock Exchange. At the end of 1999, there were 3,025 domestic and non-US companies listed on the NYSE. In addition to the Composite Index, there are also indexes representing industrial, transportation, utility, and finance stocks.

Standard & Poor's Stock Price Indexes

In 1923, Standard & Poor's Corporation published a stock price index that was based on 233 stocks and it included 26 subgroup indexes. In 1957, the coverage was expanded to include 500 stocks broken down into 95 subgroups. The four main groups that are the industrials, rails utilities, and the 500-stock composite – commonly called the Standard & Poor's 500 Stock Index, or the S&P 500. The S&P 500 represents the largest 500 publicly traded companies, and it represents a wide variety of industries.

Stock price performance

As shown in Table 4.1, stock prices measured by the various indexes have increased sharply over the years – some more than others depending on the composition of stocks that they measure. The tech-heavy Nasdaq performed best over the 1990–2000 period. Stated otherwise, the stock market rewarded the growth stocks more than other sectors of the market.

Table 4.1 also shows some of the short-term volatility of stock prices. From July 2000 to April 7, 2001, the Nasdaq average declined from 4,018 to 1,720, a 57% decline. The S&P 500 declined 23%, while the other measures also declined, but not as sharply. Collectively, these figures reveal that the stock market consists of different groups of stocks represented by the various averages that exhibit widely different financial behavior.

Foreign stock markets

Many investors are familiar with stock markets in Frankfurt, Hong Kong, London, Paris, and Tokyo. These are only a few of the many overseas markets that were introduced in Chapter 2. The New York Stock Exchange web page has links to securities and commodity markets throughout the world.[17] It lists 26 markets in Asia, 62 markets in Europe, and many others in Africa, the Caribbean, North America, Pacific, and South America. International stock indexes and links for some of these markets are reported by online services, such as CNNmoney (CNNmoney.com), Bloomberg.com (www.bloomberg.com), Yahoo! Finance (http://finance.yahoo.com), and the *Financial Times* – FT.com (www.ft.com).

Table 4.1   Selected stock price indexes

Index	1990	2000	July 2000	Change 1990–2000	Change July 2000–April 7, 2001
DJIA 30 stocks	2,634	10,795	9,698	310%	−11%
Nasdaq Composite (1971=100) 5000+ stocks	374	3,784	1,720	912%	−57%
NYSE Composite (Dec. 31, 1965=50) 3,500+ stocks	181	645	582	256%	−9%
S&P 500 (1941–1942=10) 500 stocks	330	1,427	1,127	332%	−23%

Sources: *Economic Indicators* (Washington, DC: Council of Economic Advisers/US Government Printing Office, March 2001), 31; *Statistical Abstract of the United States: 1999* (Washington, DC: US Census Bureau, 1999), table 840.

The *Financial Times* and BBC Online (www.bbc.co.uk) provide analysis of these markets from the UK perspective.

CONCLUSION

Eighty million or more investors own stocks directly, or through mutual funds and retirement plans. This chapter was mostly about common stocks that represent ownership of a company. Similarly, US investors can buy ADRs in foreign companies.

The major benefits of ownership are expected capital gains and dividends. And stock prices reflect the expectation of future dividends. Because of the importance of dividends, many companies offer dividend reinvestment plans (DRIPs).

Most investors who are active in the stock market keep their stock in street-name because it facilitates trading. Others use direct ownership.

Stock market performance is measured by a variety of averages and indexes. This chapter examined the Dow Jones averages, as well as the Nasdaq, and Standard & Poor's Indexes. Several sources for foreign stock market averages also were mentioned.

SELF-TEST QUESTIONS

1. What are the US stock markets doing today? To answer this question, refer to CNNmoney (CNNmoney.com), Bloomberg.com (www.bloomberg.com), and Yahoo! finance (http://finance.yahoo.com).
2. What are stocks doing in Asia? To answer this question, use the sources cited previously as well as the *Financial Times* – FT.com (www.ft.com).
3. What are the stock markets in Europe doing today? Use the same web resources to answer this question.
4. What are the major news events affecting US stock prices? Use the same web resources to answer this question.
5. Try to put these news events in the context of the dividend valuation model. How do these events affect future dividends, the growth rate of dividends, or the rate of return required by investors?
6. List ten foreign companies that have ADRs (see www.bankofny.com/adr).
7. Select any five companies in the Dow Jones Industrial Average (Box 4.1) to determine if they have DRIPs or direct stock purchase plans. Go to the EquiServe website (www.equiserve.com) and click on "Investment Plans" for an alphabetical listing of companies.
8. Compute the dividend yield for these stocks.
9. What industries have been the best performers recently? To answer this question, go to Big Charts (www.bigcharts.com) and click on "Industries."
10. What is the significance of the ex-dividend date?

NOTES

1 "The Key to Industrial Capitalism: Limited Liability," *The Economist*, December 31, 1999, 89.
2 The definition is based on that found in *Black's Law Dictionary*, 5th edn (St. Paul, MN: West Publishing, 1979). The term business corporation is used here to distinguish it from other types of corporations: civil, closely held, joint venture, not-for-profit, and so on.
3 See SEC Final Rule: Selective Disclosure and Insider Trading, 17 CFR Parts 240, 243, and 249 (www.sec.gov/rules/final/33-7881.htm).
4 These figures are the results of a 1998 share ownership study reported in the *NYSE Fact Book, 1999* (New York: New York Stock Exchange, 1999), 55 (www.nyse.com).
5 Edward N. Wolff, "The Rich Get Richer . . . and Why the Poor Don't," *The American Prospect*, February 12, 2001.
6 Dividends as a percent of corporate after-tax profits ranged from 65% in 1990 to 58% in 1998, as reported in the *Statistical Abstract of the United States: 1999* (Washington, DC: US Census Bureau, 1999).
7 Ravi Jagannathan, Ellen R. McGrattan, and Anna Scherbina, "The Declining U.S. Equity Premium," Federal Reserve Bank of Minneapolis, *Quarterly Review*, Fall 2000, 3–19.
8 NYSE Rule 235.

9   Data are from *Stocks, Bonds, Bills, and Inflation, 2000 Yearbook* (Chicago, IL: Ibbotson Associates, 2001).

10 For more information about the DTCC, see www.dtcc.com.

11 Carol Vinzant, "Wall Street Takes Another Look at Decimals," *WashingtonPost.com*, February 13, 2001, E01.

12 "SEC Orders Securities Markets to Begin Trading Decimals on July 3, 2000," Securities and Exchange Commission, news release 2000-8, www.sec.gov (visited 1/28/00).

13 Craig Karmin, "ADR Holders Find They Have Unequal Rights," *Wall Street Journal*, March 1, 2001, C1, C15.

14 For additional details see www.daimlerchrysler.com.

15 "About Settling Trades in Three Days: Introducing T+3," US Securities and Exchange Commission, www.sec.gov/consumer/plus3.htm (visited 2/13/01).

16 For additional details, see www.mcdonalds.com/corporate/investor. Many companies use EquiServe, a division of First Chicago Trust Company, to handle shareholder services, including investment plans and dividend reinvestment plans for more than 1700 companies. See www.equiserve.com, and click on "Investment Plans."

17 See www.nyse.com. Click on "International," then on "Global Markets."

5 Debt Securities

Key Concepts

Accrued interest
Asset-backed securities (ABS)
Bankers' acceptances
Bond
Bond equivalent yield
Call-protection clause
Century bond
Certificates of deposit (CDs)
Collateralized mortgage obligations (CMOs)
Collateral trust bond
Commercial paper
Conversion price
Conversion rate
Conversion value
Convertible bond
Coupon rate
Credit rating
Current yield
Debenture
Default risk
Discount (price)
EE bonds (savings bonds)
Eurodollar CDs (Euro CDs)
Face amount
Federal agency securities
Federal Deposit Insurance Corporation (FDIC)
Federal Financing Bank
First mortgage bond

General mortgage bond
General obligation (GO) (municipal) bond
Government-sponsored enterprises (GSEs)
HH bonds (savings bonds)
I bonds (savings bonds)
Interest-only (IO) securities
Interest rate risk
Investment grade (credit rating)
Junk bonds
Liquidity
Municipal bonds
Note (debt security)
Par value
Premium (price)
Principal amount
Principal-only (PO) securities
Repurchase agreements (repos)
Revenue (municipal) bond
Securitization
Separate trading of registered interest and principal securities (STRIPS)
Tax-equivalent yield
Tranches
Treasury bills
Treasury bonds
Treasury inflation protected securities (TIPS)
Treasury notes
Yield to call
Yield to maturity
Zero coupon bonds

This chapter examines debt securities. Debt securities arise because organizations borrow funds to finance their activities. Business concerns borrow to finance plant, equipment, and for other purposes. Governments borrow to finance day-to-day activities, roads, schools, and so on.

Dealing with debt securities is complex because there are many different types of debt instruments, different maturities, thousands of issuers who range from companies to domestic and foreign governments, and other differences. Four categories of debt securities markets are examined in this chapter: (1) corporate debt, (2) federal government and agency securities, (3) state and local government securities, and (4) bank debt securities. Non-US government debt securities are not considered here.

CORPORATE DEBT
Short-term money market instruments

Corporations, including financial institutions, may try to match the maturities of their assets to the maturities of the debts used to fund them. Thus, firms may finance short-term assets, such as accounts receivable, by issuing short-term unsecured promissory notes called **commercial paper**. Similarly, banks issue **bankers' acceptances** in connection with international trade finance. They also sell large negotiable **certificates of deposit (CDs)** of $100,000 or more to fund their lending activity. Large dollar-denominated CDs issued by banks outside the US are called **Eurodollar CDs** or **Euro CDs**. **Repurchase agreements (repos)** are agreements between financial institutions to sell and then buy back securities at predetermined prices. These large-denomination securities are bought by financial institutions, including brokerage firms, that may sell them in smaller parcels to individual investors.

Intermediate-term notes

A **note** is an intermediate-term debt security that may have a maturity of 1 to 10 years, but that is up to the issuer. The main difference between a note and a bond is the maturity. Bonds are long-term debt.

Basic features of long-term debt

A **bond** is a long-term credit instrument that promises to pay principal and interest on predetermined dates. Most corporate bonds have a maturity of 15 to 20 years. However, Coca-Cola, Walt Disney, and others have issued bonds with a maturity of 100 years. Such long-term bonds are called **century bonds**.

Corporate bonds are usually issued in multiples of $1,000 or $5,000 principal amounts. The **principal (face) amount** is also called the **par value**. Bonds usually pay interest twice per year. The interest rate is sometimes referred to as the **coupon rate** because investors used to have to cut coupons off the bonds in order to collect the interest from the paying agent.

When investors buy interest-bearing bonds, they must pay the current price plus **accrued interest**, the interest earned since the last interest payment or date of issue. If the last interest payment was June 1, and the bond was bought for delivery on July 15, the accrued interest would be determined for 1 month and 14 days. The investor will regain the interest paid to the seller when the next interest payment is made.

Zero coupon bonds pay no interest. Instead, they are sold at a discounted price, and they pay the par value at maturity. The price of a zero coupon bond is determined by discounting the present value of the face amount ($1,000) of the bond by the investor's required rate of return. Because there are no intervening interest payments, only one calculation is necessary to determine the price. For example, a company wants to issue a 10-year, $1,000 zero coupon bond at 8%. The current price and present value of that bond is $463. The bond will appreciate to $1,000 at maturity.

$$PV = FV/(1 + i)^n \qquad (5.1)$$

where

PV = present value
FV = future value
i = interest rate
n = number of periods

$$PV = 1,000/(1+0.08)^{10} = \$463$$

Yields

Three types of yields are discussed here: current yield, yield to maturity, and yield to call.

Current yield The **current yield** is the interest payment (sometime called the **coupon rate**) divided by the current market price of the bond. By way of illustration, consider an 8% bond with 15 years to maturity. This bond pays $80 interest per year ($40 twice per year) on each $1,000 of par value. If the bond is selling at par, the current yield is 8%.

$$\text{Current yield} = \frac{C}{P_0} = \frac{\$80}{\$1,000} = 8\% \qquad (5.2)$$

where

C = annual income ($) from the bond
P_0 = current market price of the bond

Interest rates paid on bonds are determined at the time of issue. Because market rates of interest change continuously, the market price of outstanding bonds adjust to reflect these changes. The price change of outstanding bonds due to changes in market rates of interest is called **interest rate risk**. If market rates of interest increase after the bond is issued, the market price of the bond will decline. The lower price increases the current yield. For example, suppose that market rates of interest increased, and the market price of the bond declined to $950. Now the current yield on the bond is 8.42% ($80/$950 = 8.42%). Conversely, if market rates of interest decline after the bond is issued, the market price of the bond will increase.

Stated otherwise, *market rates of interest and the market prices of outstanding bonds are inversely related.* If the prices of outstanding bonds sell below par, the bond is said to be selling at a **discount**. If it is selling above par, it is selling at a **premium**.

Yield to maturity If the bond is held to maturity in 15 years, the market price of the bond will advance from $950 to the $1,000 par value. When the bond matures, the bondholder will receive the $1,000 par value and the $50 difference between the purchase price and the par value. In this case, the yield to maturity (YTM) is greater than the current yield. The YTM can be *approximated* by equation 5.3.

$$\text{Yield to maturity} = \frac{C + [(F - P_0)/n]}{(F + P_0)/2} \tag{5.3}$$

where

C = annual income ($) from the bond
F = par value payable at maturity
P_0 = current market price of the bond
n = number of years to maturity

Substituting in the equation, we get:

$$\text{Yield to maturity} = \frac{\$80 + [(\$1,000 - \$950)/15]}{(\$1,000 + \$950)/2} = 8.55\%$$

The yield to maturity is the average percentage earned annually from the purchase date to the maturity date, and it includes both capital gains or losses. The *exact* yield to maturity can be determined by solving the following equation for r. Alternatively, the YTM can be found by using financial calculators, spreadsheets, or bond value tables.[1]

$$P_0 = \sum_{t=1}^{n} \frac{C/m}{(1 + r/m)^{mn}} + \frac{F}{(1 + r/m)^{mn}} \tag{5.4}$$

where

P_0 = current price of the bond
C = annual income ($) from the bond
r = yield to maturity (%)
m = number of interest payments per year, usually twice per year
F = face value of the bond payable at maturity
$\sum$ = summation over time period of n years

The exact yield to maturity (r) of the bond in the example is 0.086 or 8.6%.

$$P_0 = \sum_{t=1}^{30} \frac{\$80/2}{(1 + 0.086/2)^{30}} + \frac{\$1,000}{(1 + 0.086/2)^{30}} = 0.086$$

Yield to call Corporations may reserve the right to call in their bond issues in whole or in part when market rates of interest decline, to eliminate unfavorable contractual provisions in the bond, to force conversion of bonds that are convertible into stock, and for other reasons. Many callable bonds have a **call-protection clause** that prohibits the company from calling newly issued bonds for 5 years or longer. Such clauses require the company to pay a premium over the par value if the bond is called. The size of the premium is larger in the earlier years, and it diminishes as the bond matures. By way of illustration, consider an 8% bond selling at $950, and it is callable in 3 years at $1,120. The approximate yield to the call date may be computed by the following equation.

$$\text{Yield to call} = \frac{C + [(F_c - P_0)/n]}{(F_c + P_0)/2} \tag{5.5}$$

where

C = annual income ($) from the bond
F_c = dollar amount payable to the bondholder when the bond is called
P_0 = current market price of the bond
n = number of years to call date

The yield to call is 13.2%. Note that the yield to call is higher than the yield to maturity (YTM = 8.55%) because of the call premium ($120) and the short maturity to the call date (3 years).

$$\text{Yield to call} = \frac{\$80 + [(\$1120 - \$950)/3]}{(\$1120 + \$950)/2} = 13.2\%$$

Bond prices

Bond prices are expressed as a percentage of their par value. A price of 90 means that a $1,000 par value bond is worth $900, and 110 means that it is worth $1,100.

The prices of corporate bonds traded on the New York Stock Exchange may include fractions ($\frac{1}{2}, \frac{3}{4}, \frac{7}{8}$) to represent fractional bond prices. A $1,000 par value bond selling at $98\frac{3}{8}$ is worth $980.3750. Treasury bonds, notes, and bills use 32nds to represent fractional prices. A price of 101.01 means $101\frac{1}{32}$ % of the par value. If the par value is $10,000, the price of the bond is $10,100.0313.

Bond prices quoted elsewhere may use decimal pricing. Under this system, a quote of 97.163 means that a $1,000 par value bond is worth $971.63.

Convertible bonds

Some bonds are convertible into shares of common stock. **Convertible bonds** provide investors with the interest income and safety of a bond, and the growth opportunities of common stock.

The **conversion price** is the dollar amount of par value of the bond that is exchangeable for one share of common stock. Recall that most bonds have a par value of $1,000. Therefore, a conversion price of $50 per share is equivalent to a **conversion rate** of 20. Each bond can be converted into 20 shares of stock.

$$\text{Conversion rate} = \text{Par value of bond}/\text{Conversion price} \qquad (5.6)$$
$$20 = \$1,000/\$50$$

The **conversion value** is the current market value of the shares into which the security can be converted. Suppose that a $1,000 par value bond has a conversion rate of 40, and the stock into which it is convertible is selling at $35 per share. The conversion value of this bond is $1,400 ($40 \times \$35 = \$1,400$).

$$\text{Conversion value} = \text{Conversion rate} \times \text{Current stock price} \qquad (5.7)$$

The conversion value is the theoretical value of the bond. The actual market price can be at a premium of (above) or a discount of (below) the theoretical value. The concepts presented here with respect to convertible bonds also apply to convertible preferred stock.

Collateral

Corporate bonds can be classified on the basis of the security or collateral behind them. Bonds that are secured by liens against real estate are known as mortgage bonds. Those secured by the first mortgage on real estate are called **first mortgage bonds**. Similarly, second mortgage bonds are secured by a second mortgage. Because most lenders don't like the idea of holding a third or fourth mortgage, bonds backed by such collateral are called **general mortgage bonds**. Bonds that are backed by stocks and bonds owned by the issuing corporation are known as **collateral trust bonds**. Bonds that are backed by the general credit of the issuing corporation and have no specific liens against particular assets are called **debentures**. For the most part, debentures are issued by companies with high credit ratings. A debenture from a financially sound corporation is a safer investment than a mortgage bond from a financially weak corporation. A company's financial strength can be gauged by its credit rating.

Credit ratings

Bond **credit ratings** are determined by Moody's Investor Service and Standard & Poor's Corporation (S&P) credit rating agencies, and are listed in Table 5.1. Credit ratings by two other agencies, Duff and Phelps, and Fitch, are similar to those shown

Table 5.1 Corporate bond credit ratings

Rating	Moody's	S&P
Investment grade		
Highest quality	Aaa	AAA
High quality	Aa	AA
Upper medium quality	A	A
Medium	Baa	BBB
Junk bonds		
Speculative elements	Ba	BB
Speculative	B	B
Default possible	Caa	CCC
Highly speculative, default possible	Ca	CC
Lowest rated class of bonds	C	C

in the table. The credit ratings are based on the creditworthiness of the borrower, the type of bond, collateral, and other factors. **Investment grade** bonds are suitable for bank investments and meet the minimum standards as legal investments for trust companies and other fiduciaries. Aaa/AAA is the highest credit rating indicating the least default risk. Medium grade bonds have a Baa/BBB rating. **Junk bonds** are those with a Ba/BB or lower rating, and they are speculative in quality. Bond investors require higher returns on riskier bonds than on bonds with low default risk. If a bond with an Aaa rating yields 5.8%, one with a Baa rating might yield 6.6%.

INVESTOR INSIGHTS

CREDIT RATINGS AND BOND VALUES

Visit Moody's (www.moodys.com) and Standard & Poor's (www.standardpoor.com) to learn more about how they rate bonds, stocks, and other financial obligations. Also visit Bonds Online (www.bondsonline.com) for information about bond markets and bond prices.

GOVERNMENT SECURITIES

Treasury

The US government finances the differences between its receipts and expenses by selling Treasury bills, notes, and bonds. The minimum denomination of the marketable securities is $1,000 or multiples of $1,000. The US government also sells savings bonds that are not marketable. Savings bonds have denominations that range from $25 to $10,000.

Treasury bills Treasury bills have a maturity of 1 year or less. They are sold at a discount, and investors receive the face value when they mature. The computation of the discount is based on the actual number of days and 360 days per year. Because yields on most bonds are calculated on a 365-day basis, we must compute the bond equivalent yield on Treasury bills, and we use the following symbols.

A = days to maturity or days held
B = discount basis (%)
C = full discount per $100 maturity value
P = purchase price
S = dollar value when sold
Y = annualized bond equivalent return

The equation for the discount and the purchase price is:

$$C = (A/360) \times B$$
$$P = \$100 - C \tag{5.8}$$

By way of illustration, find the discount price for a Treasury bill due in 90 days on a 10% basis.

$C = (90/360) \times 10\% = 2.5\%$ (or 2.5% of $100 = $2.50)
$P = \$100 - C = \$100 - \$2.50$
  $= \$97.50$ (the dollar price on a 10% discount basis)

Because Treasury bills are traded on a 360-day basis, we must compute the **bond equivalent yield** which converts the yield to a 365-day basis to make it comparable to other debt securities.

$$Y = C/P \times 365/A \times 100$$
$$= \$2.50/\$97.50 \times 365/90 \times 100 = 10.40\% \tag{5.9}$$

These examples are important because they illustrate how the bond equivalent yield can differ from the yield on a discount basis. In other words, the yields on Treasury bills are slightly higher when compared to bonds.

Treasury notes and bonds Treasury notes and bonds are coupon issues. Notes have an original maturity of 10 years or less, and bond maturities range up to 30 years. In 2001, the Treasury announced that it would no longer issue 30-year bonds.

Investing in marketable Treasury securities has three major advantages. First, they are risk-free with respect to **default risk**. Default risk is when the borrower fails to pay principal or interest on its debt, or fails to meet other financial obligations. Treasury securities are backed by the full faith and credit of the United States.

Nevertheless, they are still subject to **interest rate risk** – interest rates go up and the prices of debt securities decline. The second major advantage of marketable Treasury securities is their **liquidity**. They can be sold on short-notice at their current market price. The third advantage is that they are exempt from state and local taxes.

Savings bonds The Treasury sells a variety of nonmarketable savings bonds to the public. They can be purchased and redeemed though Federal Reserve Banks and paying agents, which are mostly commercial banks and thrifts. In addition, Treasury savings bonds as well as bills, notes, and bonds can be purchased and managed online from the Treasury Bureau of Public Debt.[2]

Series **EE bonds** are issued at 50% of their face value in denominations that range from $50 to $10,000. A $50 EE bond costs $25 to buy. It can earn interest for up to 30 years. However, these savings bonds can be redeemed after 5 years with no interest rate penalty. The interest rate is calculated as 90% of the 6-month averages of 5-year Treasury securities yields. Series EE and I bonds generally increase in value as the interest compounds semiannually, and the interest is paid when the securities are redeemed. Series **I bonds** are issued at face value, and they earn a fixed rate of return and a semiannual inflation rate adjustment. Series **HH bonds** are current income securities that pay interest every 6 months. Series HH bonds are issued in denominations that range from $500 to $10,000, but you can't buy them for cash; you can only exchange them for Series EE/E bonds and savings notes. The Series HH bonds pay a fixed rate of interest and some issues can earn interest for up to 30 years.

INVESTOR INSIGHTS

WANT A TIP? WANT A TIP ABOUT STRIPPING?

The Bureau of Public Debt website provides information about buying savings bonds, Treasury bills, notes, and bonds. Some bonds pay interest while the principal remains at a constant, while others are sold at a discount and they appreciate over time to the principal amount. **TIPS** are **Treasury inflation protected securities** where the interest rate is adjusted over time to reflect the rate of inflation. TIPS include Series I savings bonds as well as marketable inflation-indexed notes and bonds. The website also contains a savings bond calculator, and answers to questions such as what happens if you hold savings bonds beyond final maturity.

STRIPS is the acronym for **separate trading of registered interest and principal securities**. Investors can buy stripped notes and bonds (e.g. individual interest and principal components of the securities) through financial institutions, and government securities brokers and dealers.

For more information about various types of government debt issues, see www.publicdebt.treas.gov and www.savingsbonds.gov.

Federal agency securities

Federal agencies are divided into two groups – government-owned institutions and government-sponsored enterprises. Government-owned institutions include the Defense Department, Export-Import Bank, Federal Housing Administration, Government National Mortgage Association (Ginnie Mae), Postal Service, Tennessee Valley Authority, the United States Railway Association, and others. These institutions obtain some or all of their funding through the **Federal Financing Bank**, which sells securities on their behalf. The Federal Financing Bank is part of the US Treasury.

Government-sponsored enterprises (GSEs) are privately owned corporations that receive some direction and oversight from the federal government.[3] They were created by Congress to provide funds to certain sectors of the economy, such as agriculture, real estate, and student loans. The GSEs include the Federal Home Loan Banks, Federal Home Loan Mortgage Corporation (Freddie Mac), Federal National Mortgage Association (Fannie Mae), Farm Credit Banks, Farm Credit Financial Assistance Corporation, Student Loan Marketing Association (Sallie Mae), and the Resolution Funding Corporation (REFCO).

Like other privately owned companies, GSEs sell securities to raise capital. Because they are privately owned, their securities are not explicitly guaranteed by the US government. Fannie Mae, for example, does have emergency borrowing powers from the Treasury.

Interest earned on Ginnie Mae, Fannie Mae, and Freddie Mac is taxable income. Interest earned on other Federal agency bonds is exempt from state and local taxes.

The debt securities include notes, bonds, and debentures as well as collateralized mortgage obligations. **Collateralized mortgage obligations (CMOs)** are pools of mortgage loans that have been securitized and divided into multiple maturity classes, called **tranches**, each with different risk characteristics. **Securitization** is the packaging of loans (e.g. mortgages) and then issuing marketable securities (e.g. CMOs) backed by those loans. The principal risk of CMOs is the prepayment of mortgage loans. This risk is similar to that of corporate bonds being "called," in that it deprives the investor of future earnings from that security.

Some securities dealers strip mortgage-backed securities into **interest-only (IO)** or **principal-only (PO)** securities. Holders of PO securities only receive the principal payments when the loans are repaid. Holders of IO securities only receive the interest payments. If the loans are prepaid, the interest payments stop. Thus, IOs from distant tranches are riskier than POs.

Asset-backed securities

Asset-backed securities (ABS) are certificates representing pools of assets, such as auto loans, credit card receivables, and mortgage loans. The interest and principal amounts are passed on to investors. CMOs are one type of asset-backed security.

Although most of the ABS investors are institutions, some brokerage firms sell parts of these securities to individual investors. ABS are not for unsophisticated investors who do not understand the risks associated with them.[4]

MUNICIPAL BONDS

The Municipal Securities Rulemaking Board (MSRB) was established by Congress as a self-regulatory organization (SRO) to regulate the municipal securities activities of banks and securities firms. According to the MSRB, "There are more than 80,000 governmental units that may issue municipal securities. These issuers include not only states and local governments, but also many 'authorities' that are created to carry out special functions and to issue municipal debt. These issuers have outstanding approximately 1.4 million different municipal securities ranging from simple non-callable general obligation debt to conduit financings involving complicated credit structures and multiple call features. Characteristics such as these distinguish municipal securities from US treasuries and corporate bonds, in which far fewer types of securities are issued and the securities have more standardized features."[5]

Tax exemption

One important difference between municipal bonds and other securities is that the interest earned on certain municipal bonds is exempt from federal income taxes, and in some cases from state income taxes. An investor's income tax rate determines the extent to which tax-exempt interest income is beneficial. Suppose that an investor is in the 30% federal income tax bracket and buys a 6% tax-exempt bond. The **tax-equivalent yield** on this bond, determined by equation (5.10), is 8.57%.

$$\text{Tax-equivalent yield} = \text{Tax-exempt yield}/(1 - \text{tax rate})$$
$$= 0.06/(1 - 0.30) = 8.57\% \quad\quad (5.10)$$

Those in high income tax brackets benefit more from the tax-exempt income than those in lower income tax brackets. Had the investor been in the 15% income tax bracket, the tax-equivalent yield would be 7.06%.

Types of municipal debt

General obligation bonds and revenue bonds are the two principal types of municipal bonds. **General obligation (GO) bonds** are usually backed by the full faith, credit, and taxing power of the issuer. Simply stated, they are payable from tax revenues. In contrast, **revenue bonds** are payable from some specific source of revenue other than the taxing power of the issuer. The revenues come from utilities (e.g. water, sewer, electric), housing (e.g. single family, multi-family), transportation (e.g. airport revenue, toll road), industrial (e.g. industrial developments, pollution control), or other sources.

Municipalities also issue special types of bonds (e.g. lease rental, taxable) and notes (e.g. tax anticipation notes, bond anticipation notes), and many other types of special-purpose securities.

Bank Debt Securities

Banks and savings institutions issue various types of debt securities with varying degrees of risk. Certificates of deposit (CDs), money market accounts, and savings accounts are the most common forms of bank debt. The **Federal Deposit Insurance Corporation (FDIC)** insures *deposits* up to $100,000 at federally insured banks and savings institutions if those institutions should fail. However, not all banks and savings institutions are covered by FDIC insurance.

In some cases depositors can have more than $100,000 in a bank and still be insured, if the accounts are structured properly. For example, you can have a $100,000 CD at a bank where you have $100,000 in an *individual retirement account* (IRA) and be fully insured for $200,000 by the FDIC because IRAs are insured separately from nonretirement accounts at the same bank.

Although most CDs of less than $100,000 are FDIC insured, they are not necessarily risk-free. Some CDs are callable, which means that they are exposed to interest rate risk. Suppose that you bought a 10-year CD that paid 10% interest and it is callable. If at some time in the future interest rates decline to 6%, the bank may call the CD and pay the face amount at that time. And you can reinvest those funds at the lower interest rate.

The FDIC does not insure all debt securities issued by banks. For example, Bank of America InterNotes[sm] are unsecured debt instruments issued by the Bank of America Corporation, and are not insured by the FDIC.

Investor Insights

FDIC Deposit Insurance Coverage

If you want to know more about FDIC insurance coverage, contact the FDIC, and meet EDIE. The Electronic Deposit Insurance Estimator (EDIE) is an interactive Internet site provided by the FDIC to help bankers and consumers determine if their deposits are within the $100,000 insurance limit. EDIE is accessed through http://www.fdic.gov. In addition, you can obtain a copy of the FDIC's *Your Insured Deposit* from insured banks and savings associations.

CONCLUSION

Debt securities markets are divided into four categories in this chapter: (1) corporate debt, (2) federal government and agency securities, (3) state and local government securities, and (4) bank debt securities. Most of the focus in this chapter was on bonds, which are long-term debt instruments that promise to pay principal and interest on predetermined dates, except for zero coupon bonds. Investors buy bonds for their yields, capital gains, and to convert them when that option is available. Various ways to compute bond yields were shown in the chapter.

Bonds are generally considered safer than stocks, but they are still subject to default risk and interest rate risk. Credit rating agencies provide ratings based on the creditworthiness of the issuer and other factors. The highest investment grade bonds have lower yields, and less risk than junk bonds. US government bonds are considered risk-free with respect to default risk. GSE debt securities (ABS, CMOs) are not risk-free because they are not guaranteed by the US government. Many municipal bonds have the added benefit of providing tax-exempt income.

The FDIC insures bank deposits in member banks and savings institutions up to $100,000, and in some cases for more. However, the FDIC does not insure all debt securities issued by banks. Although most CDs bought by individual investors are risk-free, some callable CDs have interest rate risk.

SELF-TEST QUESTIONS

1. What interest rates are banks paying on CDs in your market area? To answer this question, go to Bankrate.com (www.bankrate.com), and then click on "CDs/savings". Then select your state, city, and the 1-year maturity.
2. Compare the rates on CDs to those paid on Treasury securities. How do you explain the differences? Rates on Treasury securities can be found at Bloomberg.com (www.bloomberg.com) and click on "U.S. Treasuries."
3. Compare the rates on 5-year Treasury, municipal, and corporate bonds. How do you explain the differences? See Bondsonline.com (www.bondsonline.com) and then click on "Composite Bond Yields."
4. What companies have had their credit ratings changed recently? Why were they changed? See Standard & Poor's (www.standardpoor.com) and then click on "Rating New" and "Corporate Finance." Also see Moody's (www.moodys.com) and click on "Rating Actions".
5. What state and local governments have had their ratings changed? See www.moodys.com and click on "U.S. Public Finance" and then "Rating Actions."
6. What interest rates are being paid on I, EE, and HH savings bonds? What differences are there between the savings bonds? See www.publicdebt.treas.gov.

Also see www.savingsbonds.gov, then click on "Treasury Securities at a Glance," and then under "Savings Bonds" for the individual security.

7. How can you buy Treasury bills, notes, and bonds online? See www.publicdebt.treas.gov, then click on "T-Bills, Notes and Bonds."

8. What are the risks of investing in POs and IOs?

9. Which provides the higher after-tax yield, a 6% corporate bond or a 6% GO bond? Why?

10. Is your bank insured? See the FDIC website, www.fdic.gov, and then click on "Is My Bank Insured?"

NOTES

1 The yield to maturity may be calculated as the internal rate of return (IRR) on financial calculators.

2 See www.publicdebt.treas.gov for further details on savings bonds and other Treasury securities.

3 The discussion of oversight of GSEs is beyond the scope of this book. Nevertheless, the Office of Federal Housing Enterprise Oversight (OFHEO) provides oversight for Fannie Mae and Freddie Mac.

4 To learn more about ABS, see Investing in Bonds.com (www.investinginbonds.com).

5 Municipal Securities Rulemaking Board, Alexandria, VA, *REPORTS*, vol. 21, no. 1, May 3, 2001. For further information about the MSRB, see www.msrb.org.

6 Investment Companies and Mutual Funds

Key Concepts

12b-1 fee
Back-end redemption fee
Capital appreciation funds
Closed-end investment company
Contingent deferred sales charge (CDSC)
Corporate bond funds
Diversification
Equity mutual funds
Exchange traded funds (ETFs)
Expense ratio
Family of funds
Fee table
Fund complex
Government bond funds
Hedge
Hedge funds
High-yield bond funds
Hybrid mutual funds
Index fund
Investment company
Load
Load fund
Management fees
Money market funds (taxable and tax-exempt)
Mutual fund
National municipal bond funds
Net asset value (NAV)
No-load fund

Open-end investment company
Prospectus
Real estate investment trust (REIT)
Redeem (shares)
Shareholder service fee
State municipal bond funds
Strategic income funds
Taxable bond funds
Tax-free mutual funds
Total return funds
Unit investment trust
World bond funds
World equity funds
Wrap account

About 93 million shareholders had invested their funds in more than 8,500 investment companies and mutual funds in 2001. Mutual fund assets grew from about $1 trillion in 1990 to almost $7 trillion in 2000. Several factors contributed to the increased use of mutual funds. First, the liberalization of regulations of individual retirement accounts (IRAs) in 1982 encouraged the use of third parties, such as mutual funds, to manage tax deferred retirement plan assets. Second, the record economic growth of the 1990s and rising stock prices attracted investors to the market. Finally, lower sales charges encouraged investors to buy them.

TYPES OF INVESTMENT COMPANIES

Investment companies are a special type of equity security. They are corporations or trusts that sell their own shares to investors, and then invest the proceeds in stocks, bonds, and other types of securities. Investment companies are regulated by the Securities and Exchange Commission in accordance with the Investment Company Act of 1940. The 1940 Act divides investment companies into three categories: management companies, unit investment trusts, and face-amount certificates. Management companies are further divided into **open-end** and **closed-end companies**.

Mutual funds

Open-end investment companies are called **mutual funds**. They are open-end because the mutual fund can sell new shares to investors, and **redeem** (buy back) those shares from investors who want to sell them back to the fund. The shares are bought back at the **net asset value (NAV)**. In some cases deferred sales charges

Table 6.1   Open-end mutual funds, year 2000

Type of fund	Assets ($ billions)	Number of funds
Equity	3,962.3	4,395
Bond	808.0	2,210
Hybrid	349.7	525
Money market (taxable)	1,607.2	704
Money market (tax-exempt)	238.1	337
Total	6,965.3	8,171

Source: *2001 Mutual Fund Fact Book.* Copyright © 2001 Investment Company Institute. Reprinted by permission of the Investment Company Institute (www.ici.org).

(back-end load) are deducted from the NAV. Net asset value is the fund's equity divided by the number of shares outstanding (market value of assets − liabilities = equity/number of shares outstanding). The number of shares changes daily depending on the number of purchases and redemptions. Most funds compute NAV at the end of the trading day.

A group of mutual funds managed by the same investment management company is called a **family of funds**.[1] Fidelity Investments and Dreyfus Funds are examples of a family of funds.[2] Some investment management companies hire "subadvisers" to manage some or all of their funds. Fidelity Investments, for example, hires Deutsche Bank Asset Management to manage its Fidelity Index Fund.[3] SEI Corporation has all of its assets managed by subadvisers. The subadvisers may provide expertise or other services that the investment company does not have.

Each fund within the family has different investment objectives. Shareholders can switch their money into the various funds within the family. Those families that charge for switching are called *load families* and those that do not charge are called *no-load families.*

Table 6.1 reveals the four major types of mutual funds, their asset size, and numbers.

1. Equity funds (also called stock funds) account for over half of both the total assets and the number of funds.

2. Bond funds are next in terms of number of funds, followed by hybrids.

3. Hybrid funds invest a combination of stocks, bonds, and other derivative securities.

4. Stock, bond, and hybrid funds are considered long-term funds. In contrast, money market funds are considered short-term funds because they invest in securities with maturities of 1 year or less. Collectively, taxable and tax-exempt money market funds are the second largest group in terms of assets, and third largest in terms of number of funds.

Box 6.1   Open-end mutual fund investment objectives

EQUITY FUNDS
Capital appreciation funds
   Aggressive growth funds invest mainly in stocks of small, growth companies.
   Growth funds focus on well established companies.
   Sector funds invest in companies in related fields.
Total return funds
   Growth-and-income funds invest primarily in stocks of established companies with a potential for growth and a record of dividend payments.
   Income-equity funds focus more in dividends than stocks for appreciation.
World equity funds
   Emerging market funds invest in companies based in developing countries.
   Global equity funds invest in equity securities traded worldwide.
   International equity funds invest in stocks of companies located outside the US.
   Regional equity funds invest in particular geographic areas.

HYBRID FUNDS
   Asset allocation funds invest in global stocks, bonds, derivatives, etc., seeking high returns by maintaining precise weightings of asset classes.
   Balance funds invest in stocks and bonds to conserve principal, provide income, and long-term growth.
   Flexible portfolio funds invest in a variety of securities to provide a high return.
   Income-mixed funds invest in a variety of income producing securities to provide a high level of current income without regard to capital appreciation.

TAXABLE BOND FUNDS
Corporate bond funds
   Corporate bond funds (general) invest two-thirds or more of the portfolio in US corporate bonds of various maturities.
   Corporate bond funds (intermediate-term) invest two-thirds or more of their portfolio in US corporate bonds with an average maturity of 10 years or less, seeking income.
   Corporate bond funds (short-term) invest two-thirds or more of their portfolios in US corporate bonds with an average maturity of 1 to 5 years, seeking income.
High-yield funds invest two-thirds or more of their portfolios in lower rated US corporate bonds (S&P BBB, Moody's Baa).
World bond funds invest in debt securities of foreign companies and governments.
   Global bond funds (general) invest in worldwide debt securities. They may invest up to 25% in the US.
   Global bond funds (short-term) invest in worldwide debt securities with an average maturity of 1 to 5 years. They may invest up to 25% in the US.
   Other world bond funds invest two-thirds of their debt securities portfolios outside the US.
Government bond funds invest in US government bonds, seeking high income.
   Government bond funds (general) invest two-thirds of their portfolios in US government securities with no stated average maturity.

Box 6.1 Continued

Government bond funds (intermediate term) have an average maturity of 5 to 10 years.
Government bond funds (short-term) have an average maturity of 1 to 5 years.
Mortgage-backed funds invest two-thirds or more of their portfolios in mortgage-backed securities.

Strategic income funds invest in US debt securities to provide a high level of current income.

TAX-FREE BOND FUNDS

State municipal bond funds invest primarily in bonds issued by a particular state, seeking high after-tax returns for residents of those states.

State municipal bond funds (general) invest in the bonds of a single state. The average maturities exceed 5 years. Income is largely exempt from federal and state taxes for residents of those states.
State municipal bond funds (short-term) invest in the bonds of a single state. The average maturity is 1 to 5 years. Income is largely exempt from federal and state taxes for residents of those states.

National municipal bond funds invest in tax-exempt bonds issued by various states.

National municipal bond funds (general) invest in municipal bonds with an average maturity of more than 5 years.
National municipal bond funds (short-term) invest in municipal bonds with an average maturity of 1 to 5 years.

MONEY MARKET FUNDS

Taxable money market funds invest in high-grade money market securities with an average maturity of 90 days or less, seeking income and capital preservation.

Taxable money market funds (government) invest primarily in US Treasury and agency securities.
Taxable money market funds (nongovernment) invest primarily in CDs, commercial paper, and bankers' acceptances.

Tax-exempt money market funds invest in short-term municipal securities with an average maturity of 90 days or less, seeking tax-exempt income and preservation of capital.

National tax-exempt money market funds invest primarily in short-term US municipal securities.
State tax-exempt money market funds invest primarily in short-term securities issues by a single state to offer tax-free income to residents of that state.

Source: *2001 Mutual Fund Fact Book*. Copyright © 2001 Investment Company Institute. Reprinted by permission of the Investment Company Institute (www.ici.org).

The Investment Company Institute (ICI), a national association of the American Investment Company Industry, classifies funds into 33 investment objective categories.[4] These investment objectives are listed in Box 6.1.

Hedge funds

Hedge funds are a special type of private investment pool that are limited to a small number (i.e. usually less than 500 persons) of wealthy, sophisticated individual and institutional investors.[5] They can do things that are not permitted for mutual funds, such as being highly leveraged, limiting withdrawals, providing managers with manager's compensation based on performance, and other differences.

The term "hedge" in their name is a misnomer. To **hedge** means to transfer risk to another party who is willing to take on that risk. However, most hedge funds take investment positions based on changing global macroeconomic conditions, undervalued securities, or in particular industries without hedging. Some, in fact, invest in other hedge funds. Hedge funds are not suitable for the average investor.

INVESTOR INSIGHTS

THE PROSPECTUS

A open-end mutual fund **prospectus** is a legal document required by the SEC that describes the fund or funds to prospective investors. It includes information about the fund's investment objectives, policies, performance, risk, fees, and services. The basic idea behind reading the prospectus is to look before you leap – financially. One potential "show stopper" for some funds is the minimum amount of investment required to invest in that fund, which may be $1,001 or more for some funds. About 40% of mutual funds require a minimum investment of $1,000 or more. Of that total, 14% require a minimum investment of $25,001 or more. The services might include, for example, check writing, and online and telephone exchange privileges. The fee table is also interesting to read because it explains how much of your funds are used to run the fund and its services. The more that goes to them, the less you receive! Caveat emptor.

Closed-end investment companies

Closed-end investment companies differ from mutual funds in several important respects. Nevertheless, most investors refer to them as mutual funds although that is not technically correct. The first difference is that closed-end investment companies issue a fixed number of shares that investors can buy or sell in the stock market like other stocks. Accordingly, closed-end investment companies do not redeem their shares like open-end funds. Second, closed-end investment companies are traded on the stock markets like other stocks. Finally, closed-end companies may sell at a discount (below) or a premium (above) relative to their net asset values. The discounts or premiums reflect investors' expectations of earnings discounted by their required rates of return.

In 1993, the first **index funds** began trading on the American Stock Exchange, and they mimic the price and yield performance, before fees and expenses, of selected stock indexes such as the Standard & Poor's 500 stock index and the Dow Jones Industrial Average. The Standard & Poor's depository receipts are called SPDRs, or *spiders.* The comparable securities for the Dow Jones are called *diamonds.*[6] Index funds also mimic sectors such as the Dow Jones US energy, healthcare, and utilities sectors, and so on. Other index funds cover foreign market indexes.[7] More than 60 index funds are actively traded on the American Stock Exchange (Amex). Because index funds correspond to specific indexes, their stock turnover is less than that of other mutual funds, and they do not pass on as much capital gains taxes to their shareholders.

Index funds and unit investment trusts are also called **exchange traded funds (ETFs)**. ETFs represent funds that hold stocks designed to correspond to the performance of a portfolio of securities representing the broad market, a specific sector, or international markets.

Unit investment trusts

These are closed-end portfolios of securities that are generally sold to investors by brokers. Units represent an undivided interest in the portfolio. Unit holders receive a proportion share of the income generated from the trust as it is earned or liquidated.

Load and no-load funds

Sales charge The term **load** refers to sales charges. A **load fund** sales charge may not exceed 8.5% of the purchase price. Most funds charge less than the maximum load. During the 1964–98 period, the average load on equity funds declined from about 8% to under 3%.[8]

Some funds charge small front-end loads, and then charge a **"back-end" redemption fee** when the fund is sold. A **contingent deferred sales charge (CDSC)** is a redemption fee if the fund is sold within a certain period. The back-end contingent fee generally declines the longer the fund is held by the investor. It may start at 5% in the first year and gradually declines to zero in the seventh year.

A **no-load fund** is one that is sold without a sales commission, and without a 12b-1 fee (see below) of more than 0.25% per year.

Management fees Funds also charge an annual fee for managing the portfolio. A **shareholder service fee** may be charged to reimburse the fund's distributor for account service and maintenance.

Table 6.2 Sample fee table for a money market fund's annual operating expenses (% of average daily net assets)

Management fees	0.50%
Rule 12b-1 fee	0.20%
Shareholder service fee	0.05%
Other expenses	0.05%
Total	0.80%

Many funds charge a **12b-1 fee**. This fee is named for the SEC rule that allows funds to charge for distribution costs such as advertising and commissions paid to dealers. The 12b-1 fee cannot exceed 1% of the fund's average net assets per year.

Other expenses include fees paid by the funds to transfer securities, for custody, registration fees, and so on.

The fund's **expense ratio** is the sum of all of the fund's annual expenses, including the 12b-1 fee, expressed as a percentage of its average net assets. Such fees may range from 0.3% to 2.5%. The expense ratios are shown in the fund's **fee table** in the prospectus. Table 6.2 illustrates a fee table for a money market fund's annual operating expenses. As previously noted, there is a wide range in fees charged depending on the fund's objectives, size, and other factors.

An SEC study found that larger funds had lower expense ratios than smaller funds.[9] In 1999, the weighted average expense ratio was 0.72% for no-load funds and 1.17% for load funds. The expense ratios also varied by investment objective. Bond funds had the lowest ratio, 0.80%, and specialty funds had the highest, with 1.36%. The study points out that a 1% increase in a fund's annual expenses can reduce an investor's ending account balance by 18% after 20 years.

INVESTOR INSIGHTS

COMPARING MUTUAL FUND FEES

Mutual funds fees reduce investors' returns. Given the same investment in a portfolio of securities and decisions to buy and sell securities, the returns from a no-load fund would be higher than the returns from a load fund. Similarly, suppose you invested $10,000 in a fund that produced a 10% annual return before expenses and had annual operating expenses of 1.5%. After 20 years the return would be about $49,725. What would the return be if the fund had expenses of only 0.5%? The answer is $60,858 – an 18% difference. The impact of fees on returns can be found by using the SEC's Mutual Fund Cost Calculator. It is available at their website, www.sec.gov.

Ben Franklin is reported to have said "Beware of little expenses; a small leak will sink a great ship."[10] To illustrate this point, Arthur Levitt, former Chairman of the SEC, stated that a $1,000 investment made in 1950 in a mutual fund that preformed like the S&P 500 would be worth over a half a million in 2001. If the mutual fund fees amounted conservatively to a little under 2%, the investment would be worth $230,000. If the fund was not tax efficient, the investment would be worth $65,000. Levitt goes on to say that without paying attention to costs, an investor stands a better chance of making a million dollars as a contestant on the TV show *Survivor*.

Real estate investment trusts (REITs)

Real estate investment trusts are *not* investment companies. Nevertheless, they are analogous to a closed-end investment company that invests in real estate. The principal difference is that REITs make extensive use of borrowed funds while investment companies are not permitted to do so. REITs are organized as business trusts that provide real estate portfolio management for investors who lack sufficient funds to invest in large real estate projects, lack the expertise and interest in managing such projects, and who want liquidity. The boom and bust characteristics of the real estate industry are reflected in the value of their shares.

Taxes

Investors must be aware of the tax implications of mutual fund investments. Mutual funds generally distribute all of their earnings from dividends, interest, and capital gains to their shareholders who must pay taxes on them. The exception is tax-exempt bond and money market funds that invest in municipal securities. Income from these funds is exempt from federal income taxes, and in some cases from state income taxes.

Beginning in 2001, the capital gains on assets held by the fund for more than 5 years will be taxable at an 8% rate instead of the higher 10% rate. Capital losses can be used to offset other gains.

Some investors try to time the purchase of mutual fund shares in order to minimize the taxes from distributions. The decision when to distribute income depends on the type of fund. For example, index funds may have not capital gains to distribute. Money market funds declare dividends daily in order to keep their price at $1 per share. And stock and bond funds may make several distributions during the year.

Investments in certain retirement accounts (e.g. employer-sponsored 401(k) plans, IRAs) are tax deductible, and the taxes on the distributions may be tax-deferred.

INVESTOR INSIGHTS

MUTUAL FUND SCREENERS

Investors can choose mutual fund screeners from investment services such as Morningstar (www.morningstar.com) or from mutual fund families such as Fidelity Investments (www.fidelity.com). Morningstar offers a variety of mutual fund screeners covering more than 8,000 funds. They can be used to select particular types of funds, or to compare the performance of various funds. Morningstar charges a fee for some of their products and services. Quicken (www.quicken.com) is another source for free fund screeners.

Fidelity Investments provides screeners or evaluators covering over 4,500 funds, including non-Fidelity funds. Their data are provided by Morningstar. The fund screeners are based on investment type (stock, bond, hybrid), objectives, performance, and other factors. In contrast, other fund families, such as Dreyfus Funds (www.dreyfus.com) which manages over 180 different funds, focus on the performance of their own funds.

BENEFITS FOR INVESTORS

Professional management

Investment companies have certain advantages that are lacking in other types of investments. For investors who do not have the time, knowledge, or desire to analyze and manage their securities portfolios, they offer professional management. Equally important, investment company shares can be bought by investors with either small or large dollar amounts to invest.

Some brokerage firms and investment companies offer **wrap accounts** that allow investors to buy and sell funds (and other securities) for an annual fee based on the assets in their accounts rather than charging commissions on each trade, and they have access to a financial adviser to help them make decisions. This permits active investors to load funds as they desire.

Diversification

Diversification is one advantage of owning investment company shares. **Diversification** refers to investing in different companies, industries, securities, or other forms of investment whose returns are affected differently by changing economic and financial market conditions over time. One share of an investment company can represent ownership in

25 or more companies held in the investment company's portfolio. The other side of that coin is that holding too many companies – excessive diversification – may result in the investment company performing "like the whole stock market." Excessive diversification also can result from owning too many funds that invest in the same securities.

Targeted investments

Investors can take advantage of specialized investment companies that meet their particular investment objectives. For example, an investor may want to invest in Latin American companies, the pharmaceutical industry, have tax-free income, or mimic the performance of the S&P 500 stock index.

Retirement market

Mutual funds have become an increasingly popular choice in the private pension system. Employer-sponsored defined contribution plans and individual retirement accounts have contributed to the growth of investment companies.

Liquidity

Open-end mutual funds are liquid because they must redeem their shares. As previously noted, most funds calculate the redemption price (net asset value) at the end of the trading day.

Internet

Shareholders can visit most investment companies' websites to monitor the performance of their funds as well as switching funds within families. Some funds also allow their shares to be bought or sold online.

RISKS FOR INVESTORS

Investing in investment company shares is not without risks. Like other investments, they are subject to market risk, interest rate risk, credit risk, currency risk, and so on, depending on the type of fund involved. For example, high-yield (junk) bond funds by definition invest in risky and sometime illiquid assets. When interest rates rise sharply, the value of those funds declines, and some may fail.[11] Similarly, money market funds have invested in risky securities and failed.[12]

The ultimate risk of a mutual fund is failure. Some investment companies have performed so poorly that they received injections of funds from their sponsoring organizations, they were merged with other funds, or they were liquidated.[13] Most were small funds (under $80 million in assets). Community Bankers US Government Fund was a money market fund that had losses in derivatives. Caveat emptor.

MEASURING FUND PERFORMANCE

Although past performance does not guarantee comparable future results, it does provide insights about the fund's operations.

Data provided by funds

All open-end mutual funds are required to provide a prospectus which fully discloses information about their past performance. The required information includes a bar chart revealing their annual returns in each of the past 10 years, if they have existed that long. In addition, they must include a comparison for their performance over the past 1, 5, and 10 years against an appropriate market index. They also have to present a *fee table* revealing their expenses.

External reviews

As shown in Table 6.3, various websites provide performance rankings for mutual funds. Morningstar is a popular site that can be used to select and compare about 8,000 funds. Morningstar uses its "Five-Star-Rating" system to score a fund's performance, five stars being the highest rating.[14] Morningstar charges for some of its services. Lipper Analytical Services claims to be "The Experts in Fund Evaluation," and provides advice for a fee. It uses alphabetical ratings, where "A" is the best score and "E" is the worst. Some online services specialize in particular types of funds, such as iMoneyNet that focuses on money funds.

Bloomberg.com, CNNmoney, and Yahoo! Finance are online news sources that also provide mutual fund screeners, and other information that can be used to select and evaluate funds given various objectives similar to those mentioned previously.

Forbes magazine provides a fund screener that covers 11,000 funds. The screener includes funds by type, family, Forbes ratings, performance, cost and expenses, and more. Similarly, *BusinessWeek* offers a mutual fund scoreboard and other investment advice. SmartMoney.com provides investment advice, calculators, articles, and more.

Some online newspapers also have limited information about mutual funds. The *Wall Street Journal, Washington Post Online*, and the *New York Times* are three examples.

Table 6.3   Selected websites with information about mutual funds

Mutual fund rating services	Website
Morningstar	www.morningstar.com
Lipper Analytical Services	www.lipperweb.com
iMoneyNet, Inc.	www.ibcdata.com
Online news services	
Bloomberg.com	www.bloomberg.com
CNNmoney	CNNmoney.com
Yahoo! Finance	www.finance.yahoo.com
Print/online magazines	
Forbes	www.forbes.com
BusinessWeek	www.businessweek.com
SmartMoney	www.smartmoney.com
Print/online newspapers	
Wall Street Journal	www.wsj.com
Washington Post	www.washingtonpost.com
New York Times	www.nytimes.com

Last, but certainly not least, the major brokerage firms and mutual fund families, some of which are listed in the "Directory of Websites," also provide information about mutual funds, and those that they consider the best or worst in particular categories.

This list of sources providing fund screeners is not intended to be exhaustive. It is intended to show that there is a large number of websites providing information about funds, and other sources can be found by using search engines.

Conclusion

Investment companies (mutual funds) are the investment of choice for millions of individual investors for their retirement plans and personal investments. Mutual funds provide professional investment management that most investors cannot do on their own. Other benefits include diversification, targeted investments, and liquidity.

The number of mutual fund shareholder accounts increased from 62 million in 1990 to 244 million in 2000. In addition, an increasing number of businesses are taking advantage of money market mutual funds to manage their cash resources. Changes in pension laws, the aging of the population, and rising stock market prices contributed to the growth of mutual funds.

There are about 11,000 open-end and closed-end funds that offer a wide spectrum of investment objectives ranging from conservative to aggressive in every type of security and industry, domestic and foreign.

Chapter 1 of this book dealt with the suitability of investment decisions, which in the context of this chapter means that you have to know what types of funds are suitable for you before you choose one or more of the 11,000 funds. Once that decision is made, there are ample online resources available to evaluate and monitor fund performance.

SELF-TEST QUESTIONS

1. Examine Box 6.1 and select one type of mutual fund (e.g. growth fund) that meets some of your investment objectives.
2. Using the "Directory of Websites" at the end of this book, select two of the many families of mutual funds listed. Go to their websites and find a fund (from question 1) in each family that meets your objective. What information do they provide about the funds?
3. What is the net asset value of the funds? What does that mean?
4. What are 12b-1 fees? How much are they in the funds that you selected?
5. What are the sales charges for these funds?
6. How has each of these two funds performed? What does each site tell you about their performance, and fees? Which of the two funds that you selected is better?
7. Using the SEC's Mutual Fund Cost Calculator (www.sec.gov), evaluate the effect of the two mutual funds' fees on their returns over the next 10 years. Is there a difference?
8. Using one or more of the online news services or print magazines listed in Table 6.3, and their screeners, how do the two funds that you selected compare to others with the same investment objective?
9. How do the two funds you selected rank according to Morningstar and Lipper Analytical Services (see Table 6.3 for the websites)?
10. How many exchange traded funds are there? (See www.ishares.com; www.amex.com.)

NOTES

1   A group of families of funds under common management or distributorship is called a **fund complex**.
2   For more information, see www.fidelity.com and www.dreyfus.com.
3   Bridget O'Brian, "Some Fund Managers Hand Reins to 'Subadvisers,'" *Wall Street Journal*, August 31, 2001, C1, C17.
4   For information about the ICI and mutual funds, see www.ici.org.
5   For additional information about hedge funds, see William F. Osterberg and James B. Thomson, "The Truth about Hedge Funds," Federal Reserve Bank of Cleveland, *Economic Commentary*, May 1, 1999; Barry Eichengreen and Donald Mathieson, eds,

Hedge Funds and Financial Market Dynamics (Washington, DC: International Monetary Fund, Occasional Paper 166, May 1988).

6　Some index funds use the term "tracking stock," such as the "Nasdaq-100 Index Tracking Stock." The term "tracking stock" used in connection with index funds does not have the same meaning as "tracking stocks" issued by companies, such as General Motors or Walt Disney. This use of the term was discussed in connection with common stocks (Chapter 4).

7　For additional information about both US domestic and non-US index funds and exchange traded funds, see the iShares (Barclays Global Investors) website, www.ishares.com, and the Amex, www.amex.com.

8　John V. Duca, "The Rise of Stock Mutual Funds," Federal Reserve Bank of Dallas, *Southwest Economy*, January/February 2001, 1, 6–9.

9　Securities and Exchange Commission, *Report on Mutual Fund Fees and Expenses*, December 2000 (www.sec.gov/news/studies/feestudy.htm).

10　Arthur Levitt, "The Future for America's Investors – Their Rights and Obligations," US Securities and Exchange Commission, January 16, 2001.

11　For further information, see Lewis Braham, "Lessons From a Muni-Fund Nosedive," *BusinessWeek*, December 11, 2000, 127–8; "Self Help," *The Economist*, June 18, 1994, 86–7. "Mutual Fund Fiasco," *CNNmoney.com*, July 17, 2001 (CNNmoney.com, visited 7/19/01) explained how Milwaukee-based Heartland Advisors slashed the net asset value of its High-Yield Municipal Bond Fund by 70% and its High-Yield Short-Duration Municipal Fund by 44%.

12　Michael Schroeder, "Prime Suspect in the Money-Market Murder," *BusinessWeek*, October 17, 1994, 224–6.

13　Benton E. Gup, "Are Money Market Funds an Alternative for Banks?" *Journal of Institutional and Theoretical Economics*, vol. 154, March 1998, 97–104; Anne Tergesen, "Where Did My Mutual Fund Go?" *BusinessWeek*, December 18, 2000, 237–8.

14　See Ben Mattlin, "Deciphering Ratings," *On Investing*, Spring 2000, 20–5, for an explanation of the various rating systems.

PART THREE

Making Investment Decisions

7. Analyzing Investment Opportunities Online   113
8. Interpreting Financial Data   133
9. Valuation Models   153
10. Portfolio Management   171

7 Analyzing Investment Opportunities Online

Key Concepts

Beige Book
Beta
Bond screeners
Bottom-up analysis
Decline phase (life cycle)
Dividend payout ratio
Dividend valuation model
Expansion phase (life cycle)
Fundamental analysis
Imperfect competition
Intrinsic value
Life cycle
Monopoly
North American Industry Classification System (NAICS)
Oligopoly
Pioneering phase (life cycle)
Pure competition
Stabilization phase (life cycle)
Standard Industrial Classification (SIC)
Stock screeners
Sustainable competitive advantage
Systematic risk
Top-down analysis

From the individual investor's point of view, analyzing investment opportunities begins with the suitability doctrine that was presented in Chapter 1. That doctrine refers to a broker-dealer's obligation to recommend only those investments that are suitable for you. Chapter 1 also made the point that each investor must determine his or her own investment objectives and risk preferences. This chapter explains how to find investment opportunities online, and it explains part of the process of analyzing them. There is an infinite number of investment opportunities, but it is up to you to narrow them down to those that are suitable for you. The investment process does not end there. The next steps involve analyzing the companies that you selected to determine if they are viable, fairly priced, and if this is a good time to buy them. Those subjects are covered in the remaining chapters.

TOP-DOWN ANALYSIS

Before the age of investing online, investors took a traditional approach to analyzing investments – it is commonly called **fundamental analysis**. That approach is represented here in Figure 7.1 as the **top-down analysis** of securities. The basic idea of top-down analysis is to start with a company, such as IBM, and then examine the major factors that affect firms now and in the future, and then to analyze the firm and determine its intrinsic value. **Intrinsic value** is the theoretical value of a security, and it may differ from the market price. In Chapter 4, the simplified **dividend valuation model** was introduced as one method of determining intrinsic value, and it is shown here in equation 7.1. Because the model is "simplified," it is not likely that the intrinsic value and the market price will be the same. Nevertheless, the model is useful in helping us to understand fundamental analysis. For example, an increase in demand for a firm's products may lead to higher revenues and higher dividends. From the equation, it can be seen that higher dividends result in higher stock prices. Thus, when considering the fundamental factors that are about to be discussed, think about how they affect firms' future revenues and dividends.

$$P_0 = \frac{D_1}{k-g} \tag{7.1}$$

where

P_0 = current price (at time 0)
D_1 = cash dividend in time period 1
k = the rate of return required by equity investors
g = growth rate of cash dividends

Top-down analysis works well when analyzing a small number of securities. We examine top-down analysis first, so that you understand the various factors affecting intrinsic value. Then we are going to reverse the process and do bottom-up analysis, which is more suitable for online investors. We are not starting with the online stock, bond, or mutual fund screeners because the top-down analysis also provides an understanding of some of the variables used in the screeners.

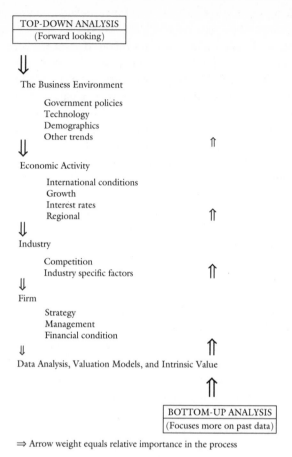

Figure 7.1   Top-down/bottom-up analysis

Major factors affecting firms are beyond their control

An important insight from top-down analysis is that the major factors affecting firms are beyond their control. The major factors affecting the demand for firms' products and services include, but are not limited to, the business environment, economic activity, and industry factors.

Business environment *Government policies* – such as defense spending, deregulation, environmental controls, and Medicare – will benefit some firms and harm others. By way of illustration, since federal spending is a limited dollar amount, an increase in spending on missile defense will help defense contractors, but what is spent on missiles cannot be spent on Medicare. Therefore, selected defense contractors will benefit from the spending, but firms involved with Medicare, housing, road building, etc. will receive less government funds.

In terms of *deregulation*, the Gramm-Leach-Bliley Act of 1999 allowed combinations of banks, securities firms, and insurance companies. The passage of the law sanctioned the merger of insurance company Travelers and Citicorp bank to form Citigroup. And it contributed to other mergers and acquisitions in those industries. For example, Regions Financial Corporation was primarily a bank until it formed a financial holding company and acquired Morgan Keegan Inc., a securities firm, and Rebsamen Insurance Company.

Changes in *technology*, such as the development of the Internet and wireless communications, are driving the growth of telecommunications, creating new opportunities for e-commerce, and new ways to invest funds. That's what this book is about.

Think about the industries affected by changes in *demographics* – the aging population, increased immigration, and more females in the labor force. These changes affect healthcare, housing, retailers, and many other industries.

Economic activity The state domestic and international economic activity affects the demand for firms' products and subsequently their revenues. Information about the state of the economy is available online. The Board of Governors of the Federal Reserve System (www.federalreserve.gov) publishes the "Beige Book" in connection with their Federal Open Market Committee Meetings.[1] The **Beige Book** outlines the current economic conditions in the various federal reserve districts. Current economic indicators are published online by the US Census Bureau in their "Census Economic Briefing Room" (www.census.gov). Figure 7.2 is an example of such data.[2]

If the economy is strong and growing, firms tend to prosper. When it falters, companies fail. By way of illustration, consider Midway Airlines, a regional air carrier which declared bankruptcy in 2001. The airline was expanding its fleet of aircraft, but when the economy slowed in 2001, there was a calamitous drop in business in their high-yielding business air travel on which they depended, plus there were increased fuel costs.[3] The external factors went against them and they went bankrupt.

Some products, such as automobiles, clothing, and televisions that were traditionally made by US firms are increasingly being imported, reflecting the increase in globalization. The growth of the North American Free Trade Zone (NAFTA), the European Union, the free trade area Mercosur in Latin America, and the Association of Southeast Asian Nations (ASEAN) are further evidence of globalization.

Changes in Federal Reserve interest rate policies have both short-run and long-run macroeconomic affects. We know from the dividend valuation model (equation 7.1) that, in the short-term, an increase in interest rates will adversely affect stock prices. In the long-term, it may reduce the demand for firms' products that would adversely affect their earnings, dividends, and their stock prices.

While the discussion has focused on global and macroeconomic changes, some companies are strictly regional. The electric power problems in California in 2001

Census Economic Briefing Room

Economic Indicator Calendar Census Bureau Economic Programs

		Previous	Current
CHART: Manufacturers' new orders	**Manufacturers' Shipments, Inventories, and Orders** New orders for manufactured goods in September decreased $7.4 billion or 2.3 percent to $318.1 billion. (Released November 4, 2002)	-0.4 % change August 2002	-2.3 % change September 2002
	Source: U.S. Bureau of the Census		
CHART: Value of Construction Put in Place	**Construction Spending** Total construction activity for September 2002 ($836.7 billion) was 0.6 percent above the revised August 2002 ($831.5 billion).	-0.7 % change August 2002	0.6 % change September
	Source: U.S. Bureau of the Census		
CHART: Homeownership Chart	**Homeownership** The homeownership rate in the third quarter 2002 (68.0 percent) was not significantly different from the third quarter 2001 rate (68.1 percent). The homeownership rate in the South was lower than one year ago, while rates in other regions were statistically unchanged from rates one year ago.	68.1 percent 3rd Qtr 2001	68.0 percent 3rd Qtr 2002
	Source: U.S. Bureau of the Census		
CHART: New Home Sales	**New Home Sales** Sales of new one-family houses in September 2002 were at a seasonally adjusted annual rate of 1,021,000. This is 0.4% above the revised August 2002 figure of 1,017,000.	+6.4 % change August 2002	+0.4 % change September
	Source: U.S. Bureau of the Census		
CHART: Durable goods new orders	**Advance Report on Durable Goods Manufacturers' Shipments and Orders** New orders for manufactured durable goods in September decreased $10.5 billion or 5.9 percent to $167.6 billion. (Released October 25, 2002)	-0.6 % change August 2002	-5.9 % change September 2002
	Source: U.S. Bureau of the Census		
CHART: Monthly trade balance	**U.S. International Trade in Goods and Services** The Nation's international deficit in goods and services increased to $38.5 billion in August, from $35.1 billion (revised) in July, as exports decreased and imports increased.	-35.1 $ billion July 2002	-38.5 $ billion August 2002
	Source: U.S. Bureau of the Census		

Figure 7.2 Census Economic Briefing Room

		Previous	Current
Housing Starts Privately owned housing starts in September were at a seasonally adjusted annual rate of 1,843,000, up 13.3% from the revised August 2002 figure of 1,627,000.		-1.5 % change August 2002	13.3 % change September 2002
CHART: New housing starts	Source: U.S. Bureau of the Census		
Quarterly Financial Report - Retail Trade After-tax profits for large retail corporations' with assets $50 million and over averaged 2.7 cents per dollar of sales for the second quarter 2002, up 0.6 (+/- 0.1) cents from the preceding quarter. (Released: October 16, 2002. Next: January 14, 2003.)		unchanged % change 1st Qtr. 2002	0.6 changed % change 2nd Qtr. 2002
CHART: Retail Profits Per Dollar of Sales	Source: U.S. Bureau of the Census		
Manufacturing and Trade Inventories and Sales U.S. total business sales for August were $835.6 bil, up 0.2% from last month. Month -end inventories were $1,123.6 bil, down 0.1% from last month. (Released 10/15/02)		1.3 % Change in sales July 2002	0.2 % Change in sales August 2002
CHART: Total Business Sales	Source: U.S. Bureau of the Census		
Advance Retail and Food Service Sales U.S. retail and food service sales for September were $302.5 billion, down 1.2 percent from the previous month. (Released 10/11/02)		0.8 % change 09/13/2002	-1.2 % change 10/11/2002
CHART: Monthly retail sales	Source: U.S. Bureau of the Census		
Monthly Wholesale Trade: Sales and Inventories August 2002 sales of merchant wholesalers were $233.5 billion, up 0.9% from last month. End-of-month inventories were $284.5 billion, up 0.2% from last month. (10/10/02)		0.6 % change in Inv July 2002	0.2 % change in Inv August 2002
CHART: Inventories/Sales Ratios	Source: U.S. Bureau of the Census		
Quarterly Financial Report - Manufacturing, Mining and Trade Manufacturing corporations' seasonally adjusted after-tax profits averaged 3.8 cents per dollar of sales for the second quarter of 2002,up 1.3 (+/- 0.1) cents from the preceding quarter. (Released: September 13, 2002. Next Release: December 13, 2002.)		1.7 % change 1st Qtr 2002	1.3 % change 2nd Qtr 2002
CHART: Manufacturing Profits Per Dollar of Sales	Source: U.S. Bureau of the Census		
Household Income Median household income in 2001 in the United States was $42,228. This level was 2.2 percent lower than in 2000 in real terms (after adjusting for inflation). The real median income of Hispanic-origin households		$43,162 2000 Dollars 2000	$42,228 2000 Dollars 2001

Figure 7.2 Census Economic Briefing Room (contd)

CHART: Income by Race	remained unchanged at $33,565, while the income of each race group declined between 2000 and 2001. Real median household income declined 1.3 percent for households with a non-Hispanic White householder to a level of $46,305; 3.4 percent for Blacks to $29,470; and 6.4 percent for Asians and Pacific Islanders to 53,635. The real earnings of women who worked full-time, year round increased 3.5 percent, to $29,215, while men's earnings ($38,275) did not change. The resulting women's-to-men's earnings ratio is at an all-time high, 0.76.		
	Source: U.S. Bureau of the Census		

	Poverty	**Previous**	**Current**
	After falling for four consecutive years, the poverty rate rose, from 11.3 percent in 2000 to 11.7 percent in 2001. The number of poor increased also, by 1.3 million, to 32.9 million poor in 2001.	11.3 percent 2000	11.7 percent 2001
CHART: Poverty Rates	Source: U.S. Bureau of the Census		

Figure 7.2   Census Economic Briefing Room (contd) (*Source*: US Census Bureau)

that caused difficulties for their public utilities did not have the same impact on utilities in New York or Florida.

Industry It is important to understand the economic structure of industries before investing in them. One type of economic structure is **pure competition**, with many firms competing and no single firm able to influence prices. Wheat farming is a classic example of pure competition, because no one farmer can influence the price of this standardized commodity. Also consider the restaurant industry. There are more than 478,000 eating and drinking places in the US. That is about one eating and drinking place for every 600 people, and that is a very competitive market.[4] Nevertheless, some firms such as McDonald's and Burger King are able to differentiate their products.

Imperfect competition prevails in markets where various firms try to convince you that their products are better than those of their competitors. The differences can be real or imagined. The dozens of brands of beers, cereals, shampoo, and toothpaste to choose from are examples of imperfect competition.

Next there are **oligopolies**, where a few large firms dominate a market. Oligopolies tend to be capital intensive, which means that large dollar amounts are required to produce products (e.g. cars, jet engines, and steel). The high costs of entry and the complexity of production tend to restrict the number of firms in such industries.

Finally, there are **monopolies**, where one firm controls the market. Local public utilities, such a power companies, have near monopoly power. Because they are government regulated, their monopoly does not guarantee them excess profits. Also consider the pharmaceutical industry. It consists of a small number of large companies, in part because it costs so much to develop new drugs. The developmental costs of a new drug may exceed $500 million, and the process may take 5 years or longer. Once a drug is developed and approved by the government for general use, the pharmaceutical company holding the patent on the drug has a monopoly on that product for

17 or more years. That may result in large profits, or it may be short-lived because other companies can make competing products. Monopolies don't guarantee profits.

INVESTOR INSIGHTS

SIC, NAICS, AND INDUSTRY DATA

In the past, industries were classified by **Standard Industrial Classification (SIC)** codes based on the Department of Commerce's *Standard Industrial Classification Manual – 1987*. In 1997, a new classification system, the **North American Industry Classification System (NAICS)**, was adopted and it will replace SIC codes over time. A listing of the NAICS industries can be found in the *Federal Register*, April 9, 1997, or in the *North American Industry Classification System – United States, 1997*. NAICS groups establishments into 20 sectors (e.g. "Manufacturing," "Wholesale Trade," etc.) and 1,170 industries. Each sector is assigned a two-digit code (e.g. "Information" is 51) and six-digit codes are used to identify particular industries. For example, the six-digit code for "Television Broadcasting" is 513120, the 51 indicating that it is in the "Information" sector, the next digit designating the industry subsector, and so on. Further information about NAICS is available on the Census Bureau NAICS website at http://www.census.gov/epcd/www/naicssvc.htm.

SIC/NAICS codes are needed when comparing firms to make sure that they are in the same sectors, industries, and subsectors. Stated otherwise, these codes make it easier to compare apples with apples in various research publications.

Several print sources devoted to industry information and analysis include:

- *U.S. Industry & Trade Outlook* (New York: McGraw-Hill Companies, US Department of Commerce). Annual; covers all major SIC/NAICS codes.
- *Standard & Poor's Industry Surveys.* Covers 50 leading industries.

Implications

Grow or die What are the implications of the factors that we have discussed? First, *grow or die*. Everybody wants firms to grow. The President and Chief Executive Officer of a firm wants it to make more money so that he or she can get a raise. The employees want higher salaries. The shareholders want their stock to appreciate and to receive higher dividends. The community and state where the firm is located want more tax revenue and the firm to support community activities.

Firms must grow and respond to changes in the market or they will go out of business as competitors take over their markets. A firm can make an excellent product, be profitable in the short-run, and then be driven out of business because its customers' preferences shift over time. Consider how covered wagons were replaced by cars, trains and boats were replaced by planes, typewriters were replaced by computers, and coin operated telephone booths by wireless phones.

Limited control Second, firms are limited as to what they can control. They cannot control the factors in the business environment or economic activity that were previously discussed. These are some of the most important factors driving the demand for their products and services, and subsequently their revenues.

They can control their assets (what they own) and their liabilities (what they owe), and make management decisions (expand, diversify, marketing, corporate structure). But such control in and of itself does not guarantee success. To paraphrase Charles Darwin: *only the fittest firms will survive.*

One key to survival and growth is to have a sustainable competitive advantage over other firms. A **sustainable competitive advantage** can take many different forms: Coca-Cola and McDonald's have successfully used their *brand names* as a sustainable competitive advantage; Microsoft's *market power* is a sustainable competitive advantage; Wal-Mart's *size and distribution* system give it an advantage; and *patents* provide a competitive advantage.

A sustainable competitive advantage is something that is not easily copied by other firms. But it is not going to last forever. Oldsmobile was a great brand name for many years, but cars are no longer manufactured under that name. Montgomery Ward and Grants were two of the leading department stores in the US, but now they are out of business. Polaroid had a monopoly on instant photographs. Although it was a growing and profitable company, that did not guarantee continued success or survival. Polaroid's competitive advantage ended with the development of 1-hour film processing and the growth of digital photography. Polaroid declared bankruptcy in 2001.[5] Finally, consider the US Postal Service, that has a monopoly on mail service. However, changes in technology – the use of fax machines and the Internet for sending correspondence instead of mailing letters – are having an adverse effect on US Postal Service revenues and eroding the value of its monopoly.

The lesson to be learned is that having a well-managed, profitable firm is a necessary but not sufficient condition for survival. Markets are dynamic and firms must respond effectively and evolve if they are to survive. Corning is one example.

INVESTOR INSIGHTS

REINVENTING CORNING

Corning Inc. epitomizes the evolution of firms. It began in 1851 as Corning Glass Works Inc. The company perfected the manufacture of the Thomas Edison light bulbs, and it was the first firm to mass-produce television picture tubes. As a result of its hi-tech work to keep missile nose cones from burning up in the atmosphere, it developed Corning Ware, dishware that could go from the oven to the freezer without shattering. It sold that business and specialized in fiber-optics for transmitting data and creating a window of information – "Corning's innovative glass technologies help individuals access information in an increasingly more connected and mobile world. As a leading producer of LCD glass used around the world, Corning substrates are used in many of the displays for electronic devices you rely on every day, from notebook computers and desktop LCD monitors to cell phones and digital cameras."*

Corning is also involved in the genomics business through the development of gene-chips. These are glass slides with bits of genetic material attached. They are intended to be used in the development of new drugs.

"Corning's success stems from its ability to constantly re-invent itself to meet the demands of current and future markets. We're at the leading edge of the world's leading-edge technologies," says Corning President and CEO John Loose. "The possibilities for our future are endless."*

Sources: *www.corning.com (visited 8/8/01); Justin Gillis, "Corning's Latest Reinvention," *Washington Post*, May 9, 2001, E01.

Life cycle

Understanding the life cycle provides unique insights into corporate growth, survival, and financial behavior. All products, firms, and industries evolve through stages of development called a **life cycle**. Figure 7.3 illustrates a typical industry life cycle that is divided into four phases: pioneering, expansion, stabilization, and decline.

Pioneering phase We begin with a single firm that has one major product line that will either be successful, or it will fail. The price of the new product is high, and there are no profits in this phase of the life cycle because of low sales volume and high development and marketing costs. Because there are no profits, there are no dividends to be paid.

The risk to the firm, as measured by beta, is also high. **Beta** is a measure of systematic risk. **Systematic risk** is risk that is common to all stocks, and it cannot be eliminated by diversification. The average beta for all stocks in, say, the Standard & Poor's 500 stock index is 1. A beta of 1.8 is considered high, and a beta of 0.7 is low.

Expansion phase The expansion phase of the life cycle is characterized by increasing competition, declining product prices, and rising industry profits. If the product is successful, other firms enter the market and competition drives the price of the product down. For example, the first wireless telephones cost $4,200 when

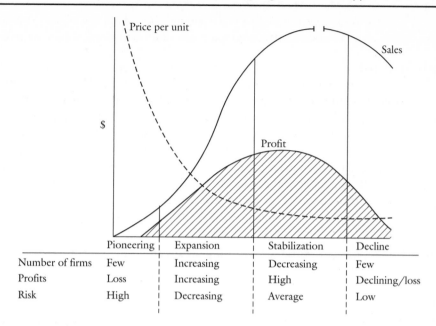

	Pioneering	Expansion	Stabilization	Decline
Number of firms	Few	Increasing	Decreasing	Few
Profits	Loss	Increasing	High	Declining/loss
Risk	High	Decreasing	Average	Low

Figure 7.3 Typical life cycle

they were introduced in 1984, and now they are given away when you buy telephone service contracts.[6] Similarly, handheld calculators cost $120 when they were introduced in 1970, and now they too are given away. VCRs cost $1,400 in 1978, and they sell for $80 today. Even more startling is that a $900 lap computer today is 13 times more powerful than a 1970 IBM mainframe that cost $4.7 million. The point here is that the price of commodity type products tends to decline as a result of competition and changes in technology.

As shown in Figure 7.3, sales revenues are increasing, but at a decreasing rate. Industry profits are increasing as well, and beta is high, but not as high as it was during the pioneering phase. As profits rise, the firms begin to pay cash dividends.

One way for successful companies to grow is by acquiring other companies. The acquisitions usually occur during the later part of the expansion phase or in the stabilization phase. For example, General Electric "made over 100 acquisitions for the fourth consecutive year and moved quickly to acquire Honeywell, whose businesses are a perfect complementary fit with our Aircraft Engines, Industrial Systems and Plastics businesses."[7] The Honeywell merger was not approved by the European Union. Nevertheless, GE acquired lots of other companies. Cisco Systems acquired more than 80 other hi-tech companies. Similarly, large pharmaceutical companies have invested in biotech firms. Roche owns 49 percent of Genentech, which is a leader in the field of genetic engineering, and Syntex Corporation, a research-oriented company.[8]

The expansion phase is a period of spectacular successes and spectacular failures. Only the fittest firms survive. The dot.com stock market bubble is one example. Dozens of dot.com business ventures entered the market around the turn of the century, but few remained by the end of 2001. Amazon.com was one of the early leaders, and a survivor.

Stabilization phase   During the stabilization phase of the life cycle, total sales continue to rise, but at a slower pace, while prices decline and industry profits in real terms fall. The number of firms continues to decline, and the **dividend payout ratio** (cash dividends/earnings) increases. Beta is about 1. By way of illustration, consider the automobile industry. During the expansion phase of the life cycle, there were about 1500 automobile companies in the US.[9] Today, only Ford, General Motors, and German-owned Chrysler[10] remain. Several foreign-owned companies are also producing cars in the US. The prices of the mass-produced cars are relatively low in real terms.

The surviving firms have the following characteristics:

1. Sufficient *capital* to finance their operations.

2. Sufficient *technology* to produce a continuous stream of new products.

3. Sufficient *scale* or size so that the products can be mass-produced at the lowest possible cost.

4. Sufficient *marketing and distribution channels* to sell, service, and finance their products.

Another aspect of firms in the stabilization phase of the life cycle is that they introduce new products to extend the duration of that phase. Consider the case of McDonald's, innovator of fast food restaurants. Its first product was a hamburger. As shown in Figure 7.4, when the growth rate of sales of hamburgers slowed, they introduced the Big Mac. When the growth rate of it slowed, they introduced Egg McMuffin, Chicken McNuggets, and other new products to increase their revenues.

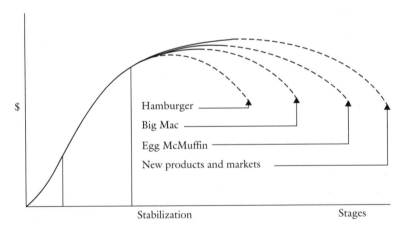

Figure 7.4   Extending the life cycle for McDonald's

Similarly, automotive manufacturers add new models to their product lines in order to maintain their revenue growth. Chrysler's PT Cruiser, the Jeep Liberty, and Dodge Ram pickups are examples of such models. The point here is that even major brands, such as McDonald's and Chrysler, must be reinvigorated with new products and services if they are to survive.

Decline phase   The decline phase of the life cycle is similar to old age in human beings. The firm or industry is over the hill and on the way out. However, there is one significant difference between humans and firms or industries. Once humans have matured, it is unlikely that they can be rejuvenated and be young again, but *rejuvenation* is possible with industries. For example, higher energy costs have contributed to the rejuvenation of the coal industry. Similarly, ceiling fans were a common means of cooling homes before central air conditioning became widespread. Then they went out of style. But when energy prices soared in the late 1970s and early 1980s, people sought ways to reduce their energy costs and once again turned to ceiling fans. Note in these examples that an external economic factor – higher energy prices – is the force that is driving the demand for coal and ceiling fans.

Firms

At the firm level, we need to understand their strategies and current developments. Many firms have websites that provide access to their annual reports, SEC filings, press releases, news stories, and current research reports. Firms also provide "financial guidance." These forward-looking statements include declarations about the expected growth rates, sales forecasts, and other specified financial items. A word of caution is in order. No forward-looking statement can be guaranteed and actual results may differ materially from those projected. Despite these limitations, such information is required reading, and is particularly useful in monitoring investments.

By way of illustration, Merck & Co., Inc. explains its strategy in its annual report, which is available online.[11] Other companies may or may not be as explicit about their strategies. Merck's strategy is to discover important new medicines through breakthrough research. And their financial goal is to be a top-tier growth company by performing over the long-term in the top quartile of leading healthcare companies.

Simply stated, research and development (R&D) is the key to Merck's success. Five medicines accounted for 57 percent of the company's pharmaceutical sales in 2000.[12] Thus, several key issues in evaluating such companies are what percentage of sales is spent on R&D, what new breakthrough medicines are coming on stream, and when do their current patents expire?

We also need to understand the financial condition of the firm, with particular emphasis on profitability, financial leverage, and other factors that are covered in the next chapter.

Finally, we use all of the information obtained in the various valuation models that are explained in Chapter 9. These valuation models are used to determine the firm's intrinsic value. If the intrinsic value is less than the market price, it may or may not be a good time to buy the stock. The timing of stock purchases or sales is covered in the technical analysis in Chapter 10.

STOCK AND BOND SCREENERS
Stock screeners

While traditional investors use the top-down analysis, online investors may choose to begin with the **bottom-up analysis** shown in Figure 7.1. The bottom-up approach starts with analyzing selected market and financial data to look for stocks that are suitable investments. The process is made easy because stock screeners are only a few clicks away. Two free online stock screeners are examined here – Yahoo! Finance and *BusinessWeek Online*. Other screeners are listed in the "Directory of Websites" at the back of this book. Stock screeners are a great way to sift through large databases to find stocks that meet selected investment criteria. They provide a starting point for analyzing securities. Some of the selection criteria used in stock screeners involves financial ratios that are covered in the next chapter.

INVESTOR INSIGHTS

SELECTED STOCK AND BOND SCREENERS

Stocks

BusinessWeek Online (www.businessweek.com). First click on "Investing," then on "Tools and Scoreboards," then on "Stock Search."

Quicken (www.quicken.com). Click on "Investing, Stocks, and Popular Searches," then click on "Stock Search."

Yahoo! Finance (finance.yahoo.com). Note: www is not used in this Internet address. Under the heading "Research & Education," click on "Stock Screener." This same site also can be used for Yahoo's bond and mutual fund screeners.

Bonds

Yahoo Bond Screener (finance.yahoo.com). Click on "Bonds."

Bonds Online (www.bondsonline.com).

For other stock, bond, and mutual fund screeners, see Stock-Screening.com (www.stock-screening.com).

Yahoo! Finance's stock screener Yahoo! Finance provides easy-to-use stock, bond, and mutual fund screeners.[13] Investors can search for stocks by selecting from the criteria shown in Figure 7.5, or they can use preset screens that cover high-volume stocks, greatest sales revenue, largest market cap, strong forecasted growth, 52-week sizzlers, and 52-week swooners.

To illustrate the use of stock screeners, we will look for a stock that is growing, profitable, and pays some dividend income. The stock screener settings begin by offering a choice of industries, or you can select "Any" industry as the first criterion. Let's start by selecting "Any" industry. The next set of choices deals with *Share Data*. We want a minimum dividend yield of 2%, and we will ignore the other criteria listed under share data, so we use the "Any" choices.

Performance is the next category. We want a stock whose price has increased 15% in the past year, and that has a minimum beta of 1 and a maximum beta of 2. Of course, past performance is no guarantee of future performance, but it does provide some useful information.

Under *Sales and Profitability* we want a profitable company and choose a minimum profit margin (net income/revenue) of 10%.

Under the *Valuation Ratios* we choose a minimum price/earnings ratio of 10 and a maximum of 30. The other criteria listed under *Valuation Ratios* will be explained in Chapter 9.

Our final criterion under *Analyst Estimates* is an estimated 5 year earnings per share (EPS) growth rate of 15% or more.

The selections are summarized below.

Selection criteria	Values
Dividend yield (dividend/price)	2%
Beta (systematic risk)	1–2
Profit margin (net income/revenue)	10%
P/E ratio (price/earnings)	10–30
5 year EPS growth rate	15%

At the bottom of the screen we click on "Find Stocks." On this day the screener selected two stocks that met our criteria – Pocahontas Bancorp (traded on Nasdaq NM, symbol PFSI) and iStar Financial Inc. (traded on NYSE, symbol SFI). Pocahontas Bancorp is a bank holding company for a federally chartered savings and loan association in Arkansas. iStar Financial is a New York-based firm that specializes as a real estate finance company, and it is taxed as a Real Estate Investment Trust (REIT). This screener provided selected financial data about these companies, and it had links to get current stock quotes, charts, news, profiles, research, SEC filings, financial data, and more. These links, in turn, go directly to the company and other sources of information.

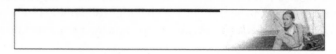

Stock Screener | Bond Screener | Fund Screener

Stock Screener

Preset Screens

· High Volume Stocks
· Greatest Sales Revenue
· Largest Market Cap
· Strong Forecasted Growth
· 52-week Sizzlers
· 52-week Swooners

Sponsored By

SmartMoney

· Investment Tools
· Free Newsletters
· Magazine Subscription

Related Resources

· Mutual Fund Center
· Financial Glossary
· Co.& Fund Index
· Top Fund Performers
· Prospectus Finder
· Fund Calculators
· Education Center

Screener Settings

Search for stocks by selecting from the criteria below. Click on the "Find Stocks" button to view the results.

Category

Industry:

> Any
> Advertising (Services)
> Aerospace & Defense (Capital Goods)
> Air Courier (Transportation)
> Airline (Transportation)

Share Data

Share Price:	Any ▼ Min	Any ▼ Max
Avg Share Volume:	Any ▼ Min	Any ▼ Max
Market Cap:	Any ▼ Min	Any ▼ Max
Dividend Yield:	2% ▼ Min	Any ▼ Max

Performance

1 Yr Stock Perf:	Up more than 15% ▼	
Beta (Volatility):	1.0 ▼ Min	2.0 ▼ Max

Sales and Profitability

Sales Revenue:	Any ▼ Min	Any ▼ Min
Profit Margin	10% ▼ Min	Any ▼ Max

Valuation Ratios

Price/Earnings Ratio:	10 ▼ Min	30 ▼ Max
Price/Book Ratio:	Any ▼ Min	Any ▼ Min
Price/Sales Ratio:	Any ▼ Min	Any ▼ Max
PEG Ratio:	Any ▼ Min	Any ▼ Max

Analyst Estimates

Est. 1 Yr EPS Growth:	Any ▼
Est. 5 Yr EPS Growth:	Up more than 15% ▼

Figure 7.5   Yahoo! Finance stock screener

Avg Analyst Rec: (1=Buy, 5=Sell)	Any
Results Display Setting	
Display info for:	Actively Screened Data
	Find Stocks

Figure 7.5 Yahoo! Finance stock screener (contd) (Reproduced with permission of Yahoo! Inc., © 2000 by Yahoo! Inc. YAHOO! and the YAHOO! logo are trademarks of Yahoo! Inc.)

BusinessWeek Online stock screener

BusinessWeek Online has three stock screeners, a *Quick Stock Search*, *Advanced Stock Search*, and BusinessWeek *50/S&P 500 Screener*. The *Advanced Stock Search* has about 70 selection criteria that include various financial ratios, daily price range percent, number of financial institutions holding the stock, the volume of stock trading over the past 30 days, comparisons of the company's growth rate to the S&P growth rate, and more. The larger number of selection criteria allows for more detailed or precise searches.

Using the same selection criteria we used in the Yahoo! search, the BusinessWeek *Advanced Stock Search* generated the following stocks:

Name (first 10 listed)	Symbol
Tele Norte (ADR)	TNE
Montana Power	MTP
Alcatel (ADR)	ALA
Medallion Financial Corp.	TAXI
iStar Financial Corp.	SFI
Nam Tai Electronics Inc.	NTAI
Enersis SA (ADR)	ENI
Pentair Inc.	PNR
Craftmade, International, Inc.	CRFT
Embratel (ADR)	EMT

Some brokerage firms provide screeners as a service to their clients. Using the same selection criteria we used in the previous two searches, the advanced stock scanner at Charles Schwab produced the following list of securities.

Name (first 10 listed)	Symbol
AGL Resources Inc.	AGT
Alexandria RE Equities	ARE
Alfa Corporation	ALFA
ALLETE, Inc.	ALE
Alliance Capital Mgt. Hldg.	AC
Alliant Energy Corp.	LNT
Altel Corporation	AT
American Bank of CT	BKC
American Financial Holdings	AMFH
Andover Bancorp, Inc.	ANDB

The lesson to be learned here is that given the same selection criteria, different stock screeners produce significantly different outputs. Because the databases used in stock screeners are updated regularly, using the same selection criteria on different days may produce different results.

Stock screeners are good tools to find stocks meeting specific financial criteria. They are a starting point, but further analysis and a determination of intrinsic value are required.

Bond screeners

Bond screeners, such as the one provided by Yahoo! Finance (finance.yahoo.com), require investors to select the type of bond (e.g. Treasury, corporate, municipal, or zero coupon), maturity, credit rating, and the amount to be invested. The minimum denomination on corporate bonds is $1,000, but it is $10,000 on some agency debt. Other screeners, such as Bonds Online (www.bondsonline.com), offer more selection criteria. Depending on the screener used, the data on the bonds selected includes the coupon, maturity, yield, price, and whether the bond is callable.

CONCLUSION

Traditional security analysis begins with a particular company in mind. The top-down approach then examines the major factors influencing the demand for that firm's products and services. Those factors include the business environment, economic activity, and industry factors including the life cycle. These are factors over which the firm has no control, but they can make or break the company. Then the firm itself is analyzed.

Online investors may choose to begin with bottom-up analysis. This is accomplished by using stock or bond screeners that allow investors to choose the market and financial data to be used by the screeners to find stocks or bonds that meet their investment criteria. Once the stocks are found, it is still necessary to evaluate the factors that affect them, their financial condition, and determine their intrinsic value.

SELF-TEST QUESTIONS

1. What are the major business environmental factors affecting Boeing, Eastman Kodak, Exxon, and Wal-Mart?
2. What is the Federal Reserve doing about interest rates? To answer this question, go to www.federalreserve.gov, and then click on "Monetary Policy."
3. Imperfect competition is the prevalent industry structure for many firms. How do companies like Starbucks and Heinz differentiate their products?
4. Do the following companies have a sustainable competitive advantage and, if so, what is it? Citigroup, Merrill Lynch, Intel.
5. General Electric is a well-known company. What lines of business is it in? What are the key points in the "Letter to Share Owners?" See www.ge.com: go to "Investors," and then to "Business" for the lines of business, and then "Annual Report" for the letter to share owners.
6. Where is General Electric in terms of the life cycle? What financial data support your view?
7. Go to the Yahoo! Finance stock screener (finance.yahoo.com) and use the same investment selection criteria presented in the text. What stocks meet those criteria?
8. Go to the following stock screeners: the *BusinessWeek Online* stock screener (www.businessweek.com) and Quicken's stock screener (www.quicken.com/investments/stocks). Use the same investment selection criteria presented in the text. What stocks meet those criteria?
9. Slightly change the selection criteria used in the previous questions. How do the stock selections differ?
10. Select a corporate bond, investing $25,000, 5 years to maturity, and best quality rating. Use the Yahoo! Finance bond screener (finance.yahoo.com; click on "Bonds") or Bonds Online (www.bondsonline.com). What bonds meet your investment criteria?

NOTES

1   Go to www.federalreserve.gov; then click on "Monetary Policy;" next click on "Beige Book."
2   See www.census.gov. Click on "Business." If the "Economic Briefing Room" is not shown, click on "More," then on the "Economic Briefing Room."

3 Martha Brannigan, "Midway Air Files for Chapter 11: To Cut 700 Workers," *Wall Street Journal*, August 15, 2001.

4 Data are from the *Statistical Abstract of the United States, 2000* (Washington, DC: US Census Bureau), table 1296 (SIC Code 58).

5 "Polaroid Files for Bankruptcy," *CNNmoney*, October 12, 2001. See CNNmoney.com (visited 10/12/01).

6 Juan Enriquez, *As the Future Catches You: How Genomics & Other Forces Are Changing Your Life, Work, Health & Wealth* (New York: Crown Publishing, 2001).

7 General Electric 2000 Annual Report, letter to share owners. See www.ge.com/annual00/letter/index.html.

8 Roche Holdings is a Swiss company that holds shares in companies that manufacture and sell pharmaceutical and chemical products. For more information see the Roche Holdings website, www.roche.com.

9 Donald L. Kemmerer and C. Clyde Jones, *American Economic History* (New York: McGraw-Hill Book Company, 1959), 325.

10 Daimler/Chrysler. See www.daimlerchrylser.com.

11 See www.merck.com.

12 Vioxx, Zocor, Cozaar/hyzaar, Fosamax, and Singulair.

13 This and other online sources of investment information contain a "Terms of Service" agreement and a "Privacy Policy" that users should understand and agree to before using their services.

8 Interpreting Financial Data

Key Concepts

Balance sheet
Basic earnings per share
Book value and tangible book value
Cash earnings
Consolidated statement of cash flows
Current assets
Current liabilities
Days of accounts payable outstanding
Days of cash and short-term investments outstanding
Days of inventory outstanding
Days of receivables outstanding
Diluted earnings per share
Dividend
Dividend payout ratio
Dividend yield
EDGAR
Financial leverage
Income statement
Internal growth rate
Leverage ratio (LR)
Liquidity
Long-term debt/equity
Market capitalization
Net income
Operating earnings
Profit margin
Pro forma earnings

Retention rate
Return on assets (ROA)
Return on equity (ROE)
Return on invested capital (ROIC)
Revenue per seat mile flown
Sales per day (SPD)
Sales per square foot
Stockholders' equity
Value spread
Weighted average cost of capital (WACC)

There are many reasons for analyzing firms' financial data. Banks do it to determine if their customers can repay loans. Auditors do it to determine if firms are following generally accepted accounting principles (GAAP). We are doing it as part of evaluating the intrinsic value of a firm. In that regard, analyzing firms' financial data is analogous to a physician giving a physical exam. Physicians perform diagnostic tests to look at the overall condition of the patient as well as for symptoms of hidden problems, such as cancer. We are going to do the same thing in a financial sense. There is no single ratio or indicator that tells us if a firm is doing well or poorly. To make that determination, we are going to consider selected financial ratios and indicators that provide insights about the firm's financial condition. Equally important, we are going to explain the significance of these measures because some are more important than others.

FINANCIAL STATEMENTS

In the past it was up to investors to obtain the financial statements of a firm, and then to interpret the data and turn them into useful information. Today, online services analyze and interpret much of the financial and market data that are available. By way of illustration, we are going to analyze Merck & Co., Inc. using selected information that is available on Quicken.com and from Merck's website. Additional financial data can be found on CNNmoney and Bloomberg, to name just a couple of sources.

- Quicken: www.quicken.com/investing

- Merck: www.merck.com; click on "About Merck," "General Information," and "Stockholder Information" for annual reports.

- CNNmoney: CNNmoney.com; enter stock symbol in "Stock Quote."

- Bloomberg: www.bloomberg.com; enter stock symbol in "Stock Quote."

A word of caution is in order. The information providers on the websites may use different methods for calculating the same financial ratio or indicator.[1] For example, the growth rate of sales may be computed as an arithmetic or compound average using annual or quarterly data. Also, some companies have different fiscal years (e.g. year-end is June 30 or December 31). Therefore, comparisons using quarterly data based on the calendar year may produce different numbers than comparisons using fiscal year-end data. The point is that there are different ways to compute the same measures; and they may differ among information providers.

With that in mind, we are going to examine Merck. "Merck & Co. Inc. is a global, research-driven pharmaceutical company that discovers, develops, manufactures, and markets a broad range of human and animal health products, directly and through joint ventures, and provides pharmaceutical benefit services through Merck-Medco Managed Care."[2]

The financial condition of a firm must be compared to other firms in the same industry. For example, suppose that revenues increase 10% per year. Is that good or bad? The answer depends on what comparable firms are doing. It's bad if the comparable firms are growing at 18% per year, and it's good if they are growing at a slower pace. Merck is considered a major drug manufacturer in the healthcare sector of the industry. Merck's growth rate of sales for 2000 was 27.6% over the previous year's while the industry grew 29.5%. Its 5-year compound growth rate of sales was 17.8% compared to the industry's 13.63%.[3]

INVESTOR INSIGHTS

EDGAR

EDGAR stands for the Securities and Exchange Commission's Electronic Data Gathering, Analysis, and Retrieval system. Publicly traded firms are required to provide the SEC with an Annual Report to Shareholders, an annual Form 10-K and quarterly Form 10-Q financial statements, and other information about their businesses. According to the SEC, "the Annual Report to Shareholders is the principal document used by most public companies to disclose corporate information to shareholders. It is usually a state-of-the-company report including an opening letter from the Chief Executive Officer, financial data, results of continuing operations, market segment information, new product plans, subsidiary activities and research and development activities on future programs." The "Form 10-K is the annual report that most reporting companies file with the Commission. It provides a comprehensive overview of the registrant's business. The report must be filed within 90 days after the end of the company's fiscal year."* Some firms combine the Annual

Report to Shareholders with their Form 10-K. The "Form 10-Q is a report filed quarterly by most reporting companies. It includes unaudited financial statements and provides a continuing view of the company's financial position during the year. The report must be filed for each of the first three fiscal quarters of the company's fiscal year and is due within 45 days of the close of the quarter."*

EDGAR can be accessed directly from the SEC (www.sec.gov) and from many company websites which have links to the SEC filings. Additionally, try FreeEDGAR (www.freeedgar.com), which also provides access to EDGAR. Finally, other websites, such as Bloomberg, CNNmoney, Quicken, and Yahoo! finance have links to EDGAR.

* For descriptions of SEC Forms, see www.sec.gov (visited 8/16/01).

Balance sheet

Merck's consolidated balance sheet is listed in Table 8.1. The **balance sheet** reflects the firm's financial condition as of a particular date (December 31, 2000). It lists what the company owns (assets) and what it owes (liabilities). The difference between the assets and the liabilities is **stockholders' equity**, which is what the stockholders own. Stockholders' equity also is called **book value**.[4] The book value of Merck at the end of 2000 was $14.8 billion. Stated otherwise, the stockholders own $14.8 billion of Merck's $39.9 billion in assets. However, Merck's stock market value, or **market capitalization** (market price times the number of shares outstanding), was $159.1 billion, a $144.3 billion dollar difference between the book value and the market value of the stock! Why the big difference?

$$\text{Stockholders' equity (book value)} = \text{Assets} - \text{Liabilities} \qquad (8.1)$$

The principal reason for the difference is that book value is a *backward-looking* measure that reflects historical accounting data as of a certain date. In contrast, market capitalization is a *forward-looking* measure that reflects the earnings potential of the firm.

Another reason for the difference is that the balance sheet does not value most intangibles,[5] such as patents, brand names (e.g. Coca-Cola), intellectual property, franchises, expertise, and so on. Patents protect the value of the new medicines Merck discovers, but they are not recognized on the balance sheet. Nevertheless, it is the expected income from the new and existing patented medicines that is reflected in the market capitalization.

Firms that depend on patents or intellectual property for their growth are different from traditional manufacturing firms such as General Motors. The major costs of

Table 8.1 Merck's consolidated balance sheet *(December 31 2000) ($ in millions)*

Assets	2000	1999
Current Assets		
Cash and cash equivalents	$2,536.8	$2,021.9
Short-term investments	1,717.8	1,180.5
Accounts receivable	5,017.9	4,089.0
Inventories	3,021.5	2,846.9
Prepaid expenses and taxes	1,059.4	1,120.9
Total current assets	13,353.4	11,259.2
Investments	4,947.8	4,761.5
Property, Plant and Equipment (at cost)		
Land	344.7	259.2
Buildings	5,481.1	4,465.8
Machinery, equipment, and office furnishings	8,576.5	7,385.7
Construction in progress	2,304.9	2,236.3
	16,707.2	14,347.0
Less allowance for depreciation	5,225.1	4,670.3
	11,482.1	9,676.7
Goodwill and Other Intangibles (net of accumulated amortization		
of $1,850.7 million in 2000 and $1,488.7 million in 1999)	7,374.2	7,584.2
Other Assets	2,752.9	2,353.3
	$39,910.4	$35,634.9
Liabilities and Stockholders' Equity		
Current Liabilities		
Accounts payable and accrued liabilities	$4,361.3	$4,158.7
Loans payable and current portion of long-term debt	3,319.3	2,859.0
Income taxes payable	1,244.3	1,064.1
Dividends payable	784.7	677.0
Total current liabilities	9,709.6	8,758.8
Long-Term Debt	3,600.7	3,143.9
Deferred Income Taxes and Noncurrent Liabilities	6,746.7	7,030.1
Minority Interests	5,021.0	3,460.5
Stockholders' Equity		
Common stock, one cent per value		
Authorized – 5,400,000,000 shares		
Issued – 2,968,355,365 shares – 2000		
– 2,968,030,509 shares – 1999	29.7	29.7
Other paid-in capital	6,265.8	5,920.5
Retained earnings	27,363.9	23,447.9
Accumulated other comprehensive income	30.8	8.1
	33,690.2	29,406.2
Less treasury stock, at cost		
660,756,186 shares – 2000		
638,953,059 shares – 1999	18,857.8	16,164.6
Total stockholders' equity	14,832.4	13,241.6
	$39,910.4	$35,634.9

developing a patent or software are on the front-end of the project. After a patent or software has been approved and developed, the marginal cost of producing additional units is very low – resulting in high profit margins. In contrast, the cost of producing cars remains relatively high and the profit margins are thin.

On the asset side of the balance sheet, there is information about **current assets**, which are those that can be converted into cash within a year. These include cash, short-term investments, accounts receivable, and inventories. We will examine how efficiently Merck manages these assets later in this chapter. The assets also include Merck's longer-term investments, property, plant and equipment, goodwill and selected intangibles.

The liability side of the balance sheet includes **current liabilities** – those due within 1 year – and longer-term debts. This brings us to **financial leverage** – the amount of debt relative to equity or assets. In 2000, Merck's long-term debt was 24% of its equity (**long-term debt/equity**). The important point here is that a single year alone does not tell the entire story. In 1996, for example, long-term debt/equity was 10%. This indicates that Merck increased its financial leverage.

$$\text{Long-term debt/Equity} = \text{Long-term debt/Stockholder's equity} \qquad (8.2)$$

Leverage also can be measured by dividing assets by equity.

$$\text{Leverage ratio} = \text{Assets/Equity} \qquad (8.3)$$

A **leverage ratio** of 1 means that every $1 of assets is financed by $1 of equity. The leverage ratio for Merck in 2000 was 2.7. More will be said about this ratio shortly.

Figure 8.1 provides a graph and a table showing how Merck's financial leverage has increased in recent years. It also provides a commentary comparing Merck's leverage to that of the industry, sector, and the S&P 500.

Income statement

Sales Merck's annual consolidated statement of income reflects its income and expenses for the entire year. Sales for 2000 were $40.36 billion, up 23.4% from the previous year (see Table 8.2).

Expenses Most of Merck's expenses were for materials and production, and marketing and administrative expenses. As previously noted, patents play a crucial role in this firm's future. New patents are the end result of spending on research and development (R&D), which has increased over the years both in absolute and relative terms (see Table 8.3).

Earnings Net income is the difference between income and expenses after taxes. In 2000, Merck reported net income of $6.82 billion, an increase of 15.6% over the previous year.

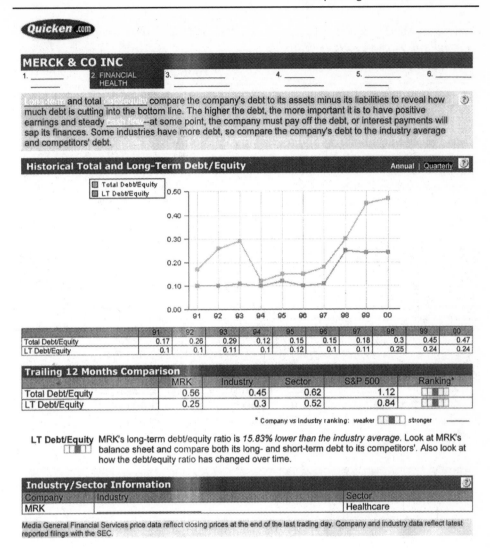

Figure 8.1   Quicken.com, Stock Evaluator, financial health of Merck & Co., Inc.

The net income divided by the number of shares of common stock outstanding is the **basic earnings per share** ($2.96). Because Merck has a large number of stock option plans outstanding, it also reports **diluted earnings per share** ($2.90). Diluted earnings per share takes into account options that can be exercised and converted into common stock.

Basic earnings per share = Net income/Number of shares of
common stock outstanding   (8.4)

Table 8.2 Merck's consolidated statement of income 2000 *(years ended December 31)* *($ in millions except per share amounts)*

	2000	1999	1998
Sales	**$40,363.2**	$32,714.0	$26,898.2
Costs, Expenses, and Other			
Materials and production	**22,443.5**	17,534.2	13,925.4
Marketing and administrative	**6,167.7**	5,199.9	4,511.4
Research and development	**2,343.8**	2,068.3	1,821.1
Acquired research	—	51.1	1,039.5
Equity income from affiliates	**(764.9)**	(762.0)	(884.3)
Gains on sales of businesses	—	—	(2,147.7)
Other (income) expense, net	**349.0**	3.0	499.7
	30,539.1	24,094.5	18,765.1
Income Before Taxes	**9,824.1**	8,619.5	8,133.1
Taxes on Income	**3,002.4**	2,729.0	2,884.9
Net Income	**$6,821.7**	$5,890.5	$5,248.2
Basic Earnings per Common Share	**$2.96**	$2.51	$2.21
Earnings per Common Share Assuming Dilution	**$2.90**	$2.45	$2.15

Table 8.3 Merck's R&D expenses

Year	R&D expense ($ billion)	R&D sales (%)
1992	1.1	11
1995	1.3	7.8
1998	2.8	10.4
2000	6.2	15.4

Source: Merck & Co., Inc., 2000 Annual Report.

$$\text{Diluted earnings per share} = \text{Net income/Number of shares assuming dilution from options} \qquad (8.5)$$

Earnings per share (EPS) is particularly important to stock analysts who provide forecasts to services such as *Thomson Financial/First Call*. If a company misses the earnings target that the analysts estimate, or that the company provides, its stock price will suffer. Analysts' estimates of EPS are widely circulated on the Internet and elsewhere for all to see. For example, as of September 2001, analysts were estimating that Merck's EPS for fiscal year 2001 would range from $3.10 to $3.16, and for 2002 it would range from $3.16 to $3.53.[6]

INVESTOR INSIGHTS

REVENUES AND EARNINGS PER SHARE

Inflated revenue: Some companies boost their earnings in the following ways. For example, a dot.com company may exchange $1 million in "banner ads" on its website with another dot.com for $1 million in ads on the other website. No money has changed hands, but both companies report $1 million in revenue and expenses.
Revenue now or later: Suppose that you close a deal with a customer to use your company's software for the next 4 years. Should all of the revenue be reported now, or should it be spread over 4 years? The SEC wants it spread over 4 years.
Adjusted earnings is also called pro forma earnings (defined below).
Basic earnings per share is usually computed by dividing income available for common stock by the number of shares outstanding. In recent years some companies have developed other measures. For example:

- *Operating earnings:* Net income less special items such as the cost of mergers or plant closings.

- *Cash earnings:* Net income ignoring amortization of goodwill from mergers.

- *Core earnings:* This refers to operating earnings, but there is no set definition for this term.

EBITDA stands for earnings before interest, taxes, depreciation, and amortization. It is a widely used form of pro forma earnings.
Pro forma earnings: Projected numbers used by technology companies that have no earnings to report. For example, Jds Uniphase reported pro forma earnings of $0.14. The GAAP earnings were −$1.13, a difference of $1.27.* Similarly, Checkfree reported pro forma earnings of −$0.04, while the GAAP earnings were −$1.17, a difference of $1.13.* There are no definitions in the accounting rules for operating earnings or pro forma earnings.

* Andy Kessler, "Creative Accounting.com," *Wall Street Journal*, July 24, 2000, A26; David Henry, "The Numbers Game," *BusinessWeek*, May 14, 2001, 100–10; Nanette Byrnes and David Henry, "Confused about Earnings," *BusinessWeek*, November 26, 2001, 77–84.

EPS and financial leverage   Merck increased its financial leverage in recent years. To illustrate the effect of financial leverage on EPS, consider the data presented in Table 8.4 below. The data represent a firm with no financial leverage, a firm with average financial leverage, a bank with high leverage, and a firm with extremely high financial leverage, such as Fannie Mae (FNM – NYSE stock symbol). FNM is a

Table 8.4 Understanding financial leverage

	No leverage	Average leverage	Banks – high leverage	FNM – extremely high leverage
Assets	$100	$100	$100	$100
Debt	0	30	90	97
Equity	100	70	10	3
Total	$100	$100	$100	$100
Leverage ratio	1×	1.4×	10×	33×
Total revenue	Earnings per share	Earnings per share	Earnings per share	Earnings per share
$100	$1	$1	$1	$1
$200	$1	$2.43	$11	$34
$50	$0.50	$0.29	Default; can't pay interest (−$40)	Default; can't pay interest (−$47)

Assumptions for Table 8.4:
1. Debt and equity represent both the dollar amount and the number of securities.
2. Each bond earns $1 interest.
3. No taxes.

private, shareholder-owned company operating under a federal government charter. It specializes in providing mortgage funds to financial institutions.[7]

For simplicity, suppose that each firm has $100 in assets. Debt and equity represent both the dollar amount and the number of securities. The assets can be financed by debt or equity. The firm with no leverage is financed entirely by equity, and at the other extreme FNM has $97 debt and $3 in equity. Each bond earns $1 interest, and there are no taxes. The leverage ratios (assets/equity) range from 1 to 33. Recall that Merck's leverage ratio was 2.7, which is slightly above average. However, consider FNM's leverage ratio of 33 – it is supporting $33 dollars of assets for every $1 of equity!

If we assume that total revenue is $100, then each firm will earn $1 per share. If the total revenue doubles to $200, the firm with no leverage will earn $2 per share, while FNM will earn $34 per share (($200 − $97)/3 = $34). But what happens when total revenues fall to $50? The table reveals the firm with no leverage will earn $0.50, the average firm will earn $0.29 per share, and the bank and FNM will not be able to cover their interest payments and they default on their debts.

This demonstrates that the higher the degree of financial leverage, the greater the impact of a change in total revenue on EPS. When total revenues are rising, the highly leveraged firms benefit the most. When revenues fall, the highly leveraged firms are in financial jeopardy. Many firms in the stabilization phase of the life cycle that was discussed in the previous chapter tend to increase their financial leverage in order to enhance their earnings growth.

Table 8.5 Analysis of cash flow statement patterns

Pattern no.	CF from operating	CF from investing	CF from financing	Explanation
1	+	+	+	*Profitable from operations,* sale of assets, building up cash
2	+	−	−	*Profitable from operations,* buying fixed assets, paying debts or paying owners
3	+	+	−	*Profitable from operations,* selling fixed assets, paying debts or paying owners
4	+	−	+	*Profitable from operations,* borrowing to expand
5	−	+	+	Operating shortfall covered by sale of fixed assets and borrowing on shareholder contributions
6	−	−	+	Operating shortfall and purchase of fixed assets financed by new debt or owners
7	−	+	−	Operating shortfall and payment to debt and/or stockholders financed by sale of fixed assets
8	−	−	−	Operating shortfall, using cash reserve to pay creditors and/or investors

Consolidated statement of cash flows

The **consolidated statement of cash flows** summarizes the sources and uses of funds. The term cash flow is a misnomer because the statement includes the disposition of cash, other funds, and noncash expenses such as depreciation. This statement is part of Merck's financial statements presented in their annual report.

The statement of cash flows is divided into three major parts: (1) cash flows from operating activities, (2) cash flows from investing activities, and (3) cash flows from financing activities. The cash flows can be positive (+) dollar amounts or negative (−) dollar amounts. There are eight possible patterns (+, −) of operating, investing, and financing cash flows, and they are depicted in Table 8.5 along with their interpretation.[8] In most cases, investors should look for positive cash flows from operations and negative cash flows from investing activities (this was the case for Merck). Where that pattern does not exist, they should find out why.

PROFITABILITY

Profits are the ultimate test of management's effectiveness, and they are of major concern to investors. As discussed above, EPS is a key measure of profitability. In this section we are going to examine some other important measures of profitability.

Measures of profitability

The **return on equity (ROE)** is calculated by dividing net income by common shareholders' equity. Stockholders' equity consists mainly of retained earnings and paid-in equity capital. ROE measures the return on the stockholders' investment in the company.

$$ROE = \text{Net income}/\text{Stockholders' equity} \qquad (8.6)$$

The **return on assets (ROA)** is calculated by dividing net income by total assets. It is the broadest measure of return on the firm's assets.

$$ROA = \text{Net income}/\text{Total assets} \qquad (8.7)$$

The relationship between ROE and ROA is presented in the following equation.

$$\text{Return on equity} = \text{Return on assets} \times \text{Leverage ratio} \qquad (8.8)$$
$$ROE = ROA \times LR$$
$$NI/E = NI/A \times A/E$$

where

NI = net income
E = common stockholders' equity
A = total assets

From this equation, we see that there are three ways to increase ROE. First a firm can operate more efficiently and earn more income per dollar of assets to increase its ROA. Second, it can increase its financial leverage. Recall that a leverage ratio of 1 means that every dollar of assets is financed by $1 of equity. If the ROA is 10% and the LR is 1, the ROE will be 10%.

$$ROE = ROA \times LR$$
$$10\% = 10\% \times 1$$

What happens if the firm didn't earn any more money and the ROA remains unchanged, but it increases its LR to 1.5? The ROE will increase to 15%, giving the appearance that it is more profitable. This demonstrates that ROE is affected by the degree of financial leverage.

$$ROE = ROA \times LR$$
$$15\% = 10\% \times 1.5$$

Finally, both profitability and financial leverage can increase, and result in a higher ROE.

Figure 8.2 shows Merck's ROE and ROA. Notice how the ROE increased faster than its ROA as the financial leverage increased in recent years. The figure also shows the **return on invested capital (ROIC)**. It measures how well the company did on its invested capital.

$$ROIC = \text{Return from operations/Invested capital} \qquad (8.9)$$

where

> Return from operations is net operating profits less adjusted taxes (NOPLAT).
> Invested capital is long-term debt, and common and preferred equity.

ROIC is useful in determining whether a firm is creating or destroying value. The difference between its ROIC and the **weighted average cost of capital (WACC)** is called the **value spread**.[9] Simply stated, WACC is the firm's cost of raising funds. More will be said about it in the next chapter. If the ROIC is greater than WACC, the firm is creating value because it is earning more than its cost of funds. Conversely, if ROIC is less than WACC, it is destroying value. As shown in Figure 8.2, Merck's ROIC is 37%. Suppose that Merck's WACC is 15%, then Merck's value spread is a positive 22%, which is very high.

$$\text{Value spread} = ROIC - WACC \qquad (8.10)$$

The **profit margin** measures profitability relative to sales. It is easily computed from the numbers provided in the income statement (Table 8.2). Merck's profit margin peaked in 1992 at 25.3%, and has declined steadily since then. In 2000, the profit margin was 16.9%.

$$\text{Profit margin} = \text{Net income/Sales} \qquad (8.11)$$

Collectively, the aforementioned measures indicate that Merck is a profitable firm. However, its profitability is increasing at a decreasing rate. Stated another way, the growth rate of profits has been slowing.

Dividends

The cash dividend is the only financial return that shareholders receive until they sell their stock. Merck paid cash dividends of $1.21 per share of common stock in 2000, up from $0.62 per share in 1995. However, the company's dividend payout ratio declined from 47% in 1995 to 43% in 2000. The **dividend payout ratio** is the percentage of net income paid as cash dividends to the stockholders.

$$\text{Dividend payout ratio} = \text{Cash dividend/Net income} \qquad (8.12)$$

MERCK & CO INC

1. _____ 2. _____ 3. MANAGEMENT PERFORMANCE 4. _____ 5. _____ 6. _____

Return on Equity, Return on Assets, and Return on Invested Capital are used to measure a company's profitability. Are managers successfully converting share- holders' equity, assets, and invested capital into net earnings? Compare to the industry average and competitors to gauge the company's success.

Historical ROE, ROA, and ROIC   Annual | Quarterly

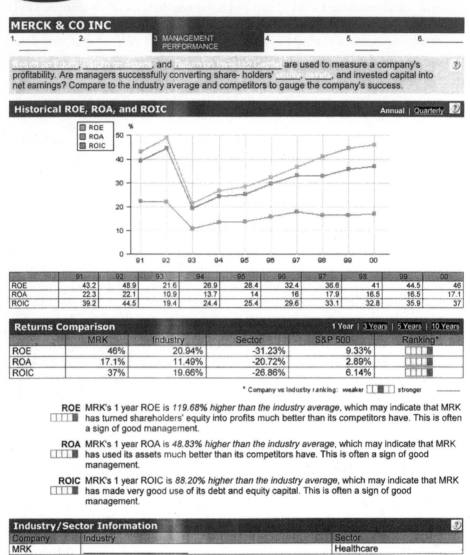

	91	92	93	94	95	96	97	98	99	00
ROE	43.2	48.9	21.6	26.9	28.4	32.4	36.6	41	44.5	46
ROA	22.3	22.1	10.9	13.7	14	16	17.9	16.5	16.5	17.1
ROIC	39.2	44.5	19.4	24.4	25.4	29.6	33.1	32.8	35.9	37

Returns Comparison   1 Year | 3 Years | 5 Years | 10 Years

	MRK	Industry	Sector	S&P 500	Ranking*
ROE	46%	20.94%	-31.23%	9.33%	
ROA	17.1%	11.49%	-20.72%	2.89%	
ROIC	37%	19.66%	-26.86%	6.14%	

* Company vs Industry ranking: weaker ☐☐■☐☐ stronger

ROE MRK's 1 year ROE is *119.68% higher than the industry average*, which may indicate that MRK has turned shareholders' equity into profits much better than its competitors have. This is often a sign of good management.

ROA MRK's 1 year ROA is *48.83% higher than the industry average*, which may indicate that MRK has used its assets much better than its competitors have. This is often a sign of good management.

ROIC MRK's 1 year ROIC is *88.20% higher than the industry average*, which may indicate that MRK has made very good use of its debt and equity capital. This is often a sign of good management.

Industry/Sector Information

Company	Industry	Sector
MRK		Healthcare

Media General Financial Services price data reflect closing prices at the end of the last trading day. Company and industry data reflect latest reported filings with the SEC.

Figure 8.2 Quicken.com, Stock Evaluator, management performance of Merck & Co., Inc.

Table 8.6   Internal growth rates

Growth rate of assets, $g = b \times$ ROA (%)	Retention rate, b	ROA
0.0	0.00	0.17
4.3	0.25	0.17
8.5	0.50	0.17
12.8	0.75	0.17
17.0	1.00	0.17

The **dividend yield** of the stock is the cash dividend divided by the price of the stock. In 2001, Merck increased its dividend to $1.37. With the stock selling at $69.50 per share, the dividend yield is 1.97%.

$$\text{Dividend yield} = \text{Cash dividend/Stock price} \qquad (8.13)$$

While the cash dividends increased steadily over the years, the payout ratio declined. This means that Merck retained a larger share of the earnings to help foster its asset growth. The internal growth rate of a firm's assets is directly related to the proportion of earnings it retains – the **retention rate**, b ($b = 1 -$ dividend payout ratio). The **internal growth rate** (g) is equal to the firm's return on assets (ROA) multiplied by its retention rate.

$$\text{Internal growth rate } g = b \times \text{ROA} \qquad (8.14)$$

Table 8.6 shows how a firm's dividend policy affects the growth rate of its assets. For simplicity, assume that the firm is financed entirely by equity. If the firm pays out all of its earnings as cash dividends, the internal growth rate of assets will be zero. It achieves the maximum internal growth rate of 17% when it retains all of its earnings. Merck has a dividend payout ratio of 43%, which means that its retention rate is 57% ($1 - 0.43$). Given its ROA of 17%, the internal growth rate is about 8%.

EFFICIENCY AND LIQUIDITY

The beginning of this chapter used the analogy that financial analysis was like a physical exam. The previous section examined the financial health of the firm – its profitability. This section examines how efficiently the firm is using its current assets and managing current liabilities. In addition, these ratios provide some insights about the firm's **liquidity** – the ability to meet its short-term financial obligations. Equally important, they serve as early warning indicators of financial distress. If a firm is having problems with its cash, receivables, inventories, and payables in the short term, it may not survive the long run.

To simplify the examination process, we measure the number of days of receivables, inventories, accounts payable, and cash that are outstanding. In other words, all of the measures are in the number of "days outstanding" rather than turnover ratios. The number of "days outstanding" is easy to calculate and to interpret. The first step is to determine **sales per day (SPD)**.

$$SPD = \text{Sales revenue}/365 \qquad (8.15)$$

Accounts receivable

Sales revenue drives corporate growth. The other side of that coin is that a sale is not complete until the funds are collected. The uncollected funds are represented by accounts receivable. Using data from Merck's balance sheet and income statement we compute the SPD and then the **days of receivables outstanding**.

$$\text{Days of receivables outstanding} = \text{Accounts receivable}/SPD \qquad (8.16)$$

During the 1998–2000 periods, Merck's sales revenues per day increased sharply from $73.7 million to $110.6 million. It took the firm about 45 days to collect on its sales. The firm is consistent in its collection policy.

Year	2000	1999	1998
Sales per day (SPD) ($ millions)/365	$40,363/365 = $110.6	$32,714/365 = $89.7	$26,898/365 = $73.7
Days of accounts receivable outstanding	$5,017.9/SPD = 45.4 days	$4,089.0/SPD = 45.6 days	$3,374.1/SPD = 45.8 days

Inventories

The **days of inventory outstanding** is determined by dividing the inventory by SPD. As shown below, Merck increased its efficiency by sharply reducing the number of days of inventory that it keeps on hand from 35.6 days to 27.3 days.

$$\text{Days of inventory outstanding} = \text{Inventory}/SPD \qquad (8.17)$$

Year	2000	1999	1998
Days of inventory outstanding	$3,021/SPD = 27.3 days	$2,847/SPD = 31.7 days	$2,624/SPD = 35.6 days

Accounts payable

The **days of accounts payable outstanding** is determined by dividing the accounts payable by SPD. The data reveal that Merck is paying its bills faster. It may be doing this to take advantage of discounts for early payments, or to avoid the penalties for late payments.

Days of accounts payable outstanding = Accounts payable/SPD   (8.18)

Year	2000	1999	1998
Days of accounts payable outstanding	$4,361/SPD = 39.4 days	$4,158/SPD = 46.4 days	$3,682/SPD = 50.0 days

Cash and short-term investments

Cash and short-term investments are a firm's most liquid assets. The **days of cash and short-term investments outstanding** is determined by dividing the sum of both by SPD. The data suggest that Merck has ample short-term funds on hand to meet its short-term needs. If it needs more, it is in good enough financial shape to borrow funds.

Days of cash and short-term investments outstanding
= (Cash + Short-term investments)/SPD   (8.19)

Year	2000	1999	1998
Days of cash and short-term investments outstanding	$4,254/SPD = 38.5 days	$3,193/SPD = 35.6 days	$3,355.7/SPD = 45.7 days

CONCLUSION

The purpose of this chapter is to introduce selected financial measures that are available online, or that can be computed easily from data that are available online, in order to determine the general financial condition of a firm. These measures include the statement of cash flows and those shown above that provide insights about a firm's profitability, financial leverage, efficiency, and liquidity. They should not be construed as providing a complete and detailed financial analysis of the firm. That is beyond the scope of this book.

Finally, it should be noted that industry specific measures are important in selected industries. **Sales per square foot** of store space in the retail industry and **revenue per seat mile flown** in the airline industry are two examples of such measures.

Box 8.1 Summary of ratios and indicators

Balance sheet

$$\text{Stockholders' equity (book value)} = \text{Assets} - \text{Liabilities} \tag{8.1}$$

Financial leverage

$$\text{Long-term debt/Equity} = \text{Long-term debt/Stockholder's equity} \tag{8.2}$$

$$\text{Leverage ratio} = \text{Assets/Equity} \tag{8.3}$$

Profitability

$$\text{Basic earnings per share} = \text{Net income/Number of shares of common stock outstanding} \tag{8.4}$$

$$\text{Diluted earnings per share} = \text{Net income/Number of shares assuming dilution from options} \tag{8.5}$$

$$\text{Return on equity (ROE)} = \text{Net income/Stockholders' equity} \tag{8.6}$$

$$\text{Return on assets (ROA)} = \text{Net income/Total assets} \tag{8.7}$$

$$\text{Return on equity (ROE)} = \text{Return on assets (ROA)} \times \text{Leverage ratio (LR)} \tag{8.8}$$

$$\text{Return on invested capital (ROIC)} = \text{Return from operations/Invested capital} \tag{8.9}$$

$$\text{Value spread} = \text{ROIC} - \text{Weighted average cost of capital (WACC)} \tag{8.10}$$

$$\text{Profit margin} = \text{Net income/Sales} \tag{8.11}$$

$$\text{Dividend payout ratio} = \text{Cash dividend/Net income} \tag{8.12}$$

$$\text{Dividend yield} = \text{Cash dividend/Stock price} \tag{8.13}$$

$$\text{Internal growth rate, } g = b \times \text{ROA} \tag{8.14}$$

Box 8.1   Continued

Efficiency and liquidity

Sales per day (SPD) = Sales revenue/365 $\qquad$ (8.15)

Days of receivables outstanding = Accounts receivable/SPD $\qquad$ (8.16)

Days of inventory outstanding = Inventory/SPD $\qquad$ (8.17)

Days of accounts payable outstanding = Accounts payable/SPD $\qquad$ (8.18)

Days of cash and short-term investments outstanding
= (Cash + Short-term investments)/SPD $\qquad$ (8.19)

SELF-TEST QUESTIONS

1. How does Merck's growth rate of revenue over the past 5 and 10 years compare to that of the industry? To answer this question, go to www.quicken.com, click on "Investing," use Merck's symbol "MRK," then click on "Fundamentals."
2. How does Merck's growth rate of EPS compare over the same periods?
3. What do analysts project for Merck's EPS in the next fiscal year? To answer this question, go to www.quicken.com, click on "Investing," use Merck's symbol "MRK," then click on "Analyst Ratings."
4. Do analysts on average recommend buying, holding, or selling Merck?
5. How have earnings estimates for Merck's next fiscal year changed in recent months? To answer this question, go to the CNNmoney website, CNNmoney.com, enter MRK in "Stock Quote," then click on "Analyst Ratings."
6. What is the latest quarterly diluted EPS for Merck? What does management have to say about it? To answer this question, go to www.quicken.com, click on "Investing," use Merck's symbol "MRK," then click on "Financial Statements," and "Mgmt Discussion."
7. According to Bloomberg, what is Merck's "Market Cap" and "Dividend Yield"? To answer this question, go to www.bloomberg.com, and enter "MRK" in the "Stock Quote."
8. How has Merck's stock return compared to the S&P 500's return? Use the same screen as in the previous question.
9. What are Merck's latest profit margin, return on assets, and return on equity according to Yahoo! Finance? To answer this question, go to finance.yahoo.com, enter MRK in "Get Quote," and under "More Info," click on "Profile."
10. Go to www.smartmoney.com then click on "Stocks." Next click on "Ratings, Competition, and Key Ratios." How does the information on this site compare with the others used in the previous questions?

NOTES

1   Quicken.com is a distributor (and not a publisher) of content supplied by third parties. Quicken's Stock Evaluator uses the services of Media General Financial Services to perform the financial calculations. Quicken is owned by Intuit. See www.intuit.com.
2   Merck & Co., Inc., 2000 Annual Report, cover. The annual report is available on Merck's website: www.merck.com.
3   Data are from www.quicken.com/investments/stats (visited 8/16/01).
4   Some online financial information portals, such as Quicken and Yahoo! Finance, define book value as total assets less intangibles and less liabilities. This can be thought of as **tangible book value**.
5   The intangibles listed with goodwill are primarily customer relationships that arose in connection with the acquisition of Medco Containment Services Inc. For more details, see the annual report's "Notes to Consolidated Financial Statements," concerning goodwill and other intangibles.
6   www.quicken.com/investments/estimates (visited 8/10/01).
7   For further information, see www.fanniemae.com.
8   For additional information, see Michael T. Dugan and Benton E. Gup, "Teaching the Statement of Cash Flows," *Journal of Accounting Education*, vol. 9, 1991, 33–52.
9   The value spread multiplied by the invested capital is called economic profit, or economic value added (EVA^{TM}). EVA^{TM} is a trademark of Stern Stewart & Co. For a further discussion, see Tom Copeland, Tim Koller, and Jack Murrin, *Valuation: Measuring and Managing the Value of Companies*, 3rd edn (New York: John Wiley & Sons, Inc., 2000).

9 Valuation Models

Key Concepts

Beta
Book value
Capital asset pricing model (CAPM)
Capitalization rate
Dividend valuation models (simplified and complex)
Free cash flow (FCF)
Free cash flow valuation model
Intrinsic value
Market capitalization
Market risk premium
Most recent quarter (MRQ)
PEG ratio
Price/book ratio
Price/cash flow ratio
Price/earnings (P/E) ratio
Price/free cash flow ratio
Price/sales (P/S) ratio
Projected earnings
Rate of return on the market
Required rate of return
Risk-free rate of return
Risk premium
Systematic risk
Tangible book value
Technical analysis
Trailing twelve months (TTM)
Weighted average cost of capital (WACC)

How much is a stock worth? To answer that question, this chapter presents various financial models and valuation ratios that may be used in estimating a stock's **intrinsic value** – the theoretical value of the stock. Even if a stock appears to be undervalued, it may not be the time to buy it. This chapter also explains how investor psychology can affect stock prices.

DIVIDEND VALUATION MODELS

Simplified dividend valuation model

The simplified **dividend valuation model** was introduced in Chapters 4 and 7, and it is explained in greater depth here. According to the simplified model, the intrinsic value of a stock can be determined by the following equation.

$$P_0 = \frac{D_1}{k-g} \tag{9.1}$$

where

P_0 = current price (at time 0)
D_1 = cash dividend in time period 1
k = the rate of return required by equity investors (capitalization rate)
g = growth rate of cash dividends

By way of illustration, assume that a company is expected to pay a $2.50 dividend per share next year (D_1) and the dividend is expected to grow at an annual rate of 8%. Further assume that investors can invest in risk-free Treasury securities that yield about 10%. Because investing in the company is riskier than investing in Treasury securities, equity investors want a **risk premium** – an amount over the risk-free rate – of, say, 5 percentage points. Therefore, the **required rate of return** (also called the **capitalization rate**) in this example is 15%. The intrinsic value of the stock is:

$$P_0 = \frac{D_1}{k-g}$$

$$= \frac{2.50}{0.15-0.08} = \$35.71$$

The problem with the simplified model is that the assumption of a constant growth rate of dividends does not apply to all companies. We know from the examination of the life cycle that firms in the pioneering phase generally pay no cash dividends. As the firms mature in the expansion phase, they begin to pay small, but increasing cash dividends. Simply stated, the model does not provide good results when the growth rate of dividends varies over time.

Complex dividend valuation model

As firms mature, they tend to increase their dividend payouts. Therefore the simplified divided valuation model has limitations because it only has one growth for dividends. However, the dividend valuation model can be modified to take into account various growth rates of dividends. By way of illustration, equation 9.2 is the two-period dividend valuation model for a firm whose cash dividends are expected to grow at one rate for an explicit forecast period of time, and then at a constant rate thereafter. The model can be expanded to include more time periods reflecting the change in growth rates of dividends that occur as a firm matures.

$$P_0 = \sum_{t=1}^{n} \frac{D_0(1+g_x)^t}{(1+k)^t} + \frac{D_{n+1}}{(k-g_y)} \left[\frac{1}{(1+k)^n} \right] \tag{9.2}$$

where

D_0 = dividend in year 0 (the initial year as used here)
g_x = growth rate of dividends for n years
g_y = growth rate of dividends for years $n + 1$ and beyond
k = the rate of return required by equity investors
sigma (Σ) stands for summation over the time period

The usefulness of this or any model is highly dependent on the validity of the assumptions used. If the assumptions are wrong, the model will not give a valid estimate of intrinsic value. The dividend valuation model is based on two crucial assumptions. The first assumption is that the company will pay cash dividends now or at some predictable time in the future. If the company is never going to pay dividends, other methods of valuation are available. The second assumption is that the rate of return required by equity investors is greater than the growth rate of dividends ($k > g$). Both the capitalization rate and growth rate of dividends must be estimated correctly. The capital asset pricing model may be used to estimate the capitalization rate, and it will be explained shortly.

Example using the complex dividend valuation model

To illustrate the use of the complex dividend valuation model (equation 9.2), assume that Jupiter Industries is paying a cash dividend of $1.00 ($D_0$) this year. It is expected that the cash dividends will increase 20% per year for the next 5 years (g_x). Thereafter, dividends will increase 10% per year (g_y). Finally, the capitalization rate is 15% rate of return (k). Let's solve the problem step by step.

Step 1 The first step is to calculate the present value of the dividends for the first 5 years. Their worth today is the present value of dividends received in the future

Table 9.1 Present value calculation

	1	2	3 = 1 × 2
Years, n	Dividends $D_n = (1 + g_x)^t$	Present value of capitalization rate, $k = 0.15$	Present value of dividends ($)
0	$1.00	$PV_n = \dfrac{1}{(1+k)^n}$	
1	1.200	0.870	1.044
2	1.440	0.756	1.089
3	1.728	0.658	1.137
4	2.074	0.572	1.186
5	2.488	0.497	1.237
Total			5.69

discounted by the required rate of return. Present value calculations can be computed manually with calculators, or using computer spreadsheets. As shown in Table 9.1, the present value of the dividends to be received over the first 5 years is $5.69.

Step 2 (a) The next step is to determine the value at the end of 5 years for the remaining life of the company. This begins by computing the dividend in the 6th year. The dividend in the 6th year is the dividend in year 5 ($2.488) multiplied by 1 plus the growth rate of 10% (g_y).

$$D_6 = D_5(1+g_y)$$
$$= 2.488\ (1+0.10)$$
$$= \$2.737$$

(b) The value of the stock at the end of the 5th year (P_5) is equal to the dividend in the 6th year (D_6) divided by the capitalization rate (k) less the growth rate of dividends (g).

$$P_5 = \frac{D_6}{k-g_y}$$

$$= \frac{2.737}{0.15-0.10} = \$54.74$$

Step 3 The value of the stock at the end of the 5th year is $54.74. Now we must determine the present value of the stock at the end of the 5th year. This is accomplished by multiplying the value of stock at the end of the 5th year by the present value interest factor for that year (shown in Table 9.1).

$$54.74 \times (0.497) = \$27.21$$

Step 4 The stock's value today (P_0) equals the present value of the dividends for the first 5 years (Step 1) plus the present value of the stock at the end of 5 years (Step 3). The intrinsic value of this stock is $32.30 per share.

$$P_0 = \text{PV of dividends in years } 1\text{–}5 + \text{PV of dividends in year 6 and beyond}$$
$$= 5.69 + 27.21 = \$32.90$$

CAPITAL ASSET PRICING MODEL

The validity of the dividend valuation model depends on the correct estimation of the capitalization rate as well as other factors. The capitalization rate can be thought of as the minimum rate of return that equity investors require on a stock. It is equal to the risk-free rate of return plus beta multiplied by a market risk premium:

$$k = R_f + b \,(\text{market risk premium}) \tag{9.3}$$
$$= R_f + b \,(k_m - R_f)$$

where

k = capitalization rate (e.g. rate of return required by equity investors)
R_f = risk-free rate of return
b = beta (measure of systematic risk)
k_m = rate of return on the market

This equation is called the **capital asset pricing model (CAPM)**, and it is widely used in determining the capitalization rate. However, there has been considerable academic controversy concerning its validity. Nevertheless, it works reasonably well. The **risk-free rate of return** (R_f) is the interest rate on Treasury securities, typically 10-year bonds.[1] This amount is added to beta (b) times the **market risk premium** – the difference between the rate of return on the market (k_m) and the risk-free rate (R_f). It is the amount by which investors expect future returns to exceed the risk-free rate. The **rate of return on the market** (k_m) reflects the average return on a stock market. Table 9.2 illustrates the distribution of returns on stocks and bonds during the 1926–2000 period. The arithmetic mean difference between the returns on large company stocks and intermediate-term government bonds was 7.5% ($13.0 - 5.5 = 7.5\%$), and it was 11.8% for small company stocks. The table also reveals large standard deviations. Therefore, the rate of return on the market depends on the selection of

Table 9.2 Investment returns and risk

Investment	Annual arithmetic return (%)	Standard deviation (%)
Small company stocks	17.3	33.4
Large company stocks	13.0	20.2
Intermediate-term government bonds	5.5	5.8

Source: Ibbotson Associates, *Stocks, Bonds, Bills, and Inflation 2000 Yearbook* (Chicago, IL: 2001)

stock market indexes and time periods used to compute them. Accordingly, the risk premium will vary over time. Some academic studies estimate the equity risk premium as low as 1%.[2] In contrast, the Quicken.com Stock Evaluator assumes a 9% market risk premium and a 6% bond rate in its 15% default discount rate.[3] Investors using Quicken's Stock Evaluator can choose other rates if they wish to do so. More will be said about the Stock Evaluator in an "Investor Insights" box that follows shortly.

Beta (b) is a measure of **systematic risk** – risk that is common to all stocks and it cannot be eliminated by diversification. Beta is an index of volatility of returns on a stock relative to the returns on a market portfolio of stocks. The average beta for a market portfolio of stocks is 1. A beta of 2 implies a high degree of systematic risk, and a beta of 0.5 implies a low degree of such risk. Different stock market indexes and time periods will produce different betas. Generally speaking, investors in stocks with higher betas (higher risk) expect higher returns. We know from studying the life cycles of firms that betas tend to be high when firms are in the early stages of their life cycles, and they decrease toward 1 as the firms mature.

In summary, the required rate of return (capitalization rate) for any stock can be determined by the CAPM. In this example, the risk-free rate is 7%, the expected return on the market is 13%, and the stock has a beta of 1.5. The capitalization rate is 16%.

$$k = R_f + b \text{ (market risk premium)}$$
$$= R_f + b(k_m - R_f)$$
$$= 0.07 + 1.5(0.13 - 0.07) = 0.16 \text{ (or 16\%)}$$

Because stock market prices and interest rates change over time, the risk premiums and market rates of interest shown here for purposes of illustration may not be suitable for future periods.

DISCOUNTED CASH FLOW MODEL
Value of the firm

The dividend valuation models are used to determine the price of a stock. In contrast, the discounted cash flow model is used to determine the value of a firm. In theory, the intrinsic value of a firm is equal to the market value of its stock plus its long-term debts (equation 9.4). It follows that the **market capitalization** S (i.e. the market price of the stock times the number of shares outstanding) is equal to the value of that firm V less its debt D (equation 9.5). The price per share P_0 is computed by dividing the market capitalization S by the number of shares of common stock that are outstanding (equation 9.6).

$$V = S + D \tag{9.4}$$
$$S = V - D \tag{9.5}$$
$$\text{Price per share } P_0 = S/\text{Number of shares of common stock outstanding} \tag{9.6}$$

where

V = value of the firm (intrinsic value)
S = the firm's stock market capitalization (market value)
D = value of long-term debt (book value)

The value of the firm V can be determined by discounting expected **free cash flow (FCF)** by the firm's **weighted average cost of capital (WACC)**. For simplicity, we assume that the firm has no preferred stock. Both FCF and WACC are explained below. These concepts will next be applied to the valuation model.

$$\text{FCF} = \text{EBIT} (1 - t) + \text{Depreciation} - \text{Net investments} \tag{9.7}$$

where

EBIT = earnings before interest and taxes
Net investments = capital expenditures and increases in net working capital
t = tax rate

$$\text{WACC} = k\,(S/V) + k_d\,(1 - t)\,(D/V) \tag{9.8}$$

where

k = rate of return required by equity investors (capitalization rate)
t = tax rate
V = value of the firm (intrinsic value)
S = the firm's stock market capitalization (market value)
D = value of long-term debt (book value)

Table 9.3 illustrates the computation of WACC. We assume that a firm's target capital structure consists of 40% debt and 60% equity. The after-tax cost of debt is 5%,

Table 9.3 Weighted average cost of capital

| Security | 1 | 2 | 3 = 1 × 2 |
	Weights (%)	Component cost (%)	Weighted average (%)
Debt	40	5 (after tax)	2.0
Common stock	60	16	9.6
Totals	100		WACC = 11.6

and the cost of equity is 16%. Multiplying the weights by the component costs gives the firm's weighted average cost of capital, which is 11.6%.

Free cash flow valuation model

The free cash flow (FCF) valuation model presented here is similar to the complex dividend valuation model in that growth of FCF is projected to grow at one rate during the *forecast period*, of say 10 years, and then at another rate thereafter (e.g. the *continuing value period*). The value of the firm is equal to the present value (PV) of the FCF during the forecast period plus the present value of the price at the end of the terminal period. Next, the value of the firm's debt is subtracted from the firm value to give the intrinsic value of the equity. The intrinsic value per share is determined by dividing equity by the number of shares outstanding.

The data in Table 9.4 illustrate the use of the FCF valuation model for a hypothetical firm. The firm's FCF is expected to grow at 10% during the 10-year forecast period, and at 5% thereafter. The WACC in this example is 11.6%. The firm's FCF in year 1 is $900 million, and it is expected to grow at 10% through year 10. In year 11, the growth rate slows to 5%.

The value of the firm is $17,659,000. The firm's $500 million is debt is subtracted from the firm's value giving an intrinsic value of the equity of $17,159,000. Dividing this amount by the 150 million shares outstanding gives a price of $114.39 per share.

Firm value = PV of FCF during a forecast period + PV of price at the end of the continuing value period

$$\text{Firm value} = \sum_{t=1}^{n} \frac{\text{FCF}_t}{(1+\text{WACC})^t} + \frac{\text{FCF}_{t+1}}{(\text{WACC}-g)} \tag{9.9}$$

where

$$\text{FCF}_t = \text{free cash flow}$$
$$\text{WACC} = \text{weighted average cost of capital}$$
$$g = \text{growth rate of FCF}$$
$$\text{PV} = \text{present value}$$

Table 9.4   Firm value

Year	FCF ($ million)	Present value ($) (WACC = 11.60%)
	Growth rate @10%	
1	900	806
2	990	795
3	1089	783
4	1198	772
5	1318	761
6	1449	750
7	1594	740
8	1754	729
9	1929	718
10	2122	708
		$7,562 **Present value**
11	2228	**Growth rate 5%**
		$33,762 **Continuing value**
		$10,095 **Present value**
		$17,659 **Firm value**
		$500 **Debt**
		$17,159 **Equity**
		$114.39 **Price/share (150 million shares)**

INVESTOR INSIGHTS

QUICKEN'S STOCK EVALUATOR

The Quicken Stock Evaluator is an online tool that may be used to determine the intrinsic stock price. The intrinsic value of the firm is determined by discounting future earnings in a manner similar to that described in connection with the free cash flow valuation model. The Stock Evaluator is a two-stage model. The first stage is for a forecast period of 10 years with one earnings growth rate and one discount rate. The default discount rate is 15% (assuming a 6% bond rate and a 9% risk premium). The default rates listed here are those used in August 2001. They may change over time. Users have a choice of using the default growth rate and discount rate or supplying their own.

The second stage (continuing value) assumes that earnings will go on forever, and they are discounted at a static rate (12%) with no growth in earnings.

Like the FCF model, the intrinsic value of the firm is equal to the present value of the forecast period plus the present value of the continuing value, less the long-term debt. The intrinsic value is then divided by the number of shares outstanding to give the intrinsic stock price.

Figure 9.1 shows the Stock Evaluator for Merck & Co., Inc. Merck was discussed in the previous chapter. According to the Stock Evaluator, Merck's intrinsic value was $63.63, which is more than the market price of $57.17 at that time. The stock appears to be undervalued.

To access the Stock Evaluator, go to www.quicken.com. Then enter a stock symbol (e.g. GM, IBM) and click on "Go." Next select the "Stock Evaluator." The Stock Evaluator has a variety of screens, including "Intrinsic Value," where the model discussed here is used.

VALUATION RATIOS

The valuation ratios presented here are used to compare firms within an industry, and to compare firms and industries with the stock market. Some of the valuation ratios have multiple definitions, depending on who is providing them. This means that care must be used when comparing ratios from different sources to make sure they are compatible.

The valuation ratios are especially useful in verifying the intrinsic value that was determined using the previously described models.

Price/earnings ratio

The **price/earnings (P/E) ratio** may be calculated by dividing the current stock price by the firm's earnings for the **trailing twelve months (TTM)**, or by using **projected earnings**. Earnings are measured before extraordinary items and accounting changes. If a stock is selling for $45 and it is expected to earn $3 per share, its P/E ratio is 15.

From 1872 to 2000, the average P/E ratio for the Standard & Poor's 500 stock index was 14.5.[4] In June 2001, the P/E ratio was 33. Over time, the P/E ratio tends to revert back to the mean.

A simple rule of thumb used by some investors is that a P/E ratio, if fairly priced, will equal the firm's growth rate of earnings (G):[5]

$$P/E = G \tag{9.10}$$

Based on this rule of thumb, if a stock's P/E is 15, its growth of earnings should be about 15%. This rule of thumb works reasonably well for firms in the expansion and stabilization phases of the life cycle. If it does not work, then you have to ask why. Could it be that the stock is overvalued or undervalued? This ratio alone cannot provide the answer – it only provides clues.

For an individual stock, a high P/E ratio suggests that investors believe that it has high growth potential. Conversely, a low P/E ratio suggests slow growth. The P/E ratio can only be used if a company has positive earnings.

Quicken .com

Close this window

MERCK & CO INC

| 1. GROWTH TRENDS | 2. FINANCIAL HEALTH | 3. MANAGEMENT PERFORMANCE | 4. MARKET MULTIPLES | 5. INTRINSIC VALUE | 6. SUMMARY |

An intrinsic value/share is a hypothetical value that is based on the sum of a company's future earnings. This value can be compared to a stock's current price to help determine if a stock is overvalued or undervalued.

Calculate Intrinsic Value/Share

Initial earnings:

$ 7,185,299,968

Earnings growth rate: Explain

⦿ Analysts' avg 5 year (11.04) ▼ %

○ _____ %

Discount rate: Explain

⦿ 15.00 %

○ 1 yr T-Bill (5.00) ▼ %

[Recalc Intrinsic Value/Share] Explain

Intrinsic Value/Shr ($):   63.63
Current Price* ($):   57.17

By this calculation, MRK appears undervalued.

- **Insights:** Given the above earnings and discount rate, *MRK must grow earnings at a rate of 9.6%* annually for 10 years to justify its current stock price of $57.17. You can adjust the earnings growth rate and discount rate to see how they can dramatically alter MRK's intrinsic value per share.

- **Walk through:** If we assume initial earnings of $7.19 billion grow at a rate of 11.04%, and we discount those future earnings at a rate of 15.00%, we arrive at a net present value for the company's next 10 years of earnings of $59.6 billion. To account for potential earnings beyond the 10th year, we estimate a growth rate of 6.00%, a discount rate of 12.00%, and we arrive at a continuing value of $89.4 billion. To complete the calculation we add these two figures together, subtract the long-term debt for MRK ($4.23 billion), and divide by the outstanding shares (2.27 billion) to get a per share intrinsic value of **$63.63**.

- **Considerations:** Gauging the future growth and risk outlook of a company such as MRK, however, is more art than science. New products, management, or strategic directions can fuel growth far above historic norms. Likewise, unforeseen setbacks can cut a company's future value in half. Have MRK's earnings slowed or accelerated in the past year from its 5-year average? How fast do analysts expect it to grow in the next year or two? How great are the risks it faces? Be sure to check MRK's financials and recent news stories on the company. Also compare it to other companies in its industry.

*Quotes provided by S&P Comstock Disclaimer
Retrieved Monday, December 17, 2001 03:59 PM EST
Nasdaq quote delayed at least 15 minutes, all others at least 20 minutes.

Media General Financial Services price data reflect closing prices at the end of the last trading day. Company and industry data reflect latest reported filings with the SEC.

Figure 9.1 Quicken.com, Stock Evaluator, intrinsic value

PEG ratio

The **PEG ratio** is a stock's P/E ratio divided by its projected growth rate of earnings.

$$PEG = (P/E)/G \tag{9.11}$$

The earnings projections range from 3 to 5 years, with 5 years being the most common. The PEG ratio measures how expensive a stock is in terms of its price, earnings, and growth rate. A PEG ratio of less than 1 suggests that a stock is undervalued and it may increase in price. A PEG ratio of 1, where the P/E ratio and the growth rate are equal, suggests that the stock is fairly valued. The higher the PEG ratio, the higher the relative value of the stock. The validity of this measure depends on the accuracy of the projected earnings.

Price/sales ratio

The **price/sales (P/S) ratio** is calculated by dividing the stock market capitalization (price × shares outstanding) by the TTM total sales (or projected sales). Alternatively, it may be computed by dividing the price per share by total revenue per share.

In theory, the P/S ratio is equal to:

$$P/S = P/E \times (\text{profit margin}) \tag{9.12}$$

So, theoretically, if a firm has a P/S ratio of 1, and profit margin of 4%, the P/E ratio should be 25. If the numbers don't work out that way, further investigation is needed.

The P/S ratio is useful in evaluating companies that have no reported earnings. During the stock market bubble in 1999, the price/sales ratios for some companies were astronomical: QLT PhotoTherapeutics' ratio was 1,127.6; High Speed Access's ratio was 578.3; and Rhythms NetConnections' was 539.2. The historical median ratio for the S&P industrials was 0.9.[6]

Price/cash flow ratio

The **price/cash flow ratio** is computed by dividing the market price of the stock by the firm's cash flow (net income plus depreciation and amortization) in the TTM. Similarly, the **price/free cash flow ratio** is computed by dividing the market price of the stock by the firm's free cash flow (FCF). FCF was defined in equation 9.7. These ratios may be used for companies with both negative and positive earnings.

Price/book ratio

The **price/book ratio** compares a stock's current market price to its book value or tangible book value. **Book value** is common shareholders' equity – total assets less total liabilities in the **most recent quarter (MRQ)** – and it is usually expressed on a

Table 9.5 Valuation ratios

Valuation ratios	Merck & Co., Inc.	Industry	S&P 500
P/E ratio (TTM)	18.9	30.8	31.6
PEG ratio*	0.97	2.99	2.06
Price/sales (TTM)	2.9	5.8	3.8
Price/cash flow (TTM)	15.8	25.1	21.2
Price/free cash flow	52.2	53.5	36.4
Price/book (MRQ)	8.6	11.0	5.5
Price/tangible book (MRQ)	16.9	13.8	8.7

Source: Market Guide/ProVestor Plus Company Report, Merck & Co., Inc., December 17, 2001; *PEG ratio was computed by the author.

per share basis. **Tangible book value** is defined as total assets less intangibles and total liabilities expressed on a per share basis.

The price/book ratio assumes that asset values on a company's balance sheet reflect their current worth, and that is generally not the case for long-term assets such as real estate.

Table 9.5 illustrates these measures for Merck. The data suggest that Merck is undervalued. This is consistent with the data presented in Figure 9.1 that used a discounted cash flow model to determine Merck's intrinsic value.

Look before you leap

Knowing *when* to buy and sell stocks is as important as knowing which stocks to buy and sell. **Technical analysis** provides insights about the timing of stock purchases and sales by focusing primarily on stock prices and the volume of trades to predict future price directions and turning points. Technical analysis is used mainly by short-term traders, but it also provides useful information for longer-term investors. For example, Figure 9.2 illustrates the prices and volumes for Jds Uniphase Corp. over a 5-year period. The chart shows the rise in the stock price during the late 1990s and 2000, from about $2 per share to about $150 per share. The stock price peaked in 2000, and declined when the dot.com bubble burst. It plunged to $5.12 in the following year. If you had valued JDSU in 2001 when it was $30 per share, the declining trend in the stock price should have suggested that it was not a good buy. Thus, trends in stock prices provide insights about the timing of purchases and sales. A detailed discussion of technical analysis is beyond the scope of this book. See the following "Investor Insights" box for more information about it.

JDSU Jds Uniphase Corp   12/19/2001 1:32 PM

Last:	Change:	Open:	High:	Low:	Volume:
	☑ -0.26	8.59	8.88	8.48	15,119,000
8.60	Percent Change:	Yield:	P/E Ratio:	52 Week Range:	
	-2.93%	n/a	n/a	5.12 to 64.9375	

Figure 9.2 BigChart of JDSU

INVESTOR INSIGHTS

TECHNICAL ANALYSIS

Charts that can be customized for technical analysis are available online from http://finance.yahoo.com, www.bigcharts.com, and from other sources. The charts can be constructed to cover from 1 day up to 5 years or more. They also can be drawn as lines, bars, or candlesticks. (If you don't know what a "candlestick" chart is, look it up on the charts!) The main point about charts can be simply stated: a picture is worth a thousand words, and beauty is in the eye of the beholder.

Yahoo! Finance is one of the best online sources in terms of technical analysis because it provides overlays, technical indicators, and moving averages that are not available from other sites. It also explains many technical terms such as *Bollanger Bands* (an envelope plotted at a standard deviation around a moving average of prices) and *Money Flow Index* (an index of money flowing in and out of a security). BigCharts, which is part of CBS Martket Watch, has easy-to-use interactive charts, stock screeners, and other investment information.

INVESTOR PSYCHOLOGY

Investor psychology plays a significant role in the price swings that take place in the stock market and in the determination of stock prices. The collective views of investors are reflected by the changing groups of stocks that are in fashion at any given moment in time and by investors' reactions to domestic and international events. Thus, the stock market is always changing as investors continuously search for new and profitable investments. John Maynard Keynes summed up this aspect of investor psychology in the following statement:

> Professional investment may be likened to those newspaper competitions in which the competitors have to pick out the six prettiest faces from 100 photographs, the prize being awarded to the competitor whose choice most nearly corresponds to the average preference of the competitors as a whole. So, each competitor has to pick not those which he, himself thinks likeliest to catch the fancy of the other competitors, all of whom are looking at the same problem from the same point of view. It is not a case of picking those which average opinion rates the prettiest; we have reached the third degree where we devote our intelligence to anticipating what average opinion expects average opinion to be. And there are some, I believe, who are practicing the fourth, fifth, and higher degrees.[7]

Investor psychology is reflected in reactions of investors to news events. For example, when the President is going to make a speech in which major policy changes are to be announced, investors may withhold buying because they are waiting for the new information. Alternatively, they may sell early in anticipation of bad news.

Shocks, such as the terrorist attack on the World Trade Center on 9/11/01, have an adverse effect on stock prices, reflecting uncertainty about the future. Such shocks tend to be relatively short-lived when viewed from a historical perspective, but they seem to go on forever when it is happening. The uncertainty created at the time of the shock exacerbates the desire to sell stocks and take profits now, or to avoid further losses.

Finally, greed plays a major role in investing. The dot.com bubble of the late 1990s is an example of how investors ignored investment fundamentals in favor of the "bigger fool" theory. That theory claims that there are always some investors who are willing to pay a higher price for a stock because they believe that they can profit from the trade. It works until the bubble bursts.

CONCLUSION

The process of determining value is both an art and a science. This chapter presented dividend valuation models and discounted cash flow models that are widely used in the valuation process. Judgment is a key element in applying these models. The judgment comes into play in determining growth rates, discount rates, and other elements of the models.

The validity of the valuation models can be tested by comparing the results to the valuation ratios (P/E, PEG, etc.) that tell us how other investors value those stocks.

Even when both the valuation models and valuation ratios are in agreement, investor psychology can still result in stock market bubbles, and over- or undervaluation. Figure 9.2, looking at JDSU, is one example of such a boom-and-bust story. It also illustrates how charts are useful in looking at price trends.

SELECTED REFERENCES FOR VALUATION MODELS AND TECHNICAL ANALYSIS

Readers wanting more details about the valuation models presented here can refer to the following books:

Copeland, Tom, Tim Koller, and Jack Murrin, *Valuation: Measuring and Managing the Value of Companies*, 3rd edn (New York: John Wiley & Sons, Inc., 2000).

Damodaran, Aswath, *Investment Valuation*, 2nd edn (New York: John Wiley & Sons, Inc., 2002).

Higgins, Robert C., *Analysis for Financial Management*, 6th edn (New York: Irwin-McGraw-Hill, 2001).

For additional insights about investor psychology, see Nofsinger, John R., *The Psychology of Investing* (Upper Saddle River, NJ: Prentice Hall, 2002).

For technical analysis, see Aechlis, Stephen B., *Technical Analysis from A to Z*, 2nd edn (New York: McGraw-Hill, 2000).

SELF-TEST QUESTIONS

1. Stock prices determined by the simplified dividend growth model are sensitive to changes in the growth rate of dividends. Using that model (equation 9.1), determine the stock prices if the expected cash dividend is $2.00, the required rate of return is 15%, and the growth rates of dividends are 10%, and in the next example 5%.
2. What is the difference between the simplified and complex dividend valuation models?
3. What is the current risk-free rate that could be used in the capital asset pricing model? See http://finance.yahoo.com for the latest interest rates.
4. Select any listed stock. Go to http://www.marketguide.com/home.asp, and give the stock symbol (e.g. AOL, JDSU). In the company information box, click on "Ratio Comparisons." (Free registration is required.) How do the valuation ratios of the company that you selected compare to the industry and S&P 500?
5. Using the same stock as in the previous question, go to http://www.quicken.com, click on "Investing," and enter your stock symbol. Click on "Go," then on "Stock Evaluator," and then "Market Multiples." How do these valuation ratios compare with those in question 4?
6. While at Quicken's site, click on "Intrinsic Value." What is the intrinsic value of your stock according to this source?
7. Using the same stock as in the previous question, go to http://CNNmoney.com and enter your stock symbol. Then click on "Company Snapshot." Compare the valuation ratios here with those in questions 4 and 5.
8. On CNNmoney.com, click on "Earnings Estimates." What is the expected 5-year growth rate in earnings? How does it compare to the industry growth rate?
9. Using the same stock, go to http://finance.yahoo.com, and to www.bigcharts.com. What information do the charts tell you about whether this is the time to buy those stocks?
10. To what extent do P/E ratios reflect investor psychology?

NOTES

1 In October 2001, the Treasury Department announced that it would no longer issue 30-year bonds. Thus, the 10-year Treasury bond became the benchmark security.
2 Jay Ritter, "The Biggest Mistakes that We Teach," *Journal of Financial Research*, Summer 2002, vol. xxv, no. 2.
3 For further information and help with Stock Evaluator, see www.quicken.com/support/investments.

4 Pu Shen, "The P/E Ratio and Stock Market Performance," *Economic Review*, Federal Reserve Bank of Kansas City, Fourth Quarter 2000, 23–36.

5 For further discussion of P/E ratios, see www.datachimp.com/articles/valuation/peg.htm.

6 Robert McGough, "No Earnings? No Problem! Price-Sales Ratio Use Rises," *Wall Street Journal*, November 26, 1999, C1.

7 John Maynard Keynes, *The General Theory of Employment, Interest and Money* (New York: Harcourt Brace & World, 1936), 156.

10   **Portfolio Management**

Key Concepts

Asset allocation
Asset classes
Beta
Call option
Capital market line (CML)
Commodity
Diversification
Dominance rules (portfolios)
Efficient frontier
Efficient portfolio
Exercise price (strike price)
Expiration date (options)
Futures contracts
Hedging
Margin (futures contracts)
Options (puts and calls)
Portfolio theory
Premium (options)
Put option
Strike price (exercise price)
Systematic risk
Total risk
Unsystematic risk

Table 10.1 Possible combinations of stocks

	Total number of stocks			
	5	10	50	100
	Possible combinations			
Portfolio of five stocks	1	252	2,118,759	75,287,520

INTRODUCTION

Portfolio theory is concerned with the intelligent selection of investments where the outcome of future events cannot be predicted with complete certainty.[1] If we lived in a world of complete certainty, there would be no need for portfolio theory since the optimum portfolio would consist of a single asset with the highest return. Because we do not live in a world of complete certainty and do not have perfect foresight, we must diversify our portfolios to reduce the risk of financial loss. The extent to which investors select various types of assets (asset allocation) and diversify depends on their investment goals, investment time horizon, taxes, willingness to take on risk, and other factors. The *suitability* of investments was explained in Chapter 1, and covered those topics.

The process of managing a portfolio is neither easy nor precise because of the large number of choices facing investors. By way of illustration, suppose that an investor wants a portfolio of five stocks. If there are only five stocks from which to choose, there is only one possible combination. As shown in Table 10.1, if there are 10 stocks from which to choose, there are 252 possible combinations. If there are 100 stocks, there are 75 million combinations![2]

Since there are more than 40,000 securities from which portfolios can be formed, it is easy to understand why there are so many combinations and why some portfolios perform better than others. Because there are so many choices, investors must establish an investment strategy to reduce the number of choices to a manageable level. Even then, there is a large number of combinations. Modern portfolio theory recognizes that investors hold *multiple types of securities*, and they are more interested in the performance of their entire portfolios than that of any single security. Therefore, we must examine what happens to the notions of risk and return in the context of a portfolio. First, we will examine asset allocation.

ASSET ALLOCATION

Asset allocation refers to the mix of cash, stocks, bonds, and other investments in an investment portfolio. Table 10.2 illustrates how funds might be allocated for investors with different investment goals. The term cash, as used in the table, refers to high-quality, short-term investments such as bank deposits, money market funds,

Table 10.2 Asset allocation

Investment goals	Cash (%) (liquidity and some income)	Stocks (%) (various equity investments)	Bonds (%) (fixed-income investments)
Income	20	20	60
Income and growth	15	40	45
Growth and income	10	60	30
Primarily growth and limited income	5	70	25

and US Treasury bills. Stocks refer to equity securities, mutual funds, options, futures contracts, and so on. Bonds refer to long-term investments, including corporate and government bonds, mortgage-backed securities, guaranteed securities, and annuities.

As previously mentioned, the asset mix that is right for you depends on your investment goals, investment time horizon, taxes, willingness to take on risk, and other factors. Investment goals change over time. The financial needs of a 22-year-old investor who is beginning a career differ from those of a 60-year-old investor who is considering retiring in a few years. Thus, portfolio management and asset allocation are *dynamic*. At a minimum, portfolios should be reviewed annually to take into account changing needs and market values.

RISK AND RETURN

Table 10.3 illustrates the returns and risk (standard deviation (σ)) of stocks during the 1926–2000 period. The larger the standard deviation, the higher the degree of risk. As shown in the table, there were both large returns and large risks, and the extent to which they will be repeated in the future is only a guess. Nevertheless, we are going to focus on controlling the risk.

Systematic risk

Systematic risk is attributed to a common source, such as changing economic conditions, and it affects all stocks in the same manner. Systematic risk is measured by **beta**, a concept that was explained in Chapter 7 in connection with the product life cycle, and again in Chapter 9 in connection with the capital asset pricing model. In review, a beta of 1 means that the returns on the stock are as volatile as the returns on the market as a whole. A beta of greater than 1 means that stock returns fluctuate more than the stock

Table 10.3 Investment returns and risk (1926–2000)

Investment	Annual arithmetic return (%)	Standard deviation (σ) (%)
Small company stocks	17.3	33.4
Large company stocks	13.0	20.2

Source: Ibbotson Associates, *Stocks, Bonds, Bills, and Inflation 2000 Yearbook* (Chicago, IL: 2001).

Table 10.4 Average portfolio betas

Stock (1)	% of portfolio (2)	Beta (3)	(4) = (2) × (3)
Panel A			
A	25	0.9	0.225
B	25	1.6	0.400
C	25	1.0	0.250
D	25	0.7	0.175
			1.050 = average portfolio beta
Panel B			
A	5	0.9	0.045
B	80	1.6	1.280
C	10	1.0	0.100
D	5	0.7	0.035
			1.460 = average portfolio beta

market as a whole, and a beta of less than 1 means they fluctuate less. One characteristic of betas is that they are *nonstationary*, and they tend to revert to the mean value. This means that a beta of 1.7, for example, will revert toward a value of 1 over time. This usually matches the maturity of the firm, with mature firms having betas near 1.

Systematic risk *cannot* be eliminated by diversification because all stocks are affected in much the same manner. Nevertheless, investors change the average systematic risk of their portfolios by altering the proportions of stocks held. For example, assume that a portfolio is divided equally among four stocks, A, B, C, and D, which have the betas shown in Table 10.4, panel A. The average portfolio beta is 1.050, which means that the returns on the portfolio are slightly more volatile than the stock market.

Table 10.4, panel B shows what happens to the average portfolio beta when a greater proportion of the stocks is invested in stocks with high beta values. With this change, the average portfolio beta increased to 1.460. Thus, investors can change the composition of their stock portfolios to achieve a desired level of systematic risk.

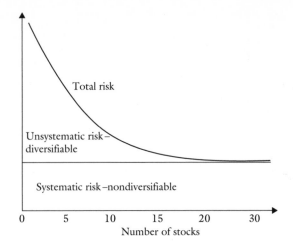

Figure 10.1 Risk

Unsystematic risk

Unsystematic risk is risk that is unique to a particular firm. It is sometimes called residual risk because it is the risk that remains after accounting for systematic risk. Unsystematic risk can occur, for example, when an earthquake in California disrupts local business activity, but firms in other parts of the country are not affected directly by that event. Similarly, a fire, labor strike, or faulty products will affect only selected firms. Because unsystematic risk is limited to particular firms, it *can* be eliminated by diversification, as will be explained shortly.

Total risk

Collectively, systematic plus unsystematic risk equals **total risk**. This is depicted in Figure 10.1. The figure shows that total risk declines as the number of stocks held in the portfolio increases. However, increasing the number of stocks beyond the point where unsystematic risk is eliminated, which is about 15–20 stocks, is superfluous. In addition, the time and effort required to manage a large number of securities can be burdensome.

The trade-off between risk and return

There is a trade-off between risk and the expected return on investments. As shown in Figure 10.2, the higher the degree of risk, the higher the expected returns. The figure is a generalization because some stocks and bonds are riskier than others.

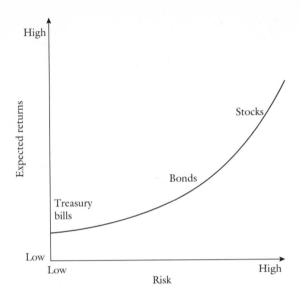

Figure 10.2 Risk vs. return

Nevertheless, investors must decide whether to focus their investments in a few high-risk securities, or to diversify. Your answer to that question depends on personal considerations that were covered in Chapter 1 dealing with the suitability of investments. Most investors prefer to diversify their investments.

DEALING WITH RISK

You can ignore risk and hope that it goes away over time, or you can do something about it. Sometimes investors don't have a choice: read the following "Investor Insights" box about the Enron employees and the losses in their 401(k) retirement accounts. For those who want to do something about risk, two strategies are presented here for dealing with it: diversification and hedging.

Diversification

Investors have to decide whether to concentrate their portfolios in a very small number of securities (or **asset classes**, such as index funds, real estate, stocks) or to diversify them. There are advantages and disadvantages to each strategy. Concentrating the portfolio in a very small number of securities is a high-risk strategy which may result in large gains – or large losses. Most investors choose diversification.

Diversification means spreading risk over a variety of companies, or other forms of investments whose returns are not perfectly positively correlated. Investing in the stocks of three automobile companies (e.g. Ford, General Motors, and Daimler/Chrysler) would *not* qualify as diversification because the stock returns from all three firms are affected similarly by the changing economic conditions – for example, if there is a recession, buyers may defer automobile purchases.

An example of stock diversification is investing in Ford (autos), Kroger (grocery), and Merck (pharmaceuticals) because the stock returns on these firms are not perfectly positively correlated. If there is a recession, people may defer buying a new car, but they still have to eat and will continue to buy food. Similarly, the extent to which they use pharmaceuticals depends more on their state of health than on factors that affect the two other firms.

The advantage of diversification is that it reduces the risk of the portfolio. The other side of the coin is that it also reduces expected returns.

INVESTOR INSIGHTS

A LESSON ABOUT DIVERSIFICATION FROM ENRON

Enron Corporation was the seventh largest firm in the US. It was the largest trader of energy (electricity, natural gas) and other services (broadband communications). The firm reported that its revenues soared from $31 billion in 1998 to $100 billion in 2000; and its stock price increased from $20 per share to $90 per share during that period. Stock analysts recommended Enron, and investors, including Enron employees who had 401(k) retirement accounts, wanted it in their portfolios. Unfortunately for investors, Enron grossly overstated its profits and understated its debts.

In December 2001, Enron filed for Chapter 11 bankruptcy protection, the largest firm ever to declare bankruptcy. It had about $13 billion in balance sheet debt and about $19 billion in off-balance-sheet debt (e.g. derivatives contracts) associated with its trading activities. Its stock price plunged from $90 per share to a few cents per share.

About 20,000 employees of Enron had most of their 401(k) retirement funds invested in Enron stock because the firm barred its employees from selling Enron shares from their retirement accounts. Because their portfolios were concentrated in Enron stock, many of the employees lost their life savings when the company's stock price collapsed. Some filed lawsuits claiming their losses to be $1 billion.

Following this disaster, President Bush proposed giving workers greater freedom to diversify their company retirement accounts. That, however, may not eliminate the concentration of employees' holdings in their employer's stock.

The lesson to be learned: *diversification reduces the risk of investing.*

Hedging

Hedging means transferring the risk of price changes to speculators who are willing to take on that risk in hopes of making a profit. Those who hedge (hedgers) do so in order to preserve (lock-in) a profit or to minimize a loss. Hedging can be accomplished in the stock market by using exchange traded options and futures contracts. The following examples are intended to illustrate the use of options and futures, but they are by no means complete explanations of the details that investors must know before using them. For further information, see the "Investor Insights" box below.

INVESTOR INSIGHTS

OPTIONS AND FUTURES

Options and futures contracts are important investment tools, in the same way that guns are tools used in hunting. When used properly, a gun is safe. However, it can hurt you when it is used improperly. The same is true for options and futures contracts. In order to learn how to use them properly, the Chicago Board of Trade (CBOT) explains what investors need to know about their products. See www.cbot.com and then under "What's Hot," click on "Getting Started." This site offers an online tutorial, publications, a glossary, and other information. It also has publications dealing with beginners' and advanced trading strategies.

Similarly, the Chicago Board Options Exchange (CBOE) has a learning center that provides insights about trading options. See www.cboe.com.

Other exchanges also provide educational information. See the "Directory of Websites" at the back of this book for their online addresses.

Options A **call option** is a contract to *buy* a specified number of shares of stock at a predetermined price (**exercise** or **strike price**) on or before a stated date (**expiration date**). A **put option** is a contract to *sell* a specified number of shares of stock at a strike price on or before the expiration date. The **premium** is the price that an option buyer pays an option writer for the rights conveyed by the option. Options are generally for 100 shares of the underlying stock. The contract conveys the *right* to the option holder to *exercise* the option during the contract period if it is to their advantage to do so. Alternatively, options can be *sold* at prices reflecting their current value, or they can *expire* unexercised.

The following cases of Sally and Bob illustrate two of the many uses of options. Sally owns 100 shares of ABC. The stock is currently selling at $65 per share, and she wants to hedge against a price decline, and at the same time benefit if the stock appreciates in value. Sally can buy a 60-day put option to sell the stock at $65 per share.

The premium is $275. If the stock declines in value, Sally will exercise the option and sell the stock at $65. If the stock appreciates in value, Sally will let the option expire without exercising it.

The option premium of $275 is the cost of this hedge. It can be thought of as the cost of insurance, and the cost of insurance deserves a comment. Most people are willing to pay the cost of life insurance and automobile liability insurance, and they hope never to collect on those policies by dying or crashing. Similarly, one must weigh the risk of financial loss against the costs and benefits of hedging for insurance. There is no right or wrong answer – it is a personal decision.

Next, we have Bob who *sold short* 100 shares of ABC at $40 per share. Bob hopes that the stock price will decline so that he can cover the short at a lower price and make a profit. However, he wants to hedge in the event the stock price rises. Bob buys a 30-day call option for $175 to hedge his position. The stock must decline in value more than 1.75 points per share ($175) before Bob can profit from the short sale. However, he is protected if the stock increases in value.

Sally and Bob's use of options was restricted to a single stock. The same concepts can be applied to options on stock market indexes such as the Standard & Poor's 500 (S&P 500) stock index and the New York Stock Exchange Composite Index. Index options representing broad groups of stocks can be used to hedge a portfolio of stocks. More than 30 different index options are actively traded, and they also include industries, such as oil services, semiconductors, and utilities.

Futures contracts   The term **futures** refers to standardized contracts to buy and receive or to sell and deliver a commodity at some future date. **Commodities** include a wide range of farm products (e.g. corn, hogs), metals (e.g. gold), currencies (e.g. Swiss Francs), and financial contracts (e.g. Treasury bonds and stock indexes, such as the Dow Jones Industrial Average).

Jack wants to hedge his portfolio of stocks and bonds against price declines. For the sake of discussion, let's assume that the composition of Jack's stock portfolio closely resembles the Dow Jones Industrial Average (DJIA). As shown in Table 10.5, Jack owns (long) $100,000 in stock. To hedge, he sells (short) an equal dollar value of futures contracts on the DJIA. The price of the contract is $10 times the DJIA. If the DJIA is 10,000, then a contract will sell for $100,000. To sell (or buy) futures contracts, Jack must make a deposit, called a **margin**, with his broker. The margin helps to ensure that Jack will perform on his contract. The initial margin requirement on the DJIA stock index contract is $5,400. (The term margin used in connection with futures contacts should not be confused with a margin account used for buying securities on credit.)

If the market value of Jack's stocks declines, the loss in the value of his stock portfolio will be offset by gains in the short position in the DJIA futures contracts. If stocks had increased in value, his gains would have been offset by losses in the futures market. Similarly, Jack can hedge his bond portfolio by selling short futures contracts on Treasury notes or bonds.[3]

Table 10.5   Hedging

Jack's stock portfolio	Futures market
Market value on March 5 = $100,000 (long)	Sells (short) $100,000 value in DJIA futures contracts
Market value on July 31 = $75,000	Buys $75,000 value in DJIA futures contracts
Portfolio loss = −$25,000	Gains on short sale = $25,000

PORTFOLIO SELECTION

After all of the previously discussed issues concerning suitability and asset allocation have been taken into account, investors must select securities that provide the best combination of risk and return. Such securities can be selected on the basis of **dominance rules**.

Dominance rules

Two dominance rules are presented here for the selection of a portfolio:

1. The security with the *least risk* is preferred to all other investments with the same rate of return.

2. The security with the *highest expected return* is preferred to all other investments with the same degree of risk.

To illustrate the application of these rules, let's examine the expected returns and risks for eight securities in Table 10.6.

Rule 1 tells us that Security D dominates Security B because they both have the same expected return (8%), but Security D has less risk ($\sigma = 4\%$) than Security B ($\sigma = 12\%$). On the basis of rule 2, Security G dominates Security F. Both securities have the same degree of risk ($\sigma = 11\%$), but G has an expected return of 11% while F's expected return is 7%. Similarly, Security A dominates Security C. H dominates E because it has a higher return for about the same degree of risk. Securities B, C, E, and F are inferior to the other securities with higher rates of return and less risk.

Efficient portfolio

A portfolio that consists of dominant securities is called an **efficient portfolio**. Figure 10.3 shows the risk and returns for the eight securities in the example. The

Table 10.6 Securities: returns and risk

Security	Expected return (%)	Risk (σ) (%)
A	5	2
B	8	12
C	4	2
D	8	4
E	6	8
F	7	11
G	11	11
H	10	7

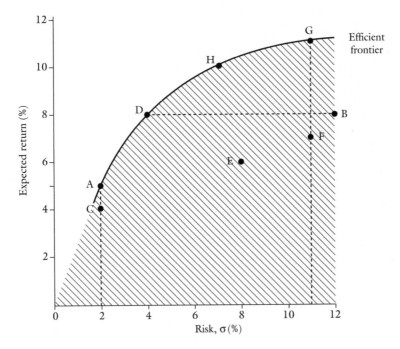

Figure 10.3 Selection of an efficient frontier

line ADHG is called an **efficient frontier**. The efficient frontier is drawn through the points that offer the best returns for each degree of risk in the set of securities under consideration.

Only eight securities were used to illustrate the concepts explained here. In reality, you may be selecting from hundreds of securities, all of which could lie in the shaded area on Figure 10.3.

Capital market line

The efficient frontier considered risky securities. Now the scope of assets is broadened to include both risk-free and risky securities. Constructing a **capital market line (CML)** provides a means for determining efficient combinations of risk-free and risky securities.

Figure 10.4 illustrates the CML. The risk-free security is represented by point R_f, which is located on the vertical axis. Point M represents a market portfolio of risky securities that is the best combination of risk and return. The expected return on the market portfolio is E_M. It is the weighted average return on all securities in the market. In other words, it is a market average portfolio. Finding the optimal combination of securities or assets is beyond the scope of this book.[4]

Two other portfolios, reflecting different degrees of risk, are illustrated by a conservative portfolio (Point L) and an aggressive portfolio (Point B). The conservative portfolio (Point L) has an expected return greater than the risk-free rate but less than the market average portfolio. The aggressive portfolio (Point B) is where investors use borrowed funds to increase the size and risk of their portfolio. Thus, the efficient CML is an efficient frontier of combinations of both risk-free and risky portfolios of securities.

All of the portfolios on the CML contain only systematic risk; that is, they are all sufficiently diversified. The diversifiable risk has been removed. Investors must decide how much systematic risk they want in their portfolios, and then select securities accordingly.

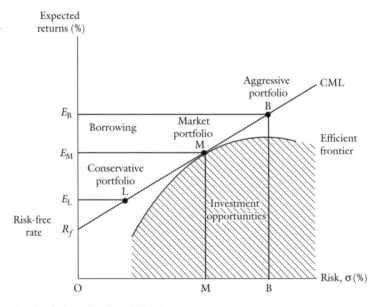

Figure 10.4 Capital market line (CML)

CONCLUSION

Prudent investing is not simply a matter of picking stocks and bonds. The process begins by determining the suitability of investments, which means taking into account investment objectives, willingness to take on risk, and other factors.

Once securities are purchased, the portfolios should be reviewed on a regular basis because investors' needs and economic conditions change over time.

This chapter stressed the need for diversification and/or hedging, which can be accomplished in a variety of ways. These include, but are not limited to, traditional diversification – which means not putting all of your eggs in one basket – and by using options and futures to hedge.

The concept of portfolio selection provides further insights about how to manage securities portfolios to get the best mix of securities or asset classes.

SELF-TEST QUESTIONS

1. What is the appropriate asset allocation for you? To find one answer, go to CNNmoney.com and click on "Calculators," where you will find "Asset Allocator." Answer the questions and it will reveal how your assets should be allocated.
2. To find another answer to question 1, go to smartmoney.com and click on "Tools." Under "Tools" and "Your Investments," you will find "Asset Allocator." Answer the questions and it will probably provide a different answer. How do the two asset allocations compare?
3. How can ETFs help with asset allocation? Go to www.amex.com and click on "Exchange Traded Funds" for answers to this question.
4. What are the most active ETFs?
5. Many banks have online investment services. Check out www.bankofamerica.com, www.citibank.com, and banks in your area. How do their services compare?
6. Systematic risk is measured by beta. Select five stocks and compare their betas. Go to www.bloomberg.com, and enter a stock symbol (such as JDSU). The beta will be listed under "Fundamentals." What is JDSU's beta? What does it mean?
7. What financial products are traded on the Chicago Board of Trade (CBOT)? Go to www.cbot.com, and click on "Financial Products."
8. Are Agency Contracts traded on the CBOT backed by the US government?
9. What index options are traded on the Chicago Board Options Exchange (CBOE)? See www.cboe.com.
10. What is "dollar cost averaging?" The answer may be found on www.datachimp.com.

NOTES

1 The original work in portfolio theory is that of Harry Markowitz, "Portfolio Selection," *Journal of Finance*, 7, March 1952, 77–91.
2 The combination C of n stocks taken x at a time can be determined as:

$$C_x^n = \frac{n!}{x! \, (n-x)!}$$

3 Futures contracts and options on the DJIA are traded on the Chicago Board of Trade. For further details, see www.cbot.com and find the description of index options under contract specifications.
4 For additional information read about the Sharpe ratio, which measures a portfolio's risk–return ratio, which is commonly used in connection with mutual funds. The Sharpe ratio is the excess return over the risk-free rate divided by its standard deviation. See www.datachimp.com and read about "Modern Portfolio Theory."

Directory of Websites

This directory presents selected websites and limited details about their content. The mutual fund sites, for example, each provide access to a large number of funds and calculators. They also rank fund performance and give other useful information. Thus, only the briefest description of each site is listed here. Because most brokerage firms provide research reports and investment recommendations as part of their service, the focus here is predominantly on websites that provide at least some free services online.

The hypertext transport protocol prefix (http:// . . .) is not shown in front of the website addresses. Equally important, note that not all addresses begin with www., which stands for World Wide Web. For example, the website address for Janus Funds is janus.com. Most of the listings are for the organizations' home pages because they are less likely to change than extensions of those addresses. If the addresses listed here are no longer valid because they have been changed, try using a search engine, such as Netscape (www.netscape.com), to find the current address for the organization that you seek.

INVESTOR INSIGHTS

INTERNET TERMINOLOGY

Bandwidth: Measure of the amount of information that can be transmitted over an Internet connection. Broadband is a high-speed connection.

Browser: Programs, such as Netscape's Navigator, that give users easy access to the Web. *See* Portals.

Chat room: Sites for online conversations about various topics. Beware of GIGO – garbage in, garbage out – and get-rich-quick schemes.

Domain: Identifies computer addresses. For example, in http://www.whitehouse.gov, the ".gov" stands for government. Similarly ".edu" is for educational institutions, ".com" for commercial firms, and ".org" is for other organizations.

Home page: A Web screen that provides an entry point to selected information about a firm, organization, products, services, links, etc. – i.e. its main website page.

Http: Hypertext transport protocol. This is the Internet standard that enables information to be transmitted over the Web. The http:// in the address http://www.whitehouse.gov indicates a Web document on a computer at the White House.

Hyperlink/link: Internet connections to other websites. Click on it and you are switched to another site.

Message board: A place to post and read online messages.

Portals: Portals are websites that are the "on ramps" to the Internet, such as America Online, Yahoo!, Quicken, and Microsoft MoneyCentral.

URL: Universal resource locator is a computer address that identifies the location and type of resources on the Web. The URL http://www.whitehouse.gov is the address for the White House.

Virus: A computer program that can infect, replicate, and spread among computer systems. Unlike a worm, a virus requires human intervention.

Worm: An independent computer program that reproduces by copying itself from one system to another while traveling from machine to machine across the network. It does not require human intervention to propagate.

American Association of Individual Investors (AAII) (Investor information and education)
www.aaii.org

American Stock Exchange (Amex) (Stock exchange)
www.amex.com
www.amextrader.com (Amex options and data)

Ameritrade Holding Corp. (Broker)
www.ameritrade.com

Bank of New York (Custodial bank; lots of information on ADRs)
www.bankofny.com/adr

Bankrate.com (Interest rates on CDs and mortgages; various calculators)
www.bankrate.com

BBC Online Homepage (British Broadcasting Corporation, for news around the world)
www.bbc.co.uk/ (go to "News," then "Business")

BigCharts (Charts of stocks prices; interactive charting)
www.bigcharts.com

Bloomberg.com (News; markets and investment information)
www.bloomberg.com

Board of Governors of the Federal Reserve System (Data; speeches; links to federal reserve banks and foreign central banks)
www.federalreserve.gov

BondMarkets.com (The Bond Market Association website, with 800 links to various debt markets, plus market news and prices)
www.bondmarkets.com

Bonds Online (Bond markets: information; research; bond screener)
www.bondsonline.com

Boston Stock Exchange (Stock exchange)
www.bostonstock.com

Bureau of Census (US government demographic and business data)
www.census.gov

Bureau of Public Debt (US government information on buying Treasury bills, notes, and bonds)
www.publicdebt.treas.gov

BusinessWeek Online (Magazine; investment advice; mutual fund scoreboard; stock reports; stock screener)
www.businessweek.com

Canadian Investor Protection Fund (CIPF) (CIPF covers customers' losses of securities and cash balances that result from the insolvency of a member firm)
www.cipf.ca/cipf.html

Cantor Financial Futures Exchange (CFFE) (Commodity exchange)
cx.cantor.com

CBS Market Watch (Domestic and foreign financial news)
www.cbs.marketwatch.com

Chicago Board of Trade (CBOT) (Commodity exchange)
www.cbot.com

Chicago Board Options Exchange (Options exchange: market data; charts; options calculator)
www.cboe.com

Chicago Mercantile Exchange (CME) (Commodity exchange)
www.cme.com

Chicago Stock Exchange (Stock exchange)
www.chicagostockex.com

Chicago Tribune (Newspaper: excellent coverage of Midwest businesses)
www.chicagotribune.com

Cincinnati Stock Exchange (Stock exchange)
www.cincinnatistock.com

CNBC.com (News; markets; investment information)
www.cnbc.com

CNNmoney (News; markets; investment information)
CNNmoney.com

Coffee, Sugar & Cocoa Exchange (CSCE) (Commodity exchange, New York Board of Trade)

www.csce.com

Commodity Exchange Inc. (Comex and New York Mercantile Exchange) (Commodity exchange)

www.nymex.com

Commodity Futures Trading Commission (CFTC) (US Government regulator of commodity futures markets)

www.cftc.gov

CSFBdirect Inc. (Credit Suisse/First Boston: investment bank; broker)

www.csfbdirect.com

www.csfb.com

Datachimp (*See* Moneychimp)

Datek Online (Broker)

www.datek.com

Dreyfus Funds (Mutual funds)

www.dreyfus.com

EquiServe (A division of First Chicago Trust Company which provides shareholder services for more than 1,700 companies – dividend reinvestment plans, stock purchases, etc.)

www.equiserve.com (click on "Investment Plans")

E*Trade (Broker)

www.etrade.com

Federal Interagency Council on Statistical Policy (Links to federal government websites for statistics and other information)

www.fedstats.gov

Federal Reserve (*See* Board of Governors of the Federal Reserve System)

Federal Reserve Bank of Chicago (Federal Reserve Bank: data)

www.frbchi.org

Federal Reserve Bank of St. Louis (Federal Reserve Bank: Federal Reserve Economic Data (FRED))

www.stls.frb.org/fred

Fidelity Investments (Mutual funds)

www.fidelity.com

Finance Site List (*Journal of Finance*; hundreds of links to investments publications, working papers, investment sites)

www.cob.ohio-state.edu/fin/journal/jofsites.htm

Financial Times (UK newspaper: excellent global coverage of markets and businesses)

www.ft.com

Fool.com (*See* Motley Fool)

Forbes.com (*Forbes* magazine: articles of interest to investors; data; calculators; mutual fund screener)

www.forbes.com

Fortune.com (*Fortune* magazine: articles (current and past); Fortune 500)
www.fortune.com
www.fortuneinvestor.com

Franklin Templeton (Mutual funds)
www.franklintempleton.com

FreeEDGAR (Data; obtain companies' financial statements and SEC filings from the SEC EDGAR database without the scrolling required when getting them from the SEC directly)
www.freeedgar.com

Gartner Group (Investment information)
www.gartner.com

GE Financial Network (Financial calculators; insurance; mortgages)
www.gefn.com

Goldman Sachs (Broker)
www.gs.com

Hoovers Online Co. (Domestic and foreign investment information)
www.hoovers.com
www.stockscreener.com (stock screener)

I/B/E/S (Earnings estimates and investment information)
www.fool.com

iMoneyNet, Inc. (Money Fund Selector: a service used to select and learn about money funds)
www.ibcdata.com

Internal Revenue Service (Income tax information; tax forms)
www.irs.gov

International Securities Exchange (ISE) (The US's first electronic options exchange (subject to SEC approval))
www.iseoptions.com

Investing in Bonds.com (The Bond Market Association: education, prices, and screens)
www.investinginbonds.com

Investment Company Institute (Trade association for mutual funds: data)
www.ici.org

Investor's Business Daily (Daily financial newspaper; subscription required)
www.investors.com

Investors Clearinghouse (Sponsored by the Alliance for Investor Education: educational articles and links)
www.investoreducation.org

iShares (Barclays Global Investors US and foreign index funds, prices, and performance)
www.ishares.com

Janus (Mutual funds)
janus.com

Kansas City Board of Trade (KCBT) (Commodity exchange)
www.kcbt.com

Kemper Funds (Mutual funds)
www.kemper.com

Library of Congress (The US government's library contains both government and other publications, including the *Congressional Record. Also see* Thomas)
www.loc.gov

Lipper Analytical Services (Experts in evaluating funds in the US, Asia, and Europe, for a fee)
www.lipperweb.com

Lycos (News; charts)
Investing.lycos.com

Market Axess (The first web-based multidealer platform for institutional trading of fixed income securities)
www.marketaxess.com

Market Guide, Inc. (Financial information; ratios; valuation model; screener; personal finance. Free registration is required for some services)
www.marketguide.com

Merrill Lynch (Broker)
www.ml.com

Minneapolis Grain Exchange (MGE) (Commodity exchange)
www.mgex.com

Moneychimp (Articles explaining basic investment concepts; calculators; links to other sites)
www.datachimp.com/
www.datachimp.com/articles

Money.com (Investment articles; information; links to other financial sites)
www.money.com

Moody's Investor Service (Credit rating agency: financial information; rating services)
www.moodys.com

Morgan Stanley Dean Witter Online (Broker)
www.online.msdw.com

Morningstar.com (News; markets and investment information; mutual funds)
www.morningstar.com

Motley Fool (Investment information)
www.fool.com

Multexinvestor (*See* Market Guide, Inc.)

Municipal Securities Rulemaking Board (MSRB) (Self-regulatory agency of the municipal securities industry)
www.msrb.org

Mutual Fund Education Alliance (Nonprofit education concerning mutual funds: links; calculators; asset allocation)
www.mfea.com

National Association of Securities Dealers (NASD) (Nasdaq Stock Market; Amex; stock prices; links to European and Asian markets; calculators; glossary of terms)
www.nasd.com
www.nasdaq.com

National Discount Brokers (Broker)
www.ndb.com

National Futures Association (Self-regulatory agency of the US futures industry)
www.nfa.futures.org

New York Cotton Exchange (NYCE) (Commodity exchange, New York Board of Trade)
www.nybot.com

New York Futures Exchange (NYFE) (Commodity exchange, accessed at New York Board of Trade)
www.nybot.com

New York Mercantile Exchange (NYME) (Commodity exchange)
www.nymex.com

New York Stock Exchange (NYSE) (Largest stock exchange: information about the exchange and listed companies; glossary)
www.nyse.com

New York Times (Newspaper: excellent business section; news and financial coverage; company information; free online subscription)
www.nytimes.com

North American Securities Administrators Association (NASAA) (Oldest international organization devoted to investor protection)
www.nasaa.org

NYBOT (Parent company of the Coffee, Sugar & Cocoa Exchange, Inc. (CSCE) and the New York Cotton Exchange (NYCE))
www.nybot.com

Oppenheimer Funds (Mutual funds)
www.oppenheimerfunds.com

Options Industry Council (Trade group for the options industry: educational material; strategies; glossary; links)
www.optionscentral.com

OTC (Research; links to investment websites for small-/microcap firms)
www.otcfn.com

Pacific Stock Exchange (Stock exchange)
www.pacificex.com

Philadelphia Board of Trade (PBOT) (Commodity exchange)
www.phlx.com

Philadelphia Stock Exchange (Stock exchange)
www.phlx.com/index.stm

Pink Sheets (OTC stock and bond quotes)
www.pinksheets.com

Prudential Insurance Company (Insurance; brokerage; banking)
www.prudential.com

Putnam Investments (Mutual funds)
www.putnaminv.com

Qualistream (International directory of banking and finance)
www.qualistream.com

Quick & Reilly (Broker; link to Fleet Web Banking)
www.quickwaynet.com

Quicken (Investment information; charts; stock and fund screeners; stock evaluators – financial analysis and intrinsic value; links to brokers and funds)
www.quicken.com

Report Gallery (Annual reports for over 2000 companies)
www.reportgallery.com

Reuters Group, PLC (Information services; international news; investments)
www.reuters.com

SalomonSmithBarney (Broker)
www.salomonsmithbarney.com

Savings Bonds (*See* Treasury Securities)

Charles Schwab & Co., Inc. (Broker)
www.schwab.com

Securities and Exchange Commission (SEC) (Government regulator of the securities markets; investor information; mutual fund fee calculator)
www.sec.gov

Securities Industry Association (SIA) (Trade group of the securities industry)
www.sia.com

Securities Investor Protection Corporation (SIPC) (Protects customers of broker-dealers registered with the United States Securities and Exchange Commission against losses caused by the financial failure of the broker-dealer)
www.sipc.org

SmartMoney.com (*SmartMoney* magazine: investment news; articles; calculators; other investment tools)
www.smartmoney.com

Standard & Poor's (Credit rating agency: financial information and rating services)
www.standardpoor.com

Stock-Screening.com (Links to various stock screeners; mutual fund screeners; charts; earning information)
www.stock-screening.com

Suretrade.com (Broker)
www.suretrade.com

TD Waterhouse (Broker)
www.tdwaterhouse.com

The Web Investor (Site map of a large directory of websites for stocks, bonds, commodities, options, futures, mutual funds, quotes, etc.)
www.thewebinvestor.com

Thomas (Library of Congress legislative information; text of bills)
thomas.loc.gov

Treasury Securities (Information about US Treasury securities, including savings bonds; bond calculator)
www.publicdebt.treas.gov
www.savingsbonds.gov

T. Rowe Price (Mutual funds)
www.troweprice.com

UBS Paine Webber, Inc. (Investment bank; broker)
www.ubspainewebber.com

UK Invest (Excellent resources for the UK markets)
www.uk-invest.com

US Census Bureau (US government agency: for current economic indicators see the Census Economic Briefing Room; it also publishes census data)
www.census.gov

US Department of Commerce (US government agency concerned with commerce: data)
www.doc.gov

Value Line (Fee-based investment information service; screeners)
www.valueline.com

The Vanguard Group (Mutual funds)
www.vanguard.com

Wall Street Journal (A leading financial newspaper, also published online)
www.wsj.com

The White House (Seat of the US government: daily press releases; budget)
www.whitehouse.gov

WWW.consumer.gov (Federal government website: click on the "Money" section for information about investing and other financial issues of concern to investors and consumers)
www.consumer.gov

Yahoo! Finance (Portal to financial services: news; data; stock screener; bond screener; fund screener)
finance.yahoo.com
biz.yahoo.com/c/u.html (stock ratings and changes)

Index

Note: Website addresses appear on page numbers given in **bold**; "n." after a page reference indicates the number of a note on that page.

5th Market Alternative Trading Hub 47
12b-1 fees 102, 103

AbnAmro Inc. 47
access to funds 38–9: *see also* liquidity
account maintenance fees 49
accounts receivable 148
accrued interest 83
acquisitions 123
Active Trading Network 47
advertising 36
aggressive growth funds 11
alternative trading systems (ATSs) 29
Amazon.com 124
American Depository Receipts (ADRs) 73–4
American Stock Exchange (Amex) 24, 25–7, 34, 102, **186**: Commodities Corporation (ACC) 31; commodity markets 30, 43n.30
American Telephone and Telegraph 32
Ameritrade Holding Corp. 49, **186**
Archipelago 28, 29
asked price 24, 73
asset-backed securities (ABS) 22, 91–2
assets: allocation 14, 172–3; classes 176; management 50
auction markets 24

back-end redemption fees 98, 102
balance sheets 136–8
bank debt securities 93
bankers' acceptances 83
Bank of America **60**, 93
Bank of New York 74, **186**
basic earnings per share 139, 141
BBC Online 78, **186**
Beige Book 116
beneficial share owners 53, 72

best execution 49–50
beta (coefficient) 14, 122, 124, 158, 173–4
bid price 11, 24, 73
BigCharts 166, 167, **186**
"Bill of Rights" for investors 36–9
blocks of stock 23: trades 50
Bloomberg.com 28, 107, 134, **186**: stocks 15, 75, 77
blue-chip stocks 10, 75
blue sky laws 39
Board of Governors of the Federal Reserve System 34, 116, **187**
boards of directors 68, 69
bond equivalent yield 89
bonds 8, 13, 21–2, 83–4, 86–7: municipal 9, 13, 92–3; screeners 126, 130
Bonds Online 88, 126, 130, **187**
book-entry (street-name) ownership 53–4, 72
book value (stockholders' equity) 136, 144, 164–5
Boston Beer Company 23
bottom-up analysis 115–30
Bowen, Matthew 58
brand names 121
brokers 6, 51
Brown and Company Online 47
bulletin boards 58
Bureau of Census 116, 117–19, **193**
Bureau of Public Debt 90, **187**
business corporations 67
business environment 115–16
BusinessWeek Online 107, 126, 129–30, **187**
buying power 56

call options 178
call-protection clauses 86

Cantor Financial Futures Exchange (CFFE, CS) 31, **187**
capital appreciation funds 99
capital asset pricing model (CAPM) 157–8
capitalization rate 154, 155
capital market 21–2: line (CML) 182
cash accounts 53–4
cash earnings 141
cash flows 143
CBS Market Watch 167, **187**
century bonds 83
certificates of deposit (CDs) 10, 13, 83, 93
Charles Schwab & Co., Inc. 4, 45, 49, 129, **192**
chat rooms 58
Checkfree 141
Chicago Board of Trade (CBOT) 31, 32, 178, **187**
Chicago Board Options Exchange 178, **187**
Chicago Mercantile Exchange (CME) 31, **187**
Cisco Systems 123
Citibank **60**
Citicorp 116
Citigroup 47, 116
Citrus Associates of the New York Cotton Exchange, Inc. (CACE) 31
closed-end investments 97, 101–2
CNNmoney 107, 134, **187**: stocks 15, 75, 74, 77
Coca-Cola Company 22, 68, 74–5, 83, 121
Coffee, Sugar & Cocoa Exchange, Inc. (CSCE) 31, **188**
collateralized mortgage obligations (CMOs) 91
collateral trust bonds 87
Comdirect UK 47
commercial paper 83
commissions 48–9
commodities 179: markets 30–2
Commodity Exchange Inc. (CEI, Comex) 31, **188**
Commodity Futures Trading Commission (CFTC) 31, 35, **188**
common stock 67–70
complaints 38, 39, 51
consolidated statement of cash flows 143
contingent deferred sales charges (CDSCs) 102
continuous markets 24
conversion: price 87; rate 87; value 87
convertible bonds 86–7
Corning Inc. 121–2

corporate bond funds 99
coupon rate 83, 84
covering the short 52
credit balances 55
credit ratings 10, 87–8
Credit Suisse/First Boston (CSFB) 60, **188**
current assets 138
current liabilities 138
current yield 84

Daimler/Chrysler 73, **80n.14**
data organization 12–13
dates: declared 70; of record 70; payable 70
day orders 52
days: of accounts payable outstanding 149; of cash and short-term investments outstanding 149; of inventory outstanding 148; of receivables outstanding 148
day trading 11–12, 48, 55
dealers 6, 23, 51
debentures 87
debit balances 55
debt securities 81–95
decimalization 50, 72–3, 86
decline phase, life cycle 122, 125
default risk 89
demographic changes 116
Depository Trust and Clearing Corporation (DTCC) 72, **80n.10**
deregulation 116
Deutsche Bank Asset Management 98
diluted earnings per share 139–40
direct ownership 71–2
direct stock purchase plans 74–5
discount 84
discounted cash flow model 158–61
diversification 14, 105–6, 176–7
dividend reinvestment plans (DRIPs) 74
dividends 68–70, 145–7: dates 70; payout ratio 124, 145; valuation models 69, 114, 154–7; yield 69, 147
domains 185
dominance rules 180
dot.com bubble 123, 168
Dow, Charles Henry 75
Dow Jones 76: averages 75–6, 78, 179; diamonds 102
down-ticks 52
Dreyfus Funds 47, 98, 105, **188**
Duff and Phelps 87

earnings per share (EPS) 139–40, 141–2, 143

EBITDA 141
economic value added (EVA) 152n.9
EDGAR 33, 135–6, **189**
EE bonds 90
efficient frontier 181
efficient portfolio 180–1
electronic communications networks (ECNs) 28–9
Electronic Data Systems 71
Enron 67, 177
EquiServe 80n.16, **188**
equity 55: mutual funds 98, 99
E*Trade 47, **188**
Eurodollar CDs 83
Eurotrade 47
excess 56
exchange traded funds (ETFs) 102
ex-dividend date 70
exercise price 178
expansion phase, life cycle 122–3
expense ratio 103
expiration date 178

face amount (par value) 68, 83
family of funds 98
Farm Credit System 22, 91
federal agency securities 91
Federal Agricultural Mortgage Corporation (Farmer Mac) 22
Federal Deposit Insurance Corporation (FDIC) 10, 93
Federal Financing Bank 91
Federal Home Loan Bank System 22, 91
Federal Home Loan Mortgage System (Freddie Mac) 22, 91, 95n.3
Federal National Mortgage Association (Fannie Mae) 22, 91, 95n.3, 141–2, **152n.7**
Federal Reserve Board 34, 53, 54, 116, **187**
fee tables 101, 103, 107
Fidelity Investments 4, 98, 105, **188**
fill or kill orders 52
financial leverage 138, 141–2, 144–5
Financial Times 77–8, **188**
first mortgage bonds 87
Fitch 87
FLEX Options 43n.30
Forbes.com 107, **188**
foreign markets 25, 26–7, 73–4, 77–8
Fortune.com 15, **189**
free cash flow (FCF) 159, 160–1, 164: valuation model 160–1

FreeEDGAR 136, **189**
freeriding 53
fundamental analysis 114
fund complex 109n.1
futures contracts 18n.12, 30, 178, 179–80

Genentech 123
General Electric 32, 75, 123
general mortgage bonds 87
General Motors (GM) 71, 76
general obligation (GO) bonds 92
globalization 116
goods 'till cancelled (GTC) orders 52
government: bond funds 99–100; policies 115–16
Government National Mortgage Association (Ginnie Mae) 91
government-sponsored enterprises (GSEs) 22, 91
Gramm-Leach-Bliley Act (1999) 47, 116
Great Crash 32
greed 168
growth stocks 11
guilder shares 73

Heartland Advisors 110n.11
hedging 101, 178–80: funds 101
HH bonds 90
high-yield (junk) bonds 10, 88, 99
Honeywell 123
hybrid mutual funds 98, 99

I bonds 90
iMoneyNet, Inc. 107, **189**
imperfect competition 119
income statement 138–42
index funds 11, 102
indirect ownership 72
individual retirement accounts (IRAs) 93, 106
industry analysis 117–20
initial public offering (IPO) 23
inside market 25
insiders 35
Insider Trading and Fraud Act (1988) 35
Instinet 28
intellectual property 136–8
Interactive Products and Services 58
interest-only (IO) securities 91
interest rates 116: risk 84, 90
Intermarket Trading System (ITS) 25, 29
internal growth rates 147
internal rates of return (IRR) 95n.1

international regulatory cooperation 39–41
International Securities Exchange (ISE) 29, **189**
intrinsic value 12, 13, 69, 114, 154, 161–2
inventories 148
investing 11: objectives 9, 10–11
Investment Advisor Act (1940) 34, 35
investment bankers 22–3
investment companies 97–109
Investment Company Act (1940) 34, 97
Investment Company Institute 7, 101, **189**
investment grade bonds 88
InvestorLine 47
iStar Financial Inc. 128

Jds Uniphase (JDSU) 141, 165, 166
joint stock companies 66
junk (high-yield) bonds 10, 88, 99

Kansas City Board of Trade (KCBT) 31, **189**
KLM Royal Dutch Airlines 73

lettered (tracking) stocks 70–1, 110n.6
leverage ratios (LRs) 138, 142, 144
Levitt, Arthur 11, 30, 104
life cycle 122–5
limited liability 67: companies (LLCs) 48
limit orders 52, 57
Lipper Analytical Services 107, **190**
liquidity 13, 24, 67, 90, 106: analysis 147–9
load 102: funds 102–4
long stock 52, 54
long-term debt/equity 12, 21–2, 83–4, 138
Long-term Equity AnticiPation Securities (LEAPS) 43n.30
lots 52

McDonald's 68, 74, **80n.16**, 121, 124
Maloney Act (1938) 34
management fees 102–4
margin 34, 55–6: accounts 54–5; calls 55, 57; futures contracts 179; requirements 48, 54–5, 56–7
marketable shares 66–7
Market Axess 30, **190**
market: capitalization 27–8, 136, 159; coefficient *see* beta; makers 23; orders 52, 57; power 121; risk *see* systematic risk; risk premium 157
Mellon Bank Corp. 47
Merck & Co., Inc. 125, **132**, 134–49, 162, 163: valuation ratios 165

Merrill Lynch & Co. 4, 49, 60, **190**
message boards 58
Microsoft 121
MidAmerica Commodity Exchange (MACE, MidAm) 31
Midway Airlines 116
Minneapolis Grain Exchange (MGE) 31, **190**
money market 10, 21, 98, 100
monitoring stocks 15
monopolies 119
Moody's Investor Service 10, 87–8, **190**
Morgan Keegan Inc. 47, 116
Morningstar.com 27, 105, 107, **190**
mortgage-backed securities 10, 87, 91
most recent quarter (MRQ) 164
municipal securities 39: bonds 9, 13, 92–3
Municipal Securities Rulemaking Board (MSRB) 39, 92, **190**
mutual funds 97–108

Nasdaq 25, 28, 52: Composite Index 76, 77, 78; Stock Market 25–8, 29–30, 34, 50
National Association of Securities Dealers (NASD) 5, 34, **191**: cash and margin accounts 53; day-trading firms 48; dispute resolution 51; short selling of stocks 52
National Futures Association (NFA) 31, 35, 41, **191**
national municipal bond funds 100
negotiated markets 28
net asset value (NAV) 97–8
net income 138
New York Cotton Exchange (NYCE) 31, **191**
New York Futures Exchange (NYFE) 32, **191**
New York Mercantile Exchange (NYME, NYMEX) 32, **191**
New York Stock Exchange (NYSE) 5, 24, **191**: bond prices 86; broker compensation 50; cash and margin accounts 53; changes 29–30; Composite Index 76–7, 78; dispute resolution 51; exchange indexes 76–7, 78; ex-dividend date 70; foreign stocks 74, 77; trading hours 28
New York Times 107, **191**
no-load funds 102–4
North American Industry Classification System (NAICS) 120

North American Securities Administrators
    Association (NASAA) 39, 48, **191**
notes (debt) 21, 83

objectives, investment 9, 10–11
odd lots 52
offered price 11
oligopolies 119
open-end investments 97
operating earnings 141
options 29, 18n.12, 35, 178–9
original maturity 21
OTC Bulletin Board (OTCBB) 28
over-the-counter (OTC) market 28
ownership of stocks 67–8, 71–2

Pacific Stock Exchange 29, **191**
participating preferreds 71
par value 68, 83
patents 121, 136–8
payment for order flow 49, 50
PEG ratio 163–4, 165
Philadelphia Board of Trade (PBOT) 32,
    191
Philadelphia Stock Exchange 27, 61n.6,
    191
Pink Sheets 28, **191**
pioneering phase, life cycle 122
Pocahontas Bancorp 127
Polaroid 121
portals 186
portfolio theory 14, 172–80
preemptive rights 71
preferred stocks 71
premium 84, 86, 178–9
price/book ratio 164–5
price/cash flow ratio 164, 165
price/earnings (P/E) ratio 162, 165
price/free cash flow ratio 164, 165
price/sales (P/S) ratio 164, 165
primary market 22–3
principal amount (par value) 68, 83
principal-only (PO) securities 91
privacy issues 59
private placement 23
profiles of investors 7, 67
profitability 143–7
profit margin 145
pro forma earnings 141
projected earnings 162
prospectuses 33, 101, 107
proxies 67–8
Prudential Insurance Company 4, **192**

psychology of investors 167–8
pure competition 119
put options 178

Quicken 105, 126, 134, 152n.1, **192**:
    Stock Evaluator 139, 146, 158, 161–2,
    163

rate of return on the market 157
real estate investment trusts (REITs) 104
Rebsamen Insurance Company 116
redemption of shares 97
red herrings 43n.33
Regions Bank/Investment Company, Inc.
    47, 116
registration of securities 33, 54
regulations 32–40
rejuvenation of industries 125
repurchase agreements (repos) 83
required rate of return (capitalization rate)
    154, 155
residual claimants 70
residual (unsystematic) risk 14, 175
Resolution Funding Corporation (REFCO)
    91
restricted accounts 56
retention rate 147
retirement planning 17
return: on assets (ROA) 144, 145, 146; on
    equity (ROE) 144–5, 146; on invested
    capital (ROIC) 145, 146; and risk 8,
    173–6
revenue bonds 92–3
revenue per seat mile flown 150
rights (stocks) 71
risk-free rate of return 157
risk premium 154, 158
risks 37, 70, 106–7: and investment
    objectives 9, 10–11; portfolio
    management 173–80; preference 9, 14;
    and returns 8, 173–6
Roche Holdings 123, **131n.8**
round lots 52

sales: per day (SPD) 148; per square foot
    150
SalomonSmithBarney 48, **192**
savings bonds 90
Schwab & Co., Inc., Charles 4, 45, 49,
    129, **192**
secondary market 23–30
secondary offering 23
second mortgage bonds 87

Securities Act (1933) 32–3
Securities and Exchange Commission (SEC)
    4, 6, 34, **192**: 12b-1 fees 103; ADRs 73;
    broker compensation 49, 50; complaints
    about brokers 51; day-trading firms 48;
    decimalization 73; EDGAR 135–6;
    investment companies 97; mutual funds
    101, 103; primary market 22; privacy
    issues 59; Reg FD 67; regulations 33–4,
    35, 39, 67; revenues 141; secondary
    market 25, 28, 29, 30; SIPC 59;
    suitability doctrine 6; "Tokyo Joe" 58
Securities Exchange Act (1934) 34
Securities Industry Association (SIA) 7,
    192
Securities Investor Protection Act (1970)
    35
Securities Investor Protection Corporation
    (SIPC) 35, 59, **192**
securitization 91
security issues 59
SEI Corporation 98
self-regulatory organizations (SROs) 30, 51
separate trading of registered interest and
    principal securities (STRIPS) 90
settlement date 53, 72
shareholder service fees 102, 103
Sharpe ratio 184n.4
Shell Transport and Trading 73
shingle theory 5–6
shocks 167–8
short sales 52
short stock 52, 54–5
short-term debt/equity 12, 21, 83
SmartMoney.com 107, **192**
Society Anonyme Corp. 58
speculative grade (junk) bonds 10, 88, 99
spreads (price) 73
stabilization phase, life cycle 122, 124–5
Standard & Poor's (S&P) 10, 69, 87–8,
    120, **192**: 500 Stock Index 77, 78, 162;
    Depository Receipts (SPDRs, spiders)
    41n.4, 102; Stock Price Indexes 77, 78
Standard Industrial Classification (SIC) 120
state municipal bond funds 100
state securities laws 39
stock exchanges 24–5, 26–7, 29
stock funds (equity mutual funds) 98, 99
stockholders' equity (book value) 136, 144,
    164–5
stock index funds 11, 102
stock markets 22–30
stocks 8, 66–79: dividends 70; screeners 15,
    126–30; splits 70

Stock-Screening.com 126, **192**
stop orders 52–3
strategic income funds 100
street-name ownership 53–4, 72
strike price 178
Student Loan Marketing Association (Sallie
    Mae) 22, 91
sustainable competitive advantage 121
Swiss e Trade 47
syndicates 22
Syntex Corporation 123
systematic risk 14, 122, 158, 173–5

T+3 trade settlement 53, 72
tangible book value 152n.4, 165
taxable bond funds 99–100
tax-equivalent yield 92
taxes 68, 91, 92, 104: suitability doctrine
    9, 13
tax-free mutual funds 100
technical analysis 165–7
technological change 116
third market makers 23
time horizons for investments 11–12
"Tokyo Joe" 58
Tokyo Stock Exchange 25
top-down analysis 114–25
total return funds 99
total risk 175
tracking stocks 70–1: index funds
    110n.6
trading 11
trailing twelve months (TTM) 162
tranches 91
Travelers 116
Treasury, US 88–90, **193**: bills 8, 10, 21,
    89; bonds 13, 22, 89–90; notes 89–90;
    Public Debt Bureau 90, **193**
Treasury inflation protected securities
    (TIPS) 90
T. Rowe Price 4, 17, **193**

UBS Paine Webber, Inc. 60, **193**
undermargined accounts 57
underwriting 23
unit investment trusts 102
unlimited liability 66
unsystematic risk 14, 175
up-ticks 52
US Census Bureau 116, 117–19, **193**
US Department of Commerce 120,
    193
Use Agreements 7–8
US Postal Service 121

valuation ratios 162–7
value spread 145
VMS Keytrade 47

Wachovia Online 47
Wall Street Journal 60, 75, 76, 107, **193**
Wal-Mart 121
Walt Disney 22, 83
warrants (stocks) 71
Washington Post Online 107, **108**
weighted average cost of capital (WACC)
    145, 159–60

world bond funds 99
World Equity Benchmark Shares (WEBS)
    41n.4
world equity funds 99
wrap accounts 50, 105

Yahoo! Finance 107, 126, 130, 167, **193**:
    stocks 75, 77, 126–9
yield: to call 85–6; to maturity (YTM)
    85

zero coupon bonds 83–4